# THE BALLAD AND THE PLOUGH

*A Portrait of the Life of the
Old Scottish Farmtouns*

# THE BALLAD AND THE PLOUGH

*A Portrait of the Life of the
Old Scottish Farmtouns*

by

## DAVID KERR CAMERON

LONDON
VICTOR GOLLANCZ LTD
1978

© David Kerr Cameron 1978
ISBN 0 575 02468 2

Printed in Great Britain at
The Camelot Press Ltd, Southampton

# CONTENTS

# LIST OF ILLUSTRATIONS

All unacknowledged photographs are by the author.

# ACKNOWLEDGEMENTS

For permission to quote and reproduce material in which they hold the copyright, the author wishes to thank the following:

Professor T. C. Smout (*A History of the Scottish People, 1560–1830*, published by Collins), pages 17, 140; George Outram (*Tales of a Highland Parish* by T. D. Miller), pages 58, 59; *The Press & Journal*, pages 77, 105, 159; the Rev. David Ogston (for allowing the inclusion of his poem "The Winner of Wars"), page 117; G. E. Fussell (*The Farmer's Tools*, published by Melrose), page 198; the Right Honourable the Earl of Airlie (for permission to quote from *Thatched with Gold*, published by Hutchinson), pages 218, 219; Dr David Buchan (*A Scottish Ballad Book*, published by Routledge & Kegan Paul), page 223; Hutchinson (*Sunset Song* by Lewis Grassic Gibbon), page 232. John Ord's *Bothy Songs & Ballads*, published in 1930 by Alexander Gardner, Paisley, is now reprinted by John Donald, Edinburgh.

For their assistance, not least for their help in locating and identifying illustrations, the author also wishes to thank: Miss M. A. Stephen, Asst. District Librarian for North Angus; Gavin Sprott, of the National Museum of Antiquities of Scotland's Country Life Archive; A. E. Truckell, Curator, Dumfries Museum; and A. Wilson, Librarian, Stranraer Library.

# INTRODUCTION

## *Stone, Lime and Legend*

BY THE MID-1800s Scotland stood at a pivotal point in her
history: she was swinging confidently away from a turbulent past
and a rural-based economy into the headier rôle of industrial
nation. Paradoxically, at that same moment she was poised, after
a century of improvements that had wholly transformed the landscape, on the brink of a new farming age: the era of the great
farmtouns. Through the next 70 or 80 years their names would
ring in the show-ring and the feeing market: famous and infamous,
some would pass into that unique balladry of the bothies and of
farmtoun men; and their stone steadings would take on the
encrustations of legend.

The farmtouns bred dour folk; strange folk often droll to the
point of eccentricity; folk with a humour so dry sometimes that
it was just this side of maliciousness; folk whose pleasures were
mainly simple and not infrequently carnal. They were people of
a special strain, resilient and enduring; in another context their
men became the backbone of regiments and their loyalty was
heavily traded in the discreet corridors of Whitehall. From the
bothies of their mud-girt farmtouns they marched through the
countryside of France with critical landsmen's eyes and gave a
coarse laugh at the Frenchman's peasant agriculture. A poor thing
it was against the well-worked fields of their own grand touns.
They paused for a moment to look, on their way to die among
strange mud—the foreign mud of Flanders or the Somme. In the
hellish fear of it, some of them forgot to die like heroes.

For they were not all brave men, the men of the farmtouns:
they were quiet men and braggarts; fine, kindly men of conscience
and men you would not have given the time of day to; among them,
though the emphasis round the touns was always on stolid brawn,
strode the occasional giant, the odd buccaneer or two whose
farming had the kind of inspired brilliance that other men could
envy but never follow. They were out of one crop and into

another before anyone else had sensed the glut of the market, or seen the outlet unexploited. It is likely that such men would have done well in anything they had set their hands to; what is undeniable is that their tenacity and special skills immensely enriched the landscape of the Scottish farmtouns. Their achievements would become their lasting memorials and their names are now interwoven with the history of the touns: James Kilpatrick of Craigie Mains of Kilmarnock (who purified the Clydesdale strain to such perfection); Amos Cruickshank (the shy Quaker bachelor who was the real founder of the Shorthorn breed); Hugh Watson of Keillor in Forfarshire (who pioneered the beef supremacy of the Aberdeen-Angus); wild Willie McCombie of Tillyfour (who carried on that lit flame and became also the first Scottish tenant farmer to sit in the House of Commons); the likeable George Hope of Fenton Barns in the Lothians (master farming tutor, who paid a high price for his presumption of trying to do likewise). When farming men look back, it is into a landscape peopled by such formidable figures.

There is a story they like to tell about the great Willie McCombie and Queen Victoria. It is a very fine story indeed and like all good stories it may gain from being only partially based on the truth. When the queen came to the farmtoun of Tillyfour, just over the hill from her beloved Balmoral, one day in 1866, it was to see the famous McCombie herd that had done the countryside so much honour. She was seated on a chair at the front of the farmhouse while the herd of Blacks was paraded past her in single file. They say that Willie, who was never a man to let an occasion go past him, sent one or two of his Aberdeen-Angus beasts round a second time so as not to short-change her majesty. But there is a further stanza to the story: Willie (it is said), a bit disappointed by the royal response, suddenly dashed from the queen's side, seized one of the beasts, the stock bull, and turned it towards the queen. Letting the beast, a particularly fine specimen, have a good look at the seated figure, he asked it: "Ken ye wha that is?"

There is another story they tell about Queen Victoria and the farmtouns; it has that same droll reluctance to be dazzled by majesty, and again it concerns the queen's stay at Balmoral, though this time the encounter was in Glenshee, then a lonely place of sheepwalks and wandering shepherds.

Having been lured by an exceptionally fine Deeside day much

farther than either she or her guests had intended, there was some doubt about whether the queen's horses were equal to the return journey in what is far from easy country. An official was therefore sent to a nearby farmtoun to beg fresh horses—only to be told by the farmer that he had but one carriage pair. With a couple of the royal horses as leaders and his fresh beasts yoked on the wheel, however, the farmer was sure her majesty could be got safely home. The official was less certain; he demurred, insisting on two pairs.

"I'll speak to the queen herself on it," said the farmer, and had stepped up to the royal coach before anybody could stop him. He explained his proposal and the queen agreed. His pair of carriage horses were yoked as he suggested and in no time the queen's carriage was on its way again. Feeling somewhat satisfied with himself, as he had every right to, the farmer went home to his supper.

"And what thought ye of her, then?" his wife asked him.

"She just did as I told her," came the reply. "She seems to be a richt sensible woman."

If time has embellished the bare facts of both stories, they nonetheless deserve to be true in their entirety. For the confrontations were apt and not in the least incongruous. It was during Victoria's reign that the Scottish farmtouns, the stone-and-lime steadings of the improved agriculture, grew into their greatness and it was with her death that most of them began the long drift into the bleakest of the depression years. The bond went deep; even on the farmtouns of the 1930s there were old men, grizzled and twisted with work, who spoke of her still with affection as the "Auld Queen". They remembered the days of the past and spoke of them whiles round a young cottar's fireside when the Hogmanay drams had gone down.

The majority of the farmtoun men were not of McCombie's kind. But lesser men though they were, they too were unique. They did not make big ripples. They used their women badly, their children abominably, sending them out to work before they could well hold a hayfork in the fear that if they did not their bairns would be past getting the hang of it and into a lifetime of criminal indolence. But they loved the land. Farming was a kind of contagion in their blood; young men who came to their farmtouns to court their daughters and would have been happy to stay snug and warm in the farmhouse parlour were taken out to march the Sabbath fields and admire the fattening steers. After supper in winter they would be taken to the byre in their Sunday suits and patent-leather boots to fork fresh bedding straw under the beasts' hooves.

Mostly, their names are forgotten now, rare characters though many of them were. They have long been lain to sleep in quiet kirkyards up and down the country these old farmtoun men, buried in a haze of drams, all rancour stopped, all debts forgiven. Tyrant farmer lies now by the bothy hell-raiser, the brief legends of their lives, the names of their old touns, hacked in the cold granite of simple stones. The moss has long obscured their names but it little matters now for those lichened stones were never their true memorials. These stood in the fields of each year's harvest: the yellow stooks lit by sunlight. Now they too are a rare sight, swept away by the coming of the combine-harvester and the days of the factory farmtoun. When they vanished from the fields like the old farmtoun men themselves, an immemorial pattern was broken and the countryside was a little more diminished.

# I

## The New Landscape

THE LANDSCAPE THE farmtoun men of the mid-1800s inherited
was itself a remarkable achievement, one in which change continued still as drainage and reclamation brought bog and moorland
increasingly under the plough, new implements were fashioned
at the forge and the new-built touns themselves began to take
their place amid the geometrically-margined fields. By that time,
Scottish farming had begun to coalesce into its constituent parts,
areas to assume their own special and unique identities as well as
their importance in the whole. Ideas flowed still; the look of the
landscape would yet be enhanced by the addition of plantations and
hedges and dykes, cultivation further improved by the drainage
yet to be done. But far from lagging behind her southern neighbour now, Scotland had drawn ahead—changed days indeed from
that time, over 100 years earlier, when the Earl of Peterborough's
daughter, coming North to lie in the young Lord Huntly's bed,
had brought some of her father's ploughs and ploughmen with
her. Long gone now the days when their legal and landed lordships
had shipped men from Dorset and Norfolk to instigate new techniques. If anything, the flow of knowledge had gone into reverse:
now it was the East Lothian farmtoun men who were being
enticed South, for that area for a time was to be the focal point
and forcing ground of farming progress as well as one of the
nation's great granaries, with Strathmore, the Carse of Gowrie
and Moray, exporting not only to England but to Holland and
Spain and Portugal. Cobbett, riding through it in the 1830s,
although he also found much to criticize, saw: ". . . such cornfields, such fields of turnips, such turnips in those fields, such
stack-yards, and such a total absence of dwelling-houses, as never,
surely, were before seen in any country upon earth." Yet little
over a century before, Defoe, with a supercilious eye, had seen
only "good soil impoverished by want of husbandry".

The pace of improvement had been staggering.

When Prince Charles Edward Stuart slipped out of hiding and safely aboard *L'Heureux* on Loch nan Uamb in 1746, he had left behind him not only a broken dream but, in the Highlands particularly, a fragmented society. Even in the Central and North-East Lowlands the whole fabric of the region's way of life had been thrown into confusion by this final fling at restoring Stuarts to the Throne. And though Sir Archibald Grant of Monymusk seems to have been able to continue uninterrupted in his improvement programme, many of the lairds had been staunch supporters of the Stuart cause and had suffered accordingly. They were either in captivity or exile; their lands had been forfeited to the Crown. In the circumstances few tenants were coming forward to fill the empty farmtouns; few seemed anxious to take up even short leases at such an unchancy time and lairds had to resort to the ancient steelbow tenure to tenant empty steadings.

In the Highlands the situation was worse; ancient fealties faded in the aftermath of Culloden, the old clan kinship was eroded by the new laird-tenant relationship which brought its own kind of bewilderment to those who had previously known loyalty only to a territory and a name.

Yet whatever the hardships that flowed from it—and they were many—if the Forty-five did nothing else it opened up the country. Good roads, essential for maintaining a military presence, were slowly strung across the face of the land, arteries of communication not only between glen and neighbouring glen, but, for the first time, between region and region. Crofter Gael from the West met Doric Scot in the East, Lothian landsman in the South. Strange compatriots they were, the dark Gael with the soft singing of his language and the man from the North-East Lowlands whose consonants had the crunch of cold chisels; the Highlander loyal and lackadaisical, master of the bold, quick skirmish but without stomach for the long-drawn struggle; the Lowlander, dour, thrifty, enduring. In time their qualities would be seen in their agriculture.

Such were the disparate elements of Scottish nationhood at a time when England was already advancing towards a new and radically-improved agriculture. And added to that separatism there was the old hatred still of things English, especially in the Highlands where the Duke of Cumberland's soldiery, in the aftermath of the Rebellion, had been guilty of brutality amounting at times to unreason. The rejection was emotional rather than considered. But again, much of what was happening in the South was utterly irrelevant in a Highlands context.

Their homely name apart, few of the new-style touns would take anything out of that turbulent earlier time—though dotted among them still were the milltouns, the watertouns, the kirktouns whose links were more solidly with the past. Their memory would be enshrined in the names of the new stone-and-lime steadings— Milltown of This, Kirktown of That—recalling those earlier farming settlements that had survived up to the end of the eighteenth century, and in some areas beyond it. These had been, as Prof. T. C. Smout in *A History of the Scottish People, 1560–1830* says: "the common unit of settlement . . . centring on the notional 'farm' the size of which was determined (initially at least) by the area that one or sometimes two or three plough teams of horses or oxen could keep under cultivation".

The "farm" would be held in joint tenancy, even up to the number of twenty, and worked usually on the old run-rig system, an ancient form of strip cultivation in which the strips or "rigs" were reallocated year by year. On the infield strips, or arable land, close to the farmtoun cluster—the lowest ground dry enough to cultivate—grew the oats and poor-quality barley, while the out-field was used as pasture ground. Again, however, the farmtoun might be held in single tenancy and worked in conjunction with sub-tenants as well as servants. It was a pattern of land-use dating from the Middle Ages and was almost universal. It was a pattern created by the plough itself and unalterable until such time as the new farmtouns perfected a system of underground drainage. The "rigs"—the raised strips of ground on which the crops were grown and whose widths in time became adapted to the needs of hand-sowing and the hand-shearing of crops—were the basic patches of pre-improvement farming; the furrows between ran off the water. It is tempting now to see that farmtoun past in the Hebridean crofting communities of later time, and certainly there are strong affinities: the run-rigs close in, the shieling or pasture they demanded at some distance. Pushing probability a little further, one might see the shape of the old farmtoun buildings in crofterdom's township clusters, each unit based on the longhouse: the byre/dwelling/barn in-line construction. But it is more likely that the ancient touns were similar to those seen by Edward Burt in the 1720s and described in his *Letters from a Gentleman in the North of Scotland*:

> A Highland town . . . is composed of a few huts for dwellings, with barns, and stables, and both the latter are of a more diminutive size than the former, all irregularly placed, some one way, some another, and at any distance look like so many heaps of dirt; these are built in glens and straths, which are the corn-countries near rivers and rivulets, and also on the sides of lakes where there is some arable land for the support of the inhabitants.

Elsewhere Burt talks of another community: ". . . with nine dwelling huts, besides a few others of a lesser size, for barns and stables. This they call a town, with a pompous name belonging to it . . .". His irritation for once is excusable; as an Englishman, his misunderstanding of the term "town" forgivable; and one can even advance a reason why he might have found the name of the settlement pompous, for it would have been natural enough for it to begin "Bal-", that tongue-rolling prefix from the Gaelic *baile*, meaning farmtoun or farmstead. Such ancient grandeur rings down to our own time in the names of countless Scottish towns and villages as well as in the names of innumerable farm-touns. The thread of history may be tenuous but it is from such a past that the term emerged to leap the centuries and embrace the steadings of the mid-1800s.

These new touns and their improved farming brought with them immense social change, as great as any they worked on the face of the land. Enclosure in the Lowlands made the shieling or out-field pasture unnecessary (since it was as much a part of protecting the growing crops from stray beasts as of any stock-grazing pattern); improved drainage and the implements that resulted for east-coast farming brought the abolition of the run-rigs with their tradition of hand-tool labour. Until these changes came the farm-toun cluster or hamlet was a rooted element of country society, a part of the sharing made necessary by the subsistence-level agriculture that made a plough, for instance, or an ox, a heavy investment. Indeed, it was common for a joint tenant of a farmtoun to own no more than the half-share of an ox—and eight were needed to pull the plough. The run-rigs were worked by the folk of the community themselves, and even the old woman with her cow out to grass had a share in the soil.

It was a parlous agriculture, in no way perfect; a system of strife and contention always. And it put no premium whatever on improvement. A man who changed his rigs with every harvest was hardly likely to manure his patches more thoroughly and take greater pains in their cultivation only to see the next holder of the rig reap the benefit. For the farmtoun clusters were co-operatives only in the labour sense; there was no sharing of crops. When a man's barley rigs failed him, he was a man alone, though it is likely that native kindliness would have kept him this side of the starvation line. Though they grazed common pasture, a man's beasts, too, were his own. If he felt that the pasture was being over-grazed, he had little incentive to reduce the number of his cattle. To have done so would have been only to open the door to another of the toun's men to buy further beasts and make up the number. And the indiscriminate mixing of the herd meant that interest in improving the breed was minimal. In such a system, intelligent men were trapped by the indifference of their neighbours; the level of agriculture was never higher than the farming of the toun's most inefficient rig-holder.

Maybe, after all, it was time for improvement. What that involved the Duke of Argyll, in his study *Scotland as it was and as it is*, written in the 1880s, makes clear:

> It was a system of which all the parts so hung together, and which as a whole was so rooted in all the routine habits of daily and yearly life, that not one stone of it could be touched without the whole structure tumbling. Any change involved a total change in the prospects and in the life of every family concerned.

The duke, of course, was writing from the position of lairdship and for the responsibility of ownership, defending the improvements that brought an end to the old farmtoun clusters and cruel dispossession for their folk. For enclosure and the single-tenant touns set in motion a new, shifting pattern of settlement; isolated units, the touns drew in itinerant labour from far around, men without roots in the community, there in May gone in November. They were a new, hardier breed of farmtoun men entirely.

The new touns rose on the riches of war and a Tory government's protectionist policy. For the landowners the wars with France had been almost a good thing. With the market to itself, home grain had soared in price and with the end of war, in 1815, the Corn Laws had been enacted to curb that renewed importation of grain that would drain some of farming's wealth. It was government by landowners for landowners: there would be no grain allowed in, from anywhere, until the home-produced crop reached a satisfactorily high price. Round the farmtouns every acre of available grassland came quickly under the plough—the farmtouns would grow rich while the townsman, as well as the farm servant, got steadily and more pitifully poor. For the policy was a divisive one, socially as well as politically. High bread prices kept up the price of factory-made goods, closing foreign markets and the long years of confrontation between landowner and factory owner ended only in 1846 with the repeal of the Corn Laws, a measure passed under the premiership of Sir Robert Peel, leader of the Tory party. Peel himself, perhaps significantly, was the son of a cotton-mill owner. His party never forgave him and shortly after, as is the usual fate of leaders who displease their peers, found a reason for getting rid of him. Yet the farmtouns, against all expectations, did not founder. Almost the contrary, for from 1840 until almost 1880 they were buoyed by the town demand that spread, with industrial prosperity, up from the factory floor. And there was another reason, overlooked all the long protectionist years: the general climatic uniformity of Europe rarely allowed one grain-growing nation to profit at another's expense.

If the farmtoun had changed, so too had its master; he was a vastly different figure from the peasant who had entered the maelstrom of the farming revolution a century before. He was a figure now of some substance, of necessity a capitalist almost as much as an agriculturist. He drank tea and lost any desire to feed his farm men at his own table; his wife, delighted, delegated the milking and took to wearing silk bonnets. They had moved into the class of low gentry. Their farmhouse had some pretension to style, a separate dwelling where once it had abutted the barn and the byre; inside, its furnishings had become more sophisticated: the homely board was put away to make way for something more seemly, a table in imported mahogany. The old box beds that had housed ancestors from their moment of entering the world until their day of leaving it were often torn out of their wall recesses and replaced by fourposters hung with lace. There was a preoccupation with trivia that hardly related at all with the hard world of work beyond the window panes. There, as reclamation and improvement of the land went on, there was a spirit of excitement still.

Yet pioneering men walked in the shadow of great events. Under the straight, even furrows of the new agriculture there was an ancient landscape; the farmtouns stood by the scenes of destiny—touns such as North Mains of Barra, in the North-East: was this not the place where a nation took its first faltering step on the road to independence as Bruce put Red Comyn to flight? Or the West Mains of Harlaw, an hour's march away: was it not here that the Highland host was turned and the future path of Scottish history determined? Jump the centuries and yet another Mains is fixed for a brief instant in the spotlight and the turbulent days of the Forty-five: the gracious farmhouse of the Mains of Mulben, in Boharm, built by its Grant lairds in 1696 as the House of Mulben, on the borders of Moray, was one day the headquarters of that dashing Jacobite Lord Lewis Gordon and almost the next moment held for King George.

They stood—stand still—these farmtouns on the canvas of history, their lands passing back to unknowable time and events only to be guessed at. Rising from their barley fields, the tall Standing Stones are a reminder of days of a deeper destiny; silent monoliths in the twilight of the quiet evening fields or against the anger of a winter sunset, they loom darkly, tokens of dim gods and shadowy deeds that unquiet the mind, a reminder of cockerel's blood dripping from the plough-beam and black dogs baying against the yellow of the moon. And there are other stones, too, in the farmtoun fields, their purpose dread and knowable still, like the Grey Stone of Cluny, a grey whinstone shape in the fields of Woodend farm. It marks the site of the long-ago barony court. From here a man's walk in life might be a short one and all uphill—to the gallows tree.

Not that all history has been so fortuitously preserved. Built into many of the byre walls of Buchan in the North-East Lowlands are stones from the burial kists of an earlier people, for in the time of land improvement the plough turned them up with a regularity that made their discovery unremarkable: in uplands Clatt a Druid's stone has been unceremoniously incorporated into a farmtoun dyke. If such things shock the preservationist, they do at least suggest one thing: the temper and single-mindedness of the men who transformed that once-barren landscape.

But not all of the past was blood. Some of the touns stood by the deeds of saintly men and their names are a reminder of it still: Chapelhall, Chapelpark, Cloisterseat and Monkshill all stand within a short distance of each other in a North-East parish, the latter indeed the scene of an act of faith in a later time when James Anderson came north from the Lothians to put 1,300 acres of Buchan under the plough. In the area from which he came stands Monkrigg, a housing development now but its new steading of 1863 typical of many of that time and area in the boom building years of the mid-1800s. In ecclesiastical origin and name you might have found their counterparts in almost any parish of the country; great or small, their stones as yet unmellowed, they would become part of the continuum of history.

# II

## *The New Touns*

THE NEW FARMTOUNS diminished in size and architectural grandeur as you travelled north from Berwick and the Border hills with their steadings in the dales and their pastures rising behind them. In the lush Lothians the proud touns stood but beyond the Forth there were fine touns still: around Stirling and the Ochils, in the Carse of Gowrie and in the land-rich Vale of Strathmore in the shelter of the Sidlaws—where, it was said, even an idiot could hardly fail to farm well—and even up in the red-lands of the Mearns where Lewis Grassic Gibbon's Chris Guthrie, looking out on that cloud-capped landscape in the early years of this century, had mirrored the thoughts and feelings of the last land-locked generation. West and South-West were the dairytouns of Ayrshire and Galloway with its mixed farming in an almost Highland setting, but northwards on the eastern shelf, the farm-touns shrank in stature and the crofts, spreading between them, began to proliferate till it was hard sometimes to tell one type of holding from the other. In the North-East sat the bare land of Buchan where the sound of the sea could be heard in every byre on a still morning, its acres soon to be a tribute to the dour, not overly-imaginative men who, down the brutish determination of their generations, would bring its unforgiving soil to grow whisky on the stalk for the distilleries of Speyside and beef on the slither-ing hoof for the fine restaurants of London. In time it would stand second only to the Lothians as a crucible of the new farming.

But where the soil in the east thinned and the coastal land crept into the crannies of the glens and the shelter of the Grampians the small places clung to a more precarious, subsistence farming and crofting. Here indeed was the distinction blurred between one holding and the next, the agriculture sometimes so far left behind by the tide of progress that when prim Presbyterian ministers came to write their parish reports for the *Second Statistical Account* they ranted whiles like hot-gospellers from the shame of it. All the same, they bred fine folk these small touns of the glens, as hardy as the Highlanders of old; by the end of their hillside harvests their men and women had faces tanned to the hue of mahogany and their sharp-boned bodies were as supple as whipcord. Beyond the Laich of Moray, Inverness and the Black Isle there was farming still, though somehow to less purpose, and over the tossing of the Pentland Firth the Orkneymen, small-holders with boats, would grow gradually into the hearts of the mainland farming folk by their astuteness and industry. Far, far to the north, where the race of sea-tides isolated him, the Shet-lander was something else: a fisherman with a plough.

Such then was the farming landscape in which the new touns stood. The geography of their fields might vary, and the backdrop to their days, but the rigour of their work differed little. They had, many of them, strange and heart-cry names that clung in the mind long after you had flung their mud from your boots. Usually, these were the small, one-pair and two-pair touns where the tenant and a single bothy-housed help managed never quite to keep up with the work: the Peatiebogs, Fernyhillocks, Braesides, Woodhollows, Gowanleas, and such-like. Their names betrayed their lowly status. Implicit in some was an irony that cannot have been unconscious: Scrapehard, Weariefauld, Stoneyvale, Clayhill —their names memorials to all the ill-luck and disaster that could ever befall a farmtoun. Yet the scrawled sight of them on an envelope was enough to bring briefly to the face of some distant post-sorting Scot a light of recognition and a smile of understand-ing as secret to the Northern mind as an ingrowing toenail.

These were, of course, the "middling" places in the farming ladder where men who had made the leap from hired cottar to crofter essayed the swaying tightrope of tenancy. Like the crofts they stood round the skirts of the big farmtouns—with their big horse teams and bands of bothy men—away from the road, away almost from *everything*, on the kind of land that nobody else wanted. For this reason, if not from the insistence of the Post Office, their names were often qualified by the inclusion of that of the big toun to which they clung. How else could anyone be sure they existed. Emphasis on location gave rise to its own kind of confusion and ignominy. There were Watersides that stood by streams so puny that even in the spring spate they would hardly have floated a child's toy boat let alone turned a mill-wheel. There

were Whinnyfolds unfringed by even the sparsest of greenery.
And though the gowans did indeed grow there, the painful thing
about Gowanlea was that it grew little else.

Men did not grow rich on such small farmtouns, only more
human; they grew into a tolerance of man's frailty and a philosophy that passed down in their lines, watering the ambitious
blood of later generations so that in time they would settle without
effort in suburbia. It was no accident that the best stories of such
men had the edge of droll irony. Some, it is true, were steely men:
they moved up, or away, or were removed in time to the asylum
or the quiet of the kirkyard, killed by the worry of it all. Few of
these low-acreage touns would survive the great era of the farmtouns as viable farming units though they would continue to
support in a special kind of slavery farming folk who had nowhere
else to go.

Great or small, the old farmtouns were as functional as a spade;
they had a bleakness of character that could leave permanent scars
on the soul. Though the rich farmlands, Perthshire, Berwickshire,
the broad acres of the Lothians and even some corners of Suther-
land and Moray, might sport touns with some degree of manorial
pretension, most of the old steadings were built in such a cold
severity of stone as to suggest places of penal servitude. In the
North-East Lowlands especially, they sometimes sat so squatly on
the landscape as barely to interrupt its contours. Yet grand or
humble, the new-built touns of the mid-1800s had this in common:
a dour dignity and a basic allegiance to that principle of design
based on the courtyard plan of the single, square-cornered "U"—
with the farmhouse itself virtually enclosing the square—or the
double-court "E" layout, sometimes abbreviated to the form
of "F". True, there were proud touns that disobeyed that principle, that had disentangled themselves from a feudal time and
the days of clay, wattle and thatch, to spawn and sprawl eclectic-
ally over some knoll or hillside. With their roots set deep in
the farming past, they had sprung probably from the original
longhouse bigging—byre/dwelling/barn—that had housed farmer,
family, beasts and a host of servants without discrimination, or
had been the cluster of outbuildings surrounding castle or mansion
house. That great North-East Lowlands improver, Sir Archibald
Grant, describes such a grouping at Monymusk, when his family
first took over the estate:

The house was an old castle with battlements and six different roofs of various hights and directions, confusedly and inconveniently combined, and all rotten, with two wings more modern, of two stories only, the half of the wendowes of the higher riseing above the roofs, with granaries, stables and houses for all the cattle, and of the vermine attending them, close adjoining, and with the heath and muire reaching in angles or goushets to the gate, and much heath near, and what land near was in culture belonging to the farmes, by which their cattle and dung were always at the door. . . .

From the tone we may assume that such close affinity with the farmtoun pleased Sir Archibald no better than it did many of the lairds of his own and a slightly later time. Growing genteel with the times, they became self-conscious about such proximity to soil and beast that supported them; they moved away to a new mansion and sequestered silence among the trees, leaving the old house, its byres and ancient associations to a tenant with the temerity to lease it. Such was social change, and the growth of one kind of farmtoun. One would not condemn their unbridled development for they often farmed, these ill-suited touns, with unimpaired reputation and even distinction. All the same, such sporadic building lacked the cohesion of design—even that special kind of grace—of the new touns of the boom building years from 1840 until nearly 1880.

The courtyarded touns of those later, frenzied years drew their inspiration, too, from a little earlier. Their example was the steadings of the late eighteenth-century improvers of Berwickshire, the Borders and the Lothians. They were the lairds' touns, Mainses and Home Farms, their classical façades almost built, it sometimes seemed, to outshine their own mansion houses—such famous touns as Saltoun Mains, Blackadder Mount, Delgatie Castle and Rosebery home farms. It was natural enough that they should have given a lead, for it was on their acres that the improving lairds propounded (or disastrously disproved) their ideas. They were the forcing grounds of the new farming as well as the Big House's own source of produce. At a time when country society was stratifying as it had never done before, such touns were often built to reflect the aggrandizement of the family with which their fortunes were linked. Of some you might indeed almost have believed that an Adam—as he had done at Culzean Castle—had paused in the passing to add austere grace to a façade or the long run of a cartshed. There is no doubt that these early steadings delighted the eye of Cobbett as he made his celebrated rounds in East Lothian in the early half of the nineteenth century: "The farm-yard is a square, with buildings on the sides of it for horses, cattle, and implements; the stack-yard is on one side of this, the stacks all in rows, and the place as big as a little town." A justification surely, if ever one were needed, for those grand farmtouns of the 1800s inheriting their name from the past.

It was from these formidable touns and the wealth of building and design advice, in book and pamphlet, in the first two decades of the century that the main spate of building and rebuilding of the middle-1800s flowed, its impetus stimulated by the now commonplace granting of longer leases to encourage a tenant, and particularly by that change of the law of entail, towards the end of the eighteenth century, which made it possible for a laird to pass down to his heirs three-quarters of the cost of such developments.

Architecturally, the humbler stone-and-lime touns of the mid-1800s showed a restraint the early lairds' touns would sometimes have done well to copy, for there were cases in the South of the kind of unseemly ostentation that would sicken the heart of a small tenant in Buchan. Domes and spires provisioned with dovecots and bearing clocks with golden dials, had soared skywards with cathedral-like grandeur; belfries had added a note of oddity rather than distinction. But even in the later touns, there erupted occasionally the kind of rebellion against linear severity that sat finials on courtyard arches like balloons on the nose of a circus seal, or gave the low conical roof of a horse-mill the relief of a golden weathercock. Yet none offended greatly—though there were steadings yet to come in the 1870s in which a foreign influence would strike a jarring note in the landscape and whose façades, in some cases, would have disgraced any respectable distillery.

It is easy enough, however, to see why their architects fell into the trap of the *outre* embellishment: that arch of the façade, the entrance to steading and courtyard, invited attention and emphasis as the focal point of the farmtoun; it was a clever designer who knew his toun's limitations.

As Cobbett suggests, the new-style steading contained all the buildings needed for the arable farming and stock-rearing of the eastern seaboard farmtoun: new long granaries ran the length of the cartshed, high from ground damp; turnip shed and straw barn butted either end of the byre in one long, low building; the hayloft, where once before bothy days, the single men of the toun had had to sleep, took its natural place above the stable— and might even have floor openings so that the horsemen, bringing their beasts in from the fields, had only to climb on to the stable forestalls to tug down their beasts' feed from it. There were high byres and low byres, but such designation had nothing to do with architectural excellence and was indicative only of the state of fattened readiness of the cattle beasts they housed, and, of course, in the savage protocol of the farmtouns, of the relative standing of men who staffed them. There were protrusions of course that marred the rectilinear grace of the farmtouns: the hump of the horse-mill that sat like an unsightly gumboil on the side of the mill-house itself, the stack by the mill-house's side when stationary steam started to power the barn-mills of the richer touns from the earlier 1800s. There was, too, the occasional oddity of a windmill as part of the steading buildings, again to drive the mill. Few of the smaller touns blemished their dour lines with such additions, however; few could afford the luxury of giving the horse-gang beasts cover; and even if there was an archway into the court, it was functionally just that. If there were none the entrance might be between piers, plain or ornamental. In fact, the entrance to the courts of the humbler touns was usually through the gap where the farmhouse separated itself from the steading, to break its courtyard square or rectangle.

The whole was a compact, coherent layout of which any time-and-method expert would have approved. Like the number of cartpends, the situation of the farmhouse gave some clue to the importance of a toun: the larger and more successful, the greater the degree of detachment, until finally the house turned its back on the daily round of work that supported it—and found refuge behind its own circle of trees. But that, of course, was the kind of disinterest the smaller touns of the North-East and South-West could never afford. Among the dairying touns of the South-West it was not uncommon to find the farmhouse facing *into* the court-yard, though most managed to face outwards without giving offence. For them life was a sad dichotomy; a schism between

honest reality and social need. Past their back doors facing into
the activity and smells of the farmtoun came the sheaves of
harvest, the loads of dung, the kye for milking, while their fronts
faced aloofly into that gentler world of tailored lawns and shingled
paths and looked out perhaps to the prospect of distant hills.
These smaller touns were the typical touns, their simpler architecture at one with the landscape, for however uncompromising
it had an instinctual quality, as though stone had absorbed the
spirit of the land, of mist and hardship, and the buildings en-
capsulated it. Perhaps that, too, is not so surprising, for farmtoun
architecture—as later showpiece touns were to demonstrate—does
not jump geographical boundaries and the men who gave the touns
their native character, the masons who built them, were men, like
other tradesmen of their time, who would take a harvest fee and
themselves lived close to the land.

Time, alas, would destroy the cohesion and pleasing conformity
of the old farmtouns, that intuitive harmony and scale that sat so
easily on the farming landscape of the late 1800s and the earlier
years of the present century. That geometrical rapport between
steadings and fields would be lost with the prefabricated building
materials of a later time, materials that drew nothing from the landscape in which they stood. The old steading stones, on the other
hand, were gathered from it: grey and pink granite, grey whinstone and, of course, sandstone that ran the gamut of colour from
yellow to an almost bitter brown. Sometimes quarried stone set
the wall margins for field rubble; stone slates sat eave by eave
with red pantiles; new stones neighboured the hallowed stone
taken sometimes from the ruins of holy places. There, set together
in a landscape where constant drizzle could sometimes be called
good weather, they mellowed with the seasons, lichened with age,
and slowly enshrined tradition and legend. The sight of the
old touns, on a distant hillside, could bring a momentary ache to
the heart for all the hardness of the life they imposed. Indeed it
was possible, as the last of the summer light touched the russet
pantiles of Fife or the Lothians or the old red sandstone of Angus,
to imagine a kindliness and warmth in their softened contours.

It was an illusory glow.

# III

## *The Pattern of Work*

THE FARMTOUN YEAR turned slowly but remorselessly on its
axis from those meridian months of September/October, which
were beginning and ending both and saw first the crescendo of
harvest and almost at once the "renewal" of ploughing while the
corn-ricks gleamed gold in the stackyard. The year unfolded from
that first moment when the plough drew a guiding furrow across the
raked stubble. And so it would continue through the days of winter;
the work of the plough unbroken except for the interruption
of carting home turnips to the beasts fattening in the winter
byre—or for the onslaught of a winter thresh-out when the farmer
judged the time right to get the best price per quarter for his oats.

As the year turned men left their ploughs in the rig and paused
briefly to toast each other in ancient salutation, "Yer guid health
and prosperity"—for the farmtoun men the link between one and
the other was indissoluble. They were mindful of the year that
was gone and of the folk to whom they were beholden for help
at "the thrash", the loan of a horse or a love-dargue, that neigh-
bourly act that did a new widow's ploughing. They were mindful
of the time to come for a man's guidwill on New Year's day was
something to count on all through the year. With their whisky
bottles in their jacket pockets they took their old incantations
round the touns in turn and drank to the danger of their health.
Men that day, the world o'er might brothers be. Worsened with
drams, men walked waist-deep into mill-dams and were instantly
sobered, or fell into cold ditches to sleep like a baby. Sober, they
went back to their ploughs, to the tending of beasts. Soon it would
be spring and seedtime. They at least were not governed by the
watch of the grieve, that boss-man of the farmtoun, but by the
whim of a greater grieve. All the same, when it arrived, seedtime
put a lightness into the step of the farmtoun men as they came
into the stables in the morning. It was time to harrow down
winter's cold furrows, to sow the oats and spring barley.

If the seed-drill gave a kind of facile precision to the operation about the big farmtouns, there were others, smaller places, even in the early years of this century, where the days took on an ancient symbolism. Their ploughmen strode the fields, hand-broadcasting the seed from a hopper hung from their shoulders. They walked these men with a solemn metronomic skill, their scatter pattern almost as precise as the machine's, knowing that nature and the bare patches of summer might yet betray them. Even men who could callously abuse their Clydesdales would pause whiles on a headland for a moment when the oats had been sown to gaze back through the centuries and muse on the precarious predicament of Man.

The preparation of ground for the root crops followed but somehow without the same heaviness of portent. Ridges were drawn and dunged on land scarified by heavy cultivator and toothed harrow but the turnip-barrow brought forth only a deep thankfulness to Jethro Tull rather than acute reflection on the cosmic place of mankind. Potatoes were planted and ridged into drills with the same unconcern. Only grain-seed, it seemed, had that magical link with human destiny.

Spring passed into summer: it was not the warmth of the days that marked its arrival but the moment when the men of the farmtouns took off their heavy sleeved waistcoats and hung them on to the headland fence-posts. They were by no means children of the sun, but then, too much shedding of clothes in the days of the old farmtouns would have been a little unseemly. As a concession to a day of strong heat they might unbutton their winceyette shirts down to the chest and roll their sleeves well past the elbow.

If the weather held and the manure did its work the turnips would soon be ready for singling. That was one of the lighter chores amid the heavy work of the farmtouns, a holiday almost for the man who was good at the work. There were ploughmen who could handle a hoe with such artistry that their skill quite bedazzled the eye and made you wonder: how was it possible to combine such speed with such deftness of touch; to leave a single plant dangling by its root-thread while thrusting the thick stand of its unwanted neighbours into oblivion.

The turnip-hoeing was gang work. It was the foreman (the first horseman) who took the lead and set the pace—and that was as

fast as he could make it. Even so, there was consolation sometimes
for the young ploughman who was good with the hoe; foremen
as they got older lost the fine touch of their youth, though they
could not admit it. Their eye-sight failed a little and rheumatism
slowed their reflexes. Besides, their legs could get tired at the end
of the day, making it easier for the rest of the gang, the grieve
among them usually, to keep up. As in so many other jobs about
the farmtoun, there was a protocol at the hoeing: they moved
down their respective drills the second horseman behind the first,
the third horseman behind him, followed by the "fourth" and so
on, down the line of precedence to the bailie (or stockman), who
would sometimes appear about mid-morning to put in his expected
stint and could usually find some urgent reason to account for
his absence in the afternoon. At the hoeing there might be time
for a chat and the telling of coarse stories, a bonhomie even
between the men and the grieve, just for once, as they took stock
of the landscape and the backward crops of neighbour touns. But
that all depended on the weather. If the turnips were late there
would be a rush to be ready for the start of the hay-making, itself
a lightsome job that often brought the womenfolk of the farmtouns
into the fields.

Even as the work of the farmtoun year went forward it was
shadowed by the future of harvest; cornfields were watched with
concern from their first tender brairding, through the bitter green
of their early promise and into the yellow of August. Then the
farmtouns waited for the grain to rustle on the stalk, to turn to
the almost-white of gold. There was an expectation about those
final days as they hung, hazed with warmth. On the small farmtouns where the work was always behind-hand binders that had
been left to rust under tarpaulins in some sheltered corner of the
steading were wheeled into the sunlight and squirted all over with
a liberality of oil seen on no other occasion. Their canvases were
belatedly checked and rushed to the saddler, who—bad-tempered
at such slackness—had to be wheedled and implored to patch
them in time. Men who had faced 50 harvests could get suddenly
terse and excited; old farmers who had a reputation for setting a
harvesting lead lost sleep from fear of losing their standing and
rose whiles in the middle of the night to count the bags of binder
twine waiting in the implement shed.

When it started it was in earnest; all at once an armada of binders

and reapers filled the fields and even farmtouns where the sowing
had been late would sometimes be flustered into cutting crops
before they were decently ripe. It took a man of strong character
to stand out against the enchantment of fine weather and the
nagging thought that it would not hold forever. If it was a kind
of festival of humanity, it was also one of manic behaviour. Kirk
elders, men with a fine charity of mind and a piousness in all
things, took suddenly to grudging God all the fine Sundays, and
the turnpike roads were filled with the flying bikes of grieves as
they ferried the broken bits of binders to the smith for instant
repair. In their anxiety, grieves behaved badly: they cursed the
horseman driving the binder, the machine's manufacturer when
it went wrong, and the ineptitude of the folk who followed it,
stooking the sheaves it had thrown. In the later Depression years
of the 1920s and '30s, on the hard-up touns, they could be eloquent
on the miserliness of the farmer who kept them working with
inadequate machines, and were sometimes sadly discomfited
when the man himself—seen only on the turnpike as he passed
in his gig to the kirk or the sales or to sit on the council—suddenly
appeared in the harvest field to take off his jacket and give a hand
with the stooking. Tinks who passed on the summer road could
be instantly recruited (with the promise of a pound or two, a bite
to eat and a bed in the barn for a week or so) where a rogue binder
had started to throw loose sheaves or even stopped binding at all.
Such disasters could put a premium on an old bandster's skill.
At harvest, as at no other time, there was a brotherhood among
men.

Once it started, the harvest would last six to eight weeks if the
days were fair, forever if it was hindered by broken weather. The
men and women of the farmtouns would be in the fields then for
ten, maybe twelve hours a day, pausing only for dinner at mid-day
(and that to rest the horses, not the folk) and for a "piece" and a
cup of tea—or a bucket of ale—brought to the field about the
middle of the afternoon. Time and the combine-harvester would
sweep away this and much else of the tradition of harvest as well
as its immemorial architecture: the stooks that stippled the landscape after the binders and reapers had finished the cutting, the
impressive stackyards of the big farmtouns.

For the cutting was only the half of it: the corn had to stand
in the stooks until it was ready to lead-in to the stackyard. Then

B

the big harvest frames were fitted to the carts and the sheaves brought home to the farmtoun—often by moonlight, for such was the haste to secure the crop while the weather held.

So the stooks became stacks.

If anything, they were even more crucial; they were the "grain-stores" until such time as the farmer could arrange a thresh-out. Their building was of critical importance to the economy of the farmtoun; if they were not water-tight the crop, and possibly the farmtoun, would be ruined. The man who could build a good, weather-tight rick was God-gifted; all sins could be forgiven him if his work was sound and the cornyard when he had finished with it was a thing of pure symmetrical delight. He was the master of line and curve who gave his farmtoun its envied reputation at harvest-time. Or made it the laughing-stock of the parish.

So it unfurled, the pattern of the year, ancient and immutable.

Potatoes were dug from their drills and gathered, to be stored in clamps in the corners of the fields like barrows of the ancient dead; turnips sat in their rows, fattening like yellow emperors—till they were plucked from them in the winter frosts to feed beasts in the byre. The days though, the cycle from ploughing to harvest, had to be in-filled too with all the other chores of the farmtoun: the transporting of new-threshed grain to the miller or the corn merchant; the seed potatoes to the South-bound trains; the ditch-clearing; the carting of peats from the moss, cottars' coal from the boat, and in summer while the touns waited for harvest there was the cart-washing, the harness-checking, the endless twining of straw rope down the length of the cattle-byre when the weather broke. But that again depended on the farmtoun: there were touns where a man would not be sent out if there were the likelihood of a shower wetting his shoulders. There were, alas, many more where he was sent forth in oilskins and would be welcome about the steading only in days of calamitous storm. All but the toughest of farm men were racked by rheumatism by the time they were 40.

But the pattern of work varied in other ways from farmtoun to farmtoun, from region to region, depending on what crops were grown; it had to be set against the wider tapestry of time and events and it changed from decade to decade with the pace of farming advance as one crop chased another out of fashion and it, in its turn, as suddenly lost its appeal. Flax was largely forsaken as the power looms ousted the country handloom weavers; there was a massive flight from wheat after the end of the boom years about 1880, and as the farmtouns found themselves unable to compete against the imports of America's prairie gold. From that time the arable acreages of the farmtouns diminished, though potatoes—a crop that brought Scotland nothing but prestige— provided, for some, a kind of safety net. Dairying, too, had but little competition from abroad and the growing school-milk market alone could make it financially a stabilizing factor. Black corn got a brief following in the 1920s and had completely lost it by the late '30s. And through it all, bold men tampered with rotations and for their impudence got away with it, taking the farmtouns a faltering step forward.

What they could not alter was the hallowed cycle of the year itself. The turn of the seasons imposed their own order on the lives of the folk of the farmtouns; it was a pattern that they measured their own days by; it was all of it older, more primordial, than the time that came on the postman's watch. The grieve might order the farmtoun day but God and the soil itself set the rhythm of the year. Though he might well have ridiculed the notion, that awareness etched itself deep into a man's soul instilling a feel for the land and its changing scene, the melancholy of a winter landscape. About a farmtoun, in time, a man came to know where he stood in the universe.

# IV

## The Farmtoun Crew

THE FARMTOUNS BRED hard men, and no wonder. They were
forever moated with the kind of mud that sucked the boots off
you and sank farm carts (coming home with their turnip-loads)
up to the axle-trees. And such discomfort apart, there was a
tyranny about the great farmtouns; their men were as firmly
shackled by the cry of a hungry beast or a week of fine weather
as any factory hand to the punch-clock at the plant gate.

The farmtoun day began before five o'clock when the bailie
(the stockman) lifted his head from the cold pillow, and dragging
on his trousers as he went, made blear-eyed for the byre, where
his beasts were already bellowing to be fed. Indeed, on dairytouns
with a milk herd the start was even earlier, with the dairy cattle-
man awake almost before some of the single men were in their
bothy beds. In the summer he was up by four while the day was
new-minted, stepping out of his cottar's house into that strangely-
still world before sunrise, a world weird without movement. That
time of the morning was like the dawn of creation or the last days
of eternity. In winter he staggered into pitch darkness, swinging
a stable lantern to light his feet through the mud of the farm road.
A good bailie, like a good shepherd, was a loner. While he was
pushing turnips by the barrowload from an adjoining shed to
silence his hungry beasts or teasing fresh bedding straw under
their hooves, the horsemen of the farmtoun slept on. They had
an hour of sleep left, a half-hour at least. Then it was time to rise,
to feed and groom their Clydesdales. The stable was warmer,
anyway, from the horses' breath and grooming the beasts gave
them an appetite before going to breakfast about a quarter to six.
Appetite was a necessary aperitif, for whether he was married and
cottared or single and bothy-housed, breakfast, like all the other
meals of the day, had a quite predictable monotony: without fail,
it would be brose, an instant-mix of oatmeal and hot water that
could make cold porridge seem like haute cuisine.

The farmtouns did not encourage slow eaters, conversation or bouts of introspection between courses: the men would be back in the stable before six. There the grieve would already be waiting them, to give his orders. And even the dark of a winter morning that made it impossible for the ploughmen to see the gate of the field let alone the straight of the furrow, brought them no respite. Until such time as it came daylight the men would be sent to the barn to thresh and later to the corn loft to put a few quarters of oats through the fanner—the corn-dresser. Both were hard tasks that took their toll of a man's stamina and made him anxious to see the first streaks of dawn drawn across the corn-loft's skylight window. It was time then to yoke the plough and cold though that might be, with the frosty air cutting into his lungs, the horseman preferred it. There was a satisfaction at the plough, in good work, in watching the way the mouldboard flung the ribbon of the furrow unbroken on to its back; there was the steadying dialogue with his pair: encouragement as well as cursing reproach for at times they had him dancing almost between the plough stilts, doing a ballet in the bottom of the furrow.

At eleven it was time to unyoke, to return to the farmtoun and give his Clydesdales their feed before going for his own bite, oatmeal again, in a fresh disguise.

"Denner" was no more a lingering affair than breakfast but at least, back in the stable, there was time to take a seat on one of the cornkists—the large chests in which the horses' oats were stored —fill pipes and take stock of the world's affairs, or what little was known of them, for until the wireless spread its influence in the 1930s as a social integrator, news was late and often garbled by the time it reached the outlying farmtouns. It came piecemeal by the postman, who had it from the merchant, who had time to read newspapers.

The afternoon's shift—a "yoking" it was called in the North-East's Buchan area—was from one o'clock until six or, in winter, until darkness made work in the fields impossible. Then the ploughmen might return to the farmtoun without incurring the cutting edge of the grieve's tongue to stable their Clydesdales for the night. For their beasts it was the end of the day; not for the men. If there was an hour to spare before suppertime, the grieve could be counted on to see that they were not idle. They would have another hour of the barn-mill before they finished and the grieve's watch released them.

Even if there were no other proof, the relentless work-pattern of the farmtoun is irrevocably, though humorously, pinned down in the bothy ballads, that unique collection of farmtoun songs with their long litany of a farm servant's grievances. "Drumdelgie", probably the best-known, quite authentically catalogues the hurry of the farm winter morning, the feeding and grooming of the horses in the stable, the snatched breakfast with pints (laces) still untied, the sweat that can be wrung from the ploughmen's shirts after an hour or so of manning the barn-mill or corn-dresser as they wait for daylight to let them out to the plough or the carting home of turnips for the feeders' byre. Its simple metre has a rhythmic thump as raw and unsophisticated as the life itself:

> Oh ken ye o' Drumdelgie toon
>   Where a' the crack lads go?
> Stra'bogie braw in a' her boun's
>   A bigger canna show.
>
> At five o'clock we quickly rise,
>   And hurry doon the stair,
> It's there to corn oor horses,
>   Likewise to straik their hair.
>
> Syne after workin' half an hour,
>   To the kitchen each one goes;
> It's there to get oor breakfast,
>   Which is generally brose.
>
> We've scarcely got oor brose weel supt,
>   And gi'en oor pints a tie,
> When the foreman cries, "Hullo, my lads!
>   The hour is drawin' nigh."
>
> At sax o'clock the mull's put on,
>   To gie us a' strait wark;
> It tak's four o' us to mak' to her,
>   Till we could wring oor sark.
>
> And when the water is put aff,
>   We hurry doon the stair,
> To get some quarters through the fan,
>   Till daylicht does appear.

When daylicht it begins to peep,
   And the sky begins to clear,
The foreman he cries oot, "My lads,
   Ye'll stay nae langer here!

There's sax o' you'll gae to the ploo,
   And twa can ca' the neeps;
And the owsen they'll be aifter you,
   Wi' strae raips roon their queets."

But when that we were gyaun furth,
   And turnin' oot to yoke,
The snaw dang on sae thick and fast
   That we were like to choke.

The frost had been so very hard,
   The ploo she widna go;
And sae oor cairtin' days commenced
   Among the frost and snow.

Oor horses bein' but young and sma',
   The shafts they didna fill,
And aften needed the saiddler lad
   To help them up the hill.

But we will sing oor horses' praise,
   Though they be young and sma';
For they ootshine the neiper anes
   That tip the road sae braw.

Sae fare ye weel, Drumdelgie,
   For I maun gang awa';
Sae fare ye weel, Drumdelgie,
   Your weety weather and a'.

Fare ye weel, Drumdelgie,
   I bid ye a' adieu;
I leave ye as I got ye—
   A maist unceevil crew.

"Drumdelgie" is typical of its kind, right down to the sour note of the ending. After all, the way they treated men could hardly bring the touns eulogies. Again, of course, it may have been that the singer simply didn't measure up to the crack lads' standards. Typical, too is the bothy poet's good word on the farmtoun's

Clydesdales in spite of the fact that they occasionally needed the encouragement of "the saiddler" (the whip). And in the bygoing he implants history without being aware of it: we know, now, that the Drumdelgie of those days must certainly have been one of the biggest touns in the Strathbogie area, with at least eight plough-men, or horsemen as they were usually called. What he doesn't tell us, alas, is the *full* strength of such a sizeable toun, and for that we have to turn to another ballad, "The Ardlaw Crew", in the same simple style; it gives the complement of Ardlaw, a farmtoun of the North-East Lowlands. The writer was a man named Gordon McQueen who was, as he says, first bailie; the account therefore is first-hand and the names, quite likely, are actually those of his farm colleagues of that time. McQueen, like many another ballad-writer, not only delineates the main individual tasks of the farmtoun men and women but gives some indication of the savage protocol of the life. Obligingly, he gives us the year of his song, a time when the farmtouns were in their heyday:

> It was in the year eighteen-eighty
>   When I put this in rhyme;
> It's nae concernin' things o' auld,
>   It's aboot the present time.
>
> It's nae concernin' things o' auld,
>   The truth I'll tell to you.
> It's jist a verse or twa you'll find
>   Aboot the Ardlaw Crew.
>
> For rhymin's grown sae common noo,
>   That the like o' me maun try
> To get a verse or twa to clink,
>   To gar the time pass by.
>
> Willie Michie is our grieve,
>   He's a very quiet man;
> He can conduct the jolly crew,
>   Wi' muckle skill and can.
>
> James Sutherland is our foreman,
>   His pair is Sharp and Sall;
> He tak's them oot in the mornin',
>   A' jist at the first call.

He tak's them oot in the mornin',
　　A' jist at the first call,
And gies them wark fae morn till nicht,
　　Till evenin' does doonfall.

Sometimes he gaes to the cart,
　　And sometimes to the ploo;
And he must haud the hemp upon the hair,
　　Or else it widna do.

James Scott he is our second man,
　　He's on the list you'll find;
He drives a pair o' young anes,
　　And follows tee behind.

Sandy Ritchie is our third man,
　　Their kickers he can bide;
He has an iron red and a gallant gray,
　　He calls them Bet and Clyde.

Clyde and Bet is an able pair,
　　And so is Sharp and Sall;
They have to do the heavy wark,
　　They're the best among them all.

John Howatt is our fourth man,
　　His pair is Dash and Dan,
He follows them through thick and thin,
　　He's a knackie little man.

George Ritchie is our fifth man,
　　He drives a pair o' broons;
He tak's them oot in the mornin'
　　And mak's them walk their roons.

Sandie Adie is our sixth man,
　　He has a chestnut and a broon;
He follows up the merry crew
　　Upon the Ardlaw Toon.

James Murison is our orra man,
　　He keeps ticht baith close and pens,
And any orra job like that,
　　Siclike as muck the hens.

For me, I am first bailie,
    It's a very sharny shift.
But Whitsunday is comin' roon
    When I can tak' the lift.

James Mowat he is our second bailie,
    He suits the berth fu' weel,
And but and ben the muckle byre
    We gar the barrows wheel.

Donald Adie is our third bailie,
    To plan he is nae slack;
But I am let to understand
    His name is in the task.

William Mutch he is our fourth bailie,
    New Pitsligo is his hame,
And he cam' doon to Ardlaw
    Some Irishmen to tame.

First on the list of the female sex,
    Her name is Maggie Broon,
She has to plan the dairy work
    Upon the Ardlaw Toon.

Next comes our housemaid,
    Her name is Katie Massie,
But I canna say muckle aboot her,
    She is only bit a lassie.

Maggie Simpson is our kitchen maid,
    She has our kail a-makin',
And wi' sae mony hungry mou's,
    She's aften busy bakin'.

Janet Barron is oor oot-woman,
    She is on the roll, oh-ty,
She has to work the ootdoor wark,
    And help to milk the kye.

But noo our gaffer's leavin',
    And nae langer we can bide;
So we'll gang to the hirin's,
    Baith Strichen and Longside.

We will traivel up to Strichen toon,
　　And then we'll tak' the rails;
And if they dinna gie's a blast,
　　We are sure to rug their tails.

So fare-ye-well to Ardlaw,
　　Nae langer we maun stay;
We will tak' oor budgets on oor back,
　　On the twenty-sixth o' May.

Now that is all I've got to say,
　　And I hope I've said naething wrang,
For I jist made it up ae day
　　Tae haud me on-thocht lang.

Composed, as McQueen confesses, to pass the time, and woefully
lacking in any kind of poetic grace or rhyming flair though it is,
the ballad gives an excellent idea of the kind and number of
people needed to run any large-sized farmtoun towards the end
of the 1800s, including the rôle of women workers, indoors and
out. Yet not all the touns were as big, or for that matter, if they
were, as willing to hire labour on such a scale. Few of the lesser
places ran to the luxury of a housemaid unless the master was
coming up in the world—or his wife was anxious that it should be
thought so; fewer still of those small farmtouns would have an
"orra man", an unfortunate designation for that handyman of a
toun who, in later years especially, became its most valued servant.

The ambiguity of his title and misunderstanding of his rôle is
largely one of linguistic confusion. The word "orra", in the old
everyday language of the ballad touns of the North-East Lowlands,
meant "trashy" or "rubbishy" (though, like most words of its
kind, it defies exact translation), "orra trock" being the con-
demnatory dismissal for the most trashy of trivia, signalling utter
worthlessness. A man accused of being an "orra creature" would
be a coarse character of foul habits and as foully spoken, a subtler
nuance of the word and one that distinguished that kind of person
from a "puir creature", whose plight was as deplorable but suffered
with dignity. Hence the uncertainty about the orra man's place—
and desirability—around a farmtoun. Here, however, the word
was used in another of its subtle applications to mean "spare" and
was free of all value judgement. In this meaning, too, it was

applied to the "orra beast"—the Clydesdale kept as a replacement and not one of a pair—to the "orra loon", and indeed to the "orra woman", if the toun had one.

Far from being the least-employable of men, the orra man, in the latter years of the great farmtouns, enjoyed a status and wages equal to that of the foreman at least. And that deservedly, for a good orra man (to compound the contradiction) was a master of all trades. He could plough a rig with the best of them, "sort" a byre-ful of cattle in the bailie's absence, put on the water wheel for the barn-mill and take over the foreman's rôle for a day or two if the first horseman fell ill. In normal times though, when he wasn't needed as a stand-in, his duties could be less onerous, and these are neatly explained in "The Ardlaw Crew", described by Gavin Greig, that prince of ballad-collectors, as one of the best of its kind illustrating the "local life and language". Besides ensuring the tidiness of the farmyard, however, the orra man was the man who had to wash out the emptied guano bags in the mill-dam and string them out to dry for return to the merchant.

There is some inkling at least of the position from which he rose in the early days of the farmtouns—and excuse perhaps for the light in which he was so often seen—in Alexander Gibson's *Under the Cruisie*, a picture of farmtoun life in the mid-1800s:

> A handy man's the "orra" man,
> 　To him nought comes amiss,
> He's seen the world—deny't who can.
> 　And sampled it I guess.
>
> Been tinker, soldier in his time,
> 　And roved the country o'er;
> Now settled in this northern clime,
> 　He'll rove again no more.

So, it seems, the orra man may have risen from a lowly rung of the ladder to his later high status in the hierarchy of the farm-touns, and if the old designation clung he had this consolation: there was recognition of his worth as one of the farmtoun crew. That was more than the "orra loon" of the North-East farmtouns could say. His status was lowly; his was the last-washed face after the supper brose, which had been served him last. To call him under-privileged would be to overstate his standing. Straight from school—the dominie having given him a day off from his lessons a week or two before to seek his first fee at the hiring fair —he was just beginning to learn the horseman's job by driving home the bailie's turnips with the orra beast, which could be relied on to do the right thing whenever he didn't. He would have to prove his worth and reach halflin status at least before he could be given the Horseman's Word with its legendary power over beast and womenfolk. But he had plenty of time, for that was a secret, under the horsemen's rules, that could not be imparted to "anyone under sixteen, nor above the age of forty-five".

Like "orra", the word "loon" is one from the world of the North-East farmtouns; in that dour countryside it applied to all young male teenagers. Yet in one respect at least the "orra loon" did have it better than his older colleague; when he had grown to the halflin age he would have the dignity of being described as such in the newspaper advertisements. "Halflin" as a term almost certainly enjoyed a lineage more ancient than "horseman"; it was probably the consonant-dropping Doric for "halfling", itself a likely corruption of the word "half-hind" from the days of the seventeenth-century farmtouns when a "whole hind" had to supply an assistant. In the Buchan area and beyond it, the halflin was known also as "the little man", right up to the 1930s in districts where change came slow-footed. The measure of course was one of rank rather than stature, like the term "little bailie", where the word "little" was used to indicate "second". Far from being puny, there were "bailie loons" (like many halflins) who were broad-shouldered, strapping youths. They came under the control of the first or head bailie who, to give droll point to the relationship, might be a small-boned man. Their titles reflected the status of their respective byres: the muckle byre and the little byre (sometimes the high byre and the low byre). In the former, the feeders' byre, beasts fattened for market at three years old, being finally "brought on" by the addition of bruised corn and oil-cake to their straw-and-turnips diet. Their replacements in the stalls of the muckle byre came from the little bailie's domain—in the homely language of the North-East Lowlands, the "stirkies' byre". Like Ardlaw of the ballad, however, big touns in this beef-rearing region often had an embarrassing plurality of bailies.

The sizeable farmtoun would have a strapper, at least up

to the 1920s. He drove the master's gig when he went from home, cleaned it, and groomed the shelt that was yoked into it. Like the bailies, he was roped in by the grieve for an afternoon "thrash", once a week or so, when the barn-mill was put on to put through a couple of corn-ricks for livestock feed and bedding. In the South-East in the early 1800s, the farmtoun crew might include a hedger, ditcher and dyker, many of these men getting the equivalent of a grieve's pay, but later this kind of work was mainly done by contract or on a day-labour basis.

Quite the most intriguing enigma of the ballads though is the recurring use of the word "crew" to describe the complement of farmtoun men, and it is tempting, not unjustifiably, to see a parallel with shipboard life in the daily existence of the men of the "improved" single-tenant touns standing each in the isolation of its own stone-dyked fields in a countryside so different from what it had lately been. Add to that the habit, apparently, of imposing fines on men who strayed from the farmtoun in the evenings without permission, and one begins to see a stronger comparison. There were fines for other things besides but, as always, there were reasons why the bothy men of any big toun were prepared to defy them and the iron discipline they were meant to impose, as the ballad "Sleepytown", in some of its verses, makes clear:

> The order was to bed at nine,
>   And never leave the town,
> And for every time we left it
>   We'd be fined half-a-crown.
>
> Knowles he was fined mony's a time,
>   But never lost the heart;
> And I mysel' was fined a pound
>   For turnin' up a cart.
>
> We never heeded Adam,
>   But aye we took the pass,
> Sometimes to buy tobacco,
>   Sometimes to see the lass.

Defiant though the tone is, it points up the separation from society that the men of the lonely farmtouns sometimes endured.

The pay certainly was not an inducement for it was never princely. Transition from the system of payment in kind was slow and uneven. In the mid-1800s, that kindly man of the Lothians, master-farmer George Hope of Fenton Barns, was paying his married ploughmen about fourteen shillings (70p) a week, with a house provided, naturally, but also with the keep of a cow and some yardage of potatoes in the field crop. This kind of concession gave way to the "perquisites" arrangement and a little later, in 1876 at the other end of the country, in the Aberdeenshire uplands of Cluny, John Strachan of Mains of Corsindae, we learn from his diary, was paying his first horseman £26 a year, with house and garden and perquisites of eight loads of peats or a ton of coal, and twelve bushels of potatoes. His second horseman about that time was getting £16 the half-year (as a bothy-housed man, presumably, without house and perquisites) and his orra man £11 5s (£11.25p). But there are indications that John Strachan, too, was a considerate man and other figures for the same region that very year point up the big differences in "bargaining" at the hiring fair. The foreman at Castlehill, a 106-acre toun just off the main Aberchirder–Netherdale road was getting £14 9s (£14.45p) the half-year with his board at the farm; the second horseman £6 2s (£6.10p); the loon £5 1s (£5.05p). He was a great one, too, for incentives was John Strachan, though he would not have recognized the industrial nuance of the word; he promised one of his men ten shillings more "if he pleased me" and that foreman was to get an extra £1 if the stacks he built at harvest-time proved watertight.

By that time though farming was approaching the end of the boom years and it is probably significant that over the hill in Torphins, in 1881, the first horseman at another farmtoun, Easter Beltie, a married man and therefore with a cottar house and the usual perquisites, was getting only £22 a year; the second horseman, a champion ploughman, £9 the half-year. In the next 50 years, the horseman's pay would double, but would never be enough to keep him comfortably in step with the prices in the country shops. In the 1930s, the married horseman (with tied cottage and the usual perquisites) would have a "fee" of about £1 a week. It would take World War II and the nation-wide Control of Engagement Order of 1940 to save the ploughman by setting his wage at £2 8s (£2.40p) a week. There would be no more haggling in the hiring market with some unscrupulous farmer who held all the best cards. After all the years of hardship, it was a king's ransom.

# V

## *The Iron Men*

THOUGH THERE WERE those who occasionally doubted it, grieves were mortal men and full of frailty. They drank when they shouldn't have and sometimes wenched unwisely. One does not wish to speak ill of them yet, it has to be admitted, they could often be rascally men. Certainly they were the hardest of the hard men of the farmtouns, and maybe they had to be for the men they had to drive so relentlessly never took kindly to subservience. They ran tyrannous touns and such was the iron of their rule that the men would wait to be spoken to; servant and grieve might almost collide as both crossed the farmtoun close, eye meet eye, but no word would be exchanged. That said, one should acknowledge the unique rôle these bossmen of the farmtouns played, not only in the success of a particular toun but also in the greater annals of improved farming. They travelled to some effect: they went South, in the early days of East Lothian's ascendancy, Henry Grey Graham reminds us in *The Social Life of Scotland in the Eighteenth Century*, along with experienced ploughmen, to instruct "English yokels to farm". And in the earlier part of the 1800s Grant of Rothiemurchus, so Elizabeth, his diarist daughter tells us in her celebrated *Memoirs of a Highland Lady*, sent a Scots grieve down to his estate in Hertfordshire to imbue some understanding there of Scottish techniques. On his Twyford estate the Strathspey laird, like so many "improvers" a lawyer and some-time MP, had

> introduced rotation crops, deep ploughing, weeding, hay made in three days, corn cut with the scythe and housed as cut, cattle stall-fed; and I remember above all a field of turnips that all, far and near, came to look and wonder at—turnips in drills and two feet apart in the rows, each turnip the size of a man's head. It was the first such field ever seen in these parts, and so much admired by two-footed animals that little was left for the

four-footed. All the lanes in the neighbourhood were strewn with the green tops cut off by the depredators. The Scotch farming made the Hertfordshire bumpkins stare during the short period it was tried by us.

Even allowing for the fact that the young Elizabeth Grant was never happier than when catching out others in their lack of sophistication, there seems to be little reason to doubt the truth of her account.

Many grieves, indeed, were quite remarkable men who would have gone far in any other career had they ever been given the opportunity of following it. More than most, the grieves have a central part in the lore of the farmtouns; some, themselves, became legendary figures. In *The Book of Bennachie*, reflecting life on and around that landmark mountain of the North-East Lowlands, Dr Maitland Mackie tells the story of a grieve who fell behindhand, or so he thought, with the muck-spreading in the days when the only muck-spreader known was the human frame. It was sore work at the best of times, dragging manure out of a midden where it had been thoroughly trampled down by court-housed beasts, but as the task of penance the grieve gave himself it became a feat of incredible strength and will. He filled 96 cart-loads of muck each day for three days, making a total in all of 288 cart-loads. Reckoning on 15 cwt a load, Dr Mackie makes the overall muck-tonnage 216. Yet even that may be a conservative estimate since the farm-cart's design was based on a one-ton capacity. Either way, the achievement is a staggering one—but typical of the exceptional feats of strength and endurance of the men of the farmtouns. In the face of it, it is comforting to hear of another grieve with the wit, one supposes, not to have attempted it. Again, as somehow do so many of the tales of the farmtouns, it concerns manure, this time in its sophisticated fertilizer form. When this arrived at one farmtoun for the first time, after years of use of guano, which had its own distinctive pungency, the grieve, opening the comparatively odourless sacks, was something less than impressed. However, he set the farm men to work, hand-spreading from shoulder-slung hoppers. It may have been that the spreading was a little too relaxed or simply that the ordering had been wrong, but near the end of the operation the grieve was confronted by one of the spreaders who confessed that though the fertilizer was now

finished there was ground still to cover. Doubtless dreading the
explosion to come, the man waited. But the grieve thought only for
a moment. "Ach, away back an' tell them to keep walking, and
keep waving their arms," he said. "It will make nae bloody
difference!"

What is surprising in view of such drollery and dedication, is
the almost total absence of the grieve from the mainstream of
bothy balladry. There is, it is true, "Kempie" the grieve of "The
Barns o' Beneuches", a caird-tongued (rough-spoken) man whose
constant seiging (raging) finally leads to his own dismissal—and,
as the old Term day approaches, the rejoicing of men he has treated
so harshly.

> My freens ane and a', I'll sing you a sang,
> If ye a' haud your weeshts, it winna tak' me lang;
> It's aboot a mannie Kempie, he's a caird-tongued fang,
>    For he rages like a deevil in the mornin'.
>
> He's a wee little mannie, wi' a fern-tickled face,
> A' the days o' your life ye ne'er saw sic a mess;
> Ye wid sweer he hid deserted fae some tinkler race
>    Afore they had got wakened in the mornin'.
>
> At the Barnyards o' Beneuches he has lang been a grieve,
> But come May the twenty-saxt he has to pad, I believe;
> For he's seiged at his men till his maister's gein him's leave,
>    For he canna get them up in the mornin'.
>
> But when he doth rise ye never heard sic a soun',
> For he'll seige ye and damn ye like ony dragoon,
> He's lang caird tongue you'd hear't roon the toon,
>    Afore he gets his breakfast in the mornin'.
>
> Dinna gang to the Barns if ye wish to be weel,
> A' the days of your life ye ne'er saw sic a chiel,
> He'll treat ye to a breakfast o' buttermilk and meal,
>    Wi' a drink o' soor ale in the mornin'.
>
> We get beef bree whiles weel seasoned wi' reek,
> Wi' three seeds o' barley, and the smell o' a leek;
> If you're nae pleased wi' that he'll nane o' yer cheek,
>    But he'll pit ye fae his toon in the mornin'.

The ballad-writer passes on to castigate the guidwife of the farmtoun in similar terms before returning to the thought that is
sustaining him through the last days of his "engagement" there:

But it's May the twenty-saxt will be here in a crack,
And we'll a' leave the Barns never mair to gang back,
We'll gang blithely doon the road like an ill-tongued pack
Singin', Kempie he can follow in the mornin'.

Such is the savour of revenge, and to be sure there were grieves
whose ways were a byword in the feeing market, who took up sly
observation posts about the steading, watch in hand, to time their
suspecting horsemen out of the stable in a morning, or who were
impervious to the cruelty of sending a sick horse to the plough. Yet
"Kempie" one suspects is too extreme an archetypal figure.

The reticence of the ballads may of course be due to a cautionary
discretion, for the grieve's power over human destiny was proverbial. Even if a horseman were not staying on at a toun at the
Term the grieve's goodwill could go with him and pave his way
home to another place; his ill-will, on the other hand, could
spread a man's reputation for poor work through the parish like a
contagion. A good grieve exploited that power, a bad grieve
abused it. If a horseman had been troublesome, the approach of
Term-time gave the grieve a chance to get even. There came the
morning, inevitably, when he stepped into the stable ready to
speak about new "engagements", for such was the farmtouns'
word for the verbal contract that would keep a man at a toun for
the next six-month or twelve-month. There were grieves who
relished the moment, who would cast dark hints in the week or so
beforehand while keeping their cards up their sleeve until the last.

In the stable, seated on their cornkists, the horsemen waited to
be approached individually. The dialogue was guarded, careful of
rebuff; it had an almost traditional pattern.

"What think you on it, then?" a man would be asked quietly,
the grieve's own casualness a quality he could well afford in the
labour-surplus market of the times. "Would you be thinking of
biding?"

The ploughman's reply would be as unconcerned, as non-
committal, for in the shrewd world of stable bargaining enthusiasm
would put him immediately at a disadvantage. His answer was
almost as carefully rehearsed.

"Maybe, maybe—it would depend. Gin there were a pound or
two in it, like———"

It was the grieve's turn again; now it was he being tested; horror

would spread on his features, bringing well-couched protest:
"Twa pounds, laddie—by God, I don't know. I doubt gin the
Maister would even listen to it——" He would shake his head; on
this day he too was an actor.

"Hillhead's men get twa-three pounds mair nor we do, ye ken."

The horseman's assertion wasn't a threat; or was it? If he were
a good man it was likely that Hilly would have noticed the quality
of his work in some roadside field, and maybe had good reports of
his character. The grieve had to take that into account while
instantly refuting the man's claim.

"God, likely—and his pigs will have wings. And anyway, even
gin it be true, just look at the auld ploughs and the poor beasts his
folk have tae work wi'——" And maybe as an afterthought: "And
out ilka day of God's weather, rain or shine. There's nae stable
work at Hillhead on a weety morning. Na, na——" The grieve
would stroke his chin, his beard, his nose, begin to fill his pipe,
cutting plug tobacco and balling it in the palm of one hand with
the heel of the other. Gaining time. "Now—gin it was just the one
pound ye were seeking——" His voice would give hope between
puffs as he lit his Stonehaven pipe.

A horseman well enough pleased with his place (or with the
servant lass) could be tempted. Besides, rarely had he the grieve's
guile or his long years of experience of bargaining.

"Ach, well then——"

"A pound more then, the half-year?" The grieve's nod
confirming his own acquiescence. "Is't a bargain?"

"It's a bargain."

So the grieve moved on, up the stable, to the next man and the
man after, having a word here a laugh there, pointedly missing a
man or two in his progress of the cornkists. In this case there would
be no word between horseman and grieve; what was clear in the
harsh tradition of that day was that they were not being "speired
tae bide". Come the day of the feeing market they would be
looking for a new toun.

The reason of course was not always a man's work but sometimes
his moral character, especially if it were a toun where the Word
was given its full weight and the farmer was an elder of the kirk,
Free or Established. So any man leaving a toun of his own will
would take the precaution of getting a character reference from
the grieve before he went: in many an old ploughman's kist, to

this day, lie those old, stilted testimonials, written often on unsuitable paper; they betray many a grieve's lack in the scholarly skills. Conversely, any advertisement in the newspaper for a new cottar man would bring to a grieve's door in an evening a string of men bearing such lines of good conduct. In the grieve's kitchen they would await their turn for an audience in the ben-end, where the fire had been specially lit, anxiously swinging their bonnets as they sat on the hard kitchen chairs. Not all of them were shy men; some while they waited took on the grieve's wife (or better still, his daughter if she were old enough) as though they had known each other all their lives. And on a wet night and for a man who had come far, and had as far to go home again, tea would be made and a friendship soldered. In the face of such kindness nervous men became garrulous and gave their inmost fears away.

Grieves were greater or lesser figures in the countryside; it all depended on the farmtoun. Where it was of some size and the farmer himself was that and nothing more, the grieve's rôle could be little more than that of an errand-boy carrying his master's orders into the stable. Where the farmer had other interests, however, commercial or civic, there was a latitude that could make his grieve a man of affairs, and the same would be the case where the master's death had left the toun to his widow. About some lairds' touns where the factor had his hands full there might be the same freedom, and dusk up and down the country saw grieves slipping into the Big House by the side door as dinner ended, like priests to a shriving. There they were shown cap in hand into the study where their vigour and foresight were commended—or their muddle-headedness damned out of hand.

Tenants of smaller farmtouns of course were their own grieves, relying on the first horseman to force the pace when mart days took them from home. There were middling-sized touns that did without a grieve even when the farmer himself took little interest. They sometimes worked on a diabolical expedient: that of making the horseman first out of the stable door in the morning foreman for the day. Bad farmtoun management though it was, it was masterly psychology; it meant that a horseman with ambition and a natural liking for power would rise early—and that his easier-going bothy companions would have to be up even earlier if they wanted to thwart him. What it never compensated for was the lack of a grieve's eye constantly on the watch for poor work or back-sliding in the care of beast or equipment.

Though it seemed that they went on forever, grieves grew old like other men. Past their prime, such was the legendary aura that could grow round them, they had whiles quietly to dissemble, to resort even to sly deception. As prowess slipped from them they pointedly began to avoid the bravado of seizing hold of a two-hundredweight sack of barley just to show the ease with which it could be handled. Or to eschew the even wilder exhibitionism of lifting down a plough from a farm cart single-handed. There are rumours even that as their arms tired and their eyesight dimmed they had extra-width hoes quietly made for themselves by the smith, in order to keep up at the turnip-hoeing. And the arm thrown round the kitchen lass's shoulders in a moment of fun became a kindly gesture, protective even, a far cry from the fires and the randy hand of youth.

If there were too many men of "Kempie's" kind, there were also grieves who were respected, and even loved. They were iron men no less, but they managed to temper it with fairness, even the odd act of kindly humanity. Such men bred their own kind of strange loyalty. There was a tradition that when a grieve left a farmtoun, or was sent from it, the horsemen he had hired home to it would go too. The result, in the language of that long-ago countryside, was a "clean toun"—that is, a toun that would start with a fresh complement of men come Term Day. Above all, what the best grieves did was to take the farmtouns into the days of their greatness, and having done so, jealously sustained their reputations. Like old soldiers, it seemed that they did not die, only faded away. But when they did their funerals were greatly attended.

# VI

## *Lonely Men of the Glens*

SHEPHERDS WERE singular men, the lonely men of the farm-touns. In the Border sheeplands and on the wilder Highland estates where the flock was the major concern, their status and wages often equalled that of a grieve; in other areas where sheep were kept as a stabilizing fringe to acres of fluctuating arable, they were regarded as little better than gangrel folk and paid as poorly. Always though, the shepherd was an isolated figure on the land-scape, a man as solitary in his way as the mole-catcher, a silhouette with his collies on some distant hillside. If he poached a little as a sideline it was as often to break the boredom between the busy seasons of lambing, shearing and dipping as from any need to fill his pot. At times, in fact, he became almost as much an outsider as any of the wandering folk of the countryside; his bothy loneli-ness could become so much a part of his life that when he finally came home to his farmtoun his overwhelming compulsion might be to turn and run—back to the hills. Such was his alienation sometimes from society. In time he could take to drink, and his teeth blackened by long years of tobacco usage and a reliance on primitive hygiene; in his hill bothy he made his porridge once a week in the big bothy pot and then poured it into the drawer of a chest, it was said—there to be cut in cold slices when he needed it.

But his loneliness bred a resilience and independence of mind. During the Disruption, that evangelical squabble that decimated the Established Church of Scotland during the 1840s, a Suther-land sheep farmer, coming on his shepherds one day as they were washing and shearing, presented them with a paper to sign. He would be back shortly, he said, to collect it. It was, in the common coercion of that time, a certificate demanding their allegiance to the Established Church of their master and doubtless they were well aware of the instant dismissals that had resulted at other farmtouns from failure to sign. They might in the circum-stances simply have left the certificate unsigned and given

themselves the benefit of a certain ambivalence, but no; they
turned the paper on its reverse side and wrote: *"We, the
undersigned, adhere to the Free Church of Scotland."*

All the same, they would come down from the hills, from their
summer bothies in the Grampians, from the hill country of the
Lammermuirs and the Cheviots of the Border, some of these
lonely men to the kirk on the Sabbath, for the lamb sales and for the
sheepdog trials, that innovation of the later 1800s that would
become in our time a televisual treat. Held up and down the
country in the late months of summer, the trials let a shepherd
show his sheepcraft to the world and allowed his collies to do the
same. Performers of calibre, like champion ploughmen, went
forward into the wider world in international competition. They
said that a good collie did his own thinking, and certainly he
sometimes had to, for the day was as much his as his shepherd's
as he gathered and guided the trials sheep through a series of
manoeuvres to the tense finale. Then, working in a marked circle
some 50 yards in diameter, he would have to select five marked
sheep from his twenty and herd them unaided into a small pen. So
different then that limelight from the lone stillness of the hills,
though even here in the arena the shepherd was a man alone as he
played out with his pawn dogs a game of patience and uncanny
anticipation.

Elsewhere, round the more modest country shows and in areas
where shepherd men were less ambitious of success and took to
the show-ring for the pure entertainment of their own folk and the
possibility of a share of the prize-money, they worked with fewer
sheep, maybe only a half-dozen, dividing them between two pens.
For a finale their dogs would pick up a further three sheep from a
fold half-a-mile away, to drove them and pen them in the arena.
There would be a sizeable flock in the fold—to make sure that the
sheep released from it were themselves unrehearsed.

It was, as somebody once said, a masterly exercise in calculating
cunning against uncomprehending stupidity. Little wonder,
surely, if the shepherd found his solace as often in the illicit
*bothan* as in Mother Kirk.

There were, of course, other occasions when he could show his
skills and enter into open and unashamed competition with
shepherds from rival farmtouns: the yearly tup fair, for instance.
Dressing the tups for their big day was like the count-down to

something in the world of haute couture: fleeces were clipped to emphasize the animals' good points and conceal their flaws, and the night before, the beasts' faces were washed and painted white and their fleeces given a finishing dust-down with sheep dip. They went into the ring like painted warriors to bring instant fame— or failure—to the man who had groomed them; a prize was the seal on his reputation, on his special magic, and like ploughing champions, he was rarely slow to celebrate that ephemeral moment of success. The day ended in drams and when morning came it was often not welcome. Conviviality broke in, too, about the start of July, when the Border shepherds met to form the parish clipping bands, the teams of shearers who converged on the farmtouns in turn—the order traditional and unvarying—to clip the flocks. That too was a kind of social occasion, like the visit of the threshing mill, when the farmer lavished hospitality and the barn rafters at the end of the clip could echo to the scraich of wild fiddles. The next day the clipping band would move on, but the young shepherds at least had had the chance to look for wives where they might not otherwise have been socially acceptable. The moment, doubtless, was sweet, and the memory of it had to last long enough when they got back to their Border hills, where they might be visited by the farmer himself only half a dozen times in the year. More frequent intrusion into their affairs would have been considered unforgivable meddling since the shepherd knew more about sheep than the farmer himself could ever hope to.

That knowledge was in-born for shepherds came down in generations. If his start in life was in the lonely cottage of the hirsel about the turn of the century, it is likely that, as his father before him, he left the parish school at twelve to herd a half-hirsel before graduating to a full hirsel, and maybe the charge of 600 ewes, in four or five years' time. His skill was implanted from childhood. Its index was the price his lambs fetched in the auction mart. Yet his essential loneness extended even into the conditions of his employment and the "bargain" he made with his farmer in the bustle of the feeing fair. Up until the early-1900s, in fact, he was set apart from the rest of the men of the farmtoun by the fact that his "fee" was a year's grazing for his own little flock. But that was a chancy way to live: disease, disaster, glut—anything —could wipe out his animals or the expected profit from them. It was the shepherds themselves who pressed for commutation to money wages, and it is a measure of their standing in the Border farmtouns that they were then paid a rate £3 or £4 a year more than that of a top horseman. Besides which, they each had one "fat sheep" a year from the flock—the choice was the shepherd's alone—as well as five extra stones of oatmeal, ostensibly to make gruel for sick sheep during the lambing season. For all that, by the start of World War II, there would be an alarming decline in the number of old-style shepherds. They were a special breed and perhaps it was unreasonable that a leisured age should expect to furnish the hills with men who never dreamed of its neon glare.

From the South and the Solway to the far North and Strathnaver, whatever their status, they had something in common: that awesome willingness to risk their own safety for the sake of their flocks. Every winter took its toll; baffled by blizzards, they lost their bearings on the hillsides they had known from boyhood and unaccountably wandered into the swirling white curtain till exhaustion claimed them and they lay down to die, their collies beside them. In the spring, when the snow had gone, they would be found, miles from the track they should have taken: in one bad year of storm alone, on a single Sunday, they buried twelve shepherds in a Moffat kirkyard.

It was no different in the Highlands. There, too, the death of a shepherd brought its own poignancy and left a shadow forever in the mind. The Rev. T. D. Miller, in his *Tales of a Highland Parish*, wrote of it:

Hardly a season passes without some poor wanderer being found on the hill or highway in his last sleep. During my ministry the feeble ray of a tallow candle might have been seen every dark winter night shining from a little window of a cottage on the hillside because the gudewife had been told that had there been a light shown there, a faithful shepherd, who had succumbed through fatigue at no great distance from her door, might have been saved.

In a year of savage storm a farmtoun could sometimes pay its rent from the price raised on the skins of smothered sheep. It was to avoid loss on that calamitous scale that the flocks of Mr Miller's parish of Glenshee, were driven down from their high grazings to the lower lands of Perthshire and Forfarshire for the winter.

The shepherds' sacrifice was a measure of the wealth that rode on the back of the Cheviot ewe, the Blackface, and their cross-breeds. That wealth was not new; sheep had been one of the main sources of revenue for the abbeys, whose wool drew the rich merchants from as far as Flanders and subsequently Florence and Venice. It was the monastic houses that gave sheep a hold on the Borders; by 1300, and probably before, there were sheep on the Cheviot hills.

It was from the South and those Border hills that the flock-masters of the Highland glens re-stocked their sheepwalks each year with Blackface lambs. They went south to the market at Lanark Moor, until the auction mart put an end to it the chief sale for the lambs bred in the Borders. Year after year, the flock-masters would return to the fair to buy from the same hirsel. It was a long, long way from Lanark Moor to Glenshee, for man and beast alike. But let Mr Miller, minister for many years in that bare glen, tell of it:

Before the advent of the railway the journey from the Highlands to Lanark was done on foot. Along with their shepherds, the flockmasters walked to Edinburgh from Glenshee, making the distance of eighty miles in two stages. After spending a night there they next day completed the remaining fifty miles to the scene of the sales. Returning with their flock of lambs they travelled by easy stages, and when night fell enclosed them in some field by the way, but never ceased to guard them with their sheepdogs; and, for the whole week, they never had their clothes off. These long journeys could only be done by men in the full vigour of life and the sustaining power of their endurance was oatmeal.

The sheep may be stupid but it was never inconsequential; it altered the whole course of Highland history; it was the instigator of one of Scotland's great social tragedies, the Clearances which continued with cynical evictions right up to the 1880s, long after the sheep itself had been discredited as a fortune-saver, and left behind them in the long Highland memory a hatred of sheep and their shepherds. Yet it had begun innocently enough. Sir John Sinclair—Agricultural Sir John—of Ulbster was the man responsible. A man with a finger in every pie and prepared always to

give the benefit of his advice whether it was asked for or not, there
is, nonetheless, no reason in this instance to suppose that Sir
John acted other than with complete sincerity and integrity. His
plan was to import the much-improved Cheviot into the North,
where the native sheep was still something of an agricultural joke
and little more than a household pet; each lamb was given a name
at birth. Never slow to set the example he wished others to follow
—and in this he was no different from the great improvers of the
Lowlands—he took north to his Caithness estates a flock of 500
breeding Cheviot ewes and their rams, and their shepherds with
them. Neither the shepherds nor the local farmers expected the
breed to survive the hard winter of those Northern moors but they
did, much to the general astonishment.

Such success might indeed have overcome all Northern resistance and brought the Cheviot sheep in as a most useful prop to the
unsteadiness of Highland farming. The tenantry, alas, were slower
to react than the British Wool Society, which now offered one of
the most amazing of farming package deals to Highland lairds: a
ready-made flock of 150 ewes and 50 rams at prices of 20 shillings
and 36 shillings respectively. It was bold, it was visionary. Sadly
it was aimed at the wrong sector; not the small farmtouns that
Sir John wanted to impress but the landlords. Many of them,
teetering on bankruptcy, seized the straw presented to them—and
in turn opened the door to the big graziers and rich flockmasters of
the South. The big sheepwalks largely failed from the lairds'
point of view; the flocks declined and the sheepwalks became deer
forests or grouse moors. But by then the crofters and small farmers
had gone, never to return. A great opportunity had been lost to
stabilize the Highlands, to knit North with South. The lairds were
discredited in the eyes of their own folk.

Yet by the early-1800s the son of a Border shepherd was already
building the roads and bridges that would help the inter-change of
ideas between Highlands and Lowlands. His name was Thomas
Telford; he was born at Westerkirk, near Langholm, in Dumfries-
shire, and buried in Westminster Abbey. Amid all his marvels of
engineering and construction work he took time to build small,
plain kirks in the lonely glens—places, one would like to think, for
those shepherds of later generations who would come down from
the hills and their summer bothies to hear the plain word of God.
He was a man, certainly, who understood shepherds and the high

price they put on their personal integrity and loyalty to their flocks. Still an unknown journeyman mason when his father died, he carved the gravestone in Westerkirk's kirkyard to a man who had lived "thirty-three years as an unblameable shepherd". It's the epitaph every shepherd would have wished for.

# VII

## *Women of the Touns*

SINCE KNOWABLE TIME and probably beyond it, from the first days of human settlement, the nurturing hand of husbandry had been woman's. Her arm wielded the sickle and turned the quern-stones or small-millstones. Arguably, the quern-stones were the early hub of civilization for they turned Man the Hunter into Man the Crop-raiser. That link with the primeval past, with its heavy symbolism, would continue in the Highland and Hebridean landscape almost up to our own time, certainly up to the 1880s, when the quern fell out of use, its end hastened— where it was not actually engineered—by the lairds, who saw their mills standing idle while the croft-wives ground their own meal to avoid the multures or mill charges. Today, that time is com- memorated in the name of a Hebridean loch: The Loch of the Querns. Into it were hurled the quern-stones smashed by the laird's ground officers; crofting progress had taken another step forward.

The sickle and the ritual of ancient harvests continued a little longer. The informative Burt in his *Letters from a Gentleman in the North of Scotland* tells us how it was, well into the 1700s. He records an Englishwoman's astonishment at seeing a wife and her mother wielding sickles amid the corn while the husband lolled fully-dressed nearby; she asked the mother-in-law the reason for such indolence, and whether she minded, only to be told that her son-in-law was a *gentleman*. Of the larger farmtouns of the Highlands in the 1720s, Burt also reported that

where there are any number of women employed in harvest- work, they all keep time together, by several barbarous tones of the voice; and stoop and rise together, as regularly as a rank of soldiers, when they ground their arms. Sometimes they are incited to their work by the sound of a bagpipe; and by either of these, they proceed with great alacrity, it being disgraceful for any one to be out of time with the sickle. They use the same tone, or piper, when they thicken the new-woven plaiding, instead of a fulling-mill.

At other times, not far from Fort William, he saw "women with a little horse-dung brought upon their backs, in creels, or baskets, from that garrison; and on their knees, spreading it with their hands upon the land, and even breaking the balls, that every part of the little spot might have its due proportion."

The years changed little in the Highlands.

Those later women of the crofts and farmtouns even wielded a lighter version of the flail in threshing the grain, and if they did not sow the seed corn, they often pulled the springtime harrows that bedded it into the ground since their subsistence economy could not run to the keep of a horse. That essential pattern was repeated, too, on the bare, wind-swept crofts of the North-East; the women of Lumphanan's Perkhill colony harvested with the sickle while their roadmen husbands broke their quota of stones by the turnpike. Hardy women, they too would not have jibbed at taking up the flail. And there is plenty of evidence to suggest that the women of the old Lowlands farmtouns were of the same breed. If one needed proof, it is amply implied by the conditions under which the cot-toun wife occupied her damp, insanitary home: she was expected to shear daily in the harvest field, to assist with winning the hay and the peats, to help with the muck-spreading, the threshing, winnowing and the cleaning of the byre and stable, as well as working the lime kiln.

It was improvement that first began to loosen the grip of such women on the land. With the new single-unit farmtouns and the end of the old ridge and furrow cultivation, they began, like the quern-stones of the Lowlands, to be seen less on the farming landscape. The immemorial pattern was broken, too, by the early dawn of farm mechanization and, even before it, by the innovation of the scythe as the cutting tool of harvest. It was the scythe that started the reversal of rôles; with it, the men of the farmtouns cut the standing corn while the women gathered. Its widening use, when it was realized that it did not, after all, shake the grain unduly, brought to an end those yearly migrations of the young girls of the Highlands and North-East from their townships to the big, earlier harvests of the South, where they sold their labour in

such shearers' markets as that at Glasgow Cross. The sickle had
been an itinerant implement, easily carried by the shearer lasses
from one farmtoun to the next; the scythe, with its sweeping blade,
was heavy, a tool of settlement; it demanded a man's strength, as
did the scythe-heuk, the enlarged sickle-type blade often favoured
as an alternative. But those Lothian "hairsts", like so much else,
would pass into the balladry of the farmtouns to leave their
memory forever tinged slightly by scandal.

Not that women disappeared from the fields. Far from it. But
their employment, as the 1800s wore on, became increasingly a
seasonal thing, and this is shown by the staffing of that well-known
Lothians farmtoun, Fenton Barns. In the 1830s, while its most
famous tenant was but a stripling of eighteen, it had in winter a
complement of seventeen men and six women, in summer an
extra eighteen women and boys. The winter figure may also be a
fairly accurate reflection of the women/men worker ratio on the
farmtouns.

Where women were employed the year round in the fields of the
South-East, their engagement might be as bondagers, an arrangement that threw the long shadow of the past on to the days of high
farming and was little more than an ameliorated version of the
conditions that harassed the cot-toun wife of earlier years. The
provision of a bondager, in the mid-1800s and much later, was
part of the ploughman's "engagement". Her help was demanded at
harvest-time, as payment for the cottage the ploughman occupied.
And there was a further very relevant proviso: that she be available
as a day outworker when needed. It was a system that raised the
black wrath of ministers and kirk elders and the acrimony of a
time growing more and more socially conscious. And it was
detested heartily by the ploughmen themselves. Yet, an effort by
the farmtoun men to end it, in the mid-1800s, failed miserably
and the distinctive dress of the bondager—a drugget skirt, blouse
(often neatly tailored), side-buttoning boots and wide-brimmed
black straw hat rimmed with red ruching—was seen in the fields of
the Southern landscape right up to World War I. Elsewhere the
employment pattern for women outworkers varied. In Angus, for
instance, where the weaving industry drew away the girls of the
region's crofts and farmtouns into its more congenial conditions
and better pay, bothies were built on the big Lothians style in an
attempt to bring single girl workers down from the North. And

Farmtoun folk: *above*, the entire crew of a 170-acre toun in Scotland's North-East in the early-1900s, including the grieve (seated on the horse-trough by the stable door), two horsemen, two bailies, an orra loon and kitchen and ben-the-house maids. *Below*, a scene that tells the story of the small touns in the depression years: the tenant's wife was more often carrying feed and water to stock than in her own kitchen and the hens scavenged among the implements that slowly gathered rust.

Summer and winter: *above*, ricking hay in the Borders in the early-1900s; the haytime was a task that brought the farmtoun wives into the fields and sunshine to lend a hand—and small boys were given the job of leading the horse. But the chill mornings of winter, when frost bit the fingers, brought only the horsemen, *below*, to cart home the turnips for the feeders' byre, where the cattle fattened for market and the bailies toiled seven days a week.

A vanished glory: *above*, proud ricks rise in a Lothians stackyard as the sheaves of harvest are led in by longcart, their sides impressively patted to perfection by the clapper carried by the man on the right. Watertight, they will await the threshing-mill. *Below*, that classic scene, as the steam threshing-mill works in the cornyard at Shaws farmtoun, near Selkirk, early this century. The threshing-mill brought an air of electric excitement to a farmtoun. Now cornyards have been ousted by the combine-harvester.

Bothy lads, eating out: suppertime at a big farmtoun, if one may judge by the well-built masonry behind the group, here posed traditionally in the way that burlesqued the hard life. As usual, the picture prominently features the brose caups, the men's individual milk flagons as well as the bothy kettle. Point of incongruity: the shiny, polished boots of the man second from left. Could he have been the strapper, the lad who drove the master's phaeton when he went to town?

Bothy lads, eating in: much more the way it was, this scene pins down the uncomfortable quality of bothy life just before the start of World War I. Taken as the bothy's occupants sit at their mid-day meal, obviously a brose, bread and milk affair, it shows (centre foreground) the bothy cooking pot and milk flagon, a horseman's kist (far right) and the common bothy bench-type seat. Two of the men wear nicky-tams, straps worn just below the knee to give breeches-style warmth, while the third has opted for leggings. The farmtoun: Gagie, Wellbank, near Dundee.

Contrasts: outside an old thatched smiddy of the 1890s at Gamrie, in Banffshire, the sleek lines of long-stilted horse ploughs. Always, the smith and his shop had a fascination for small boys, who found it far more interesting than the schoolroom. Then a busy country smith might be keeping up to 300 farmtoun Clydesdales adequately shod. But he was more than a shoeing smith and implement-mender. Obligingly, he would singe sheeps' heads for broth—or keep a wooden leg in working order.

Industrial hearth of the farmtouns: all the interior clutter of a Montrose smiddy, with two forges and numerous anvils, in the early-1900s but quite typical of all country smithies in the days when the Clydesdale was supreme and the smiths worked late to keep up with the work. The smiddy's air was fetid with the smell of hot iron and hoof parings but its forges at least kindled warmth in the bones of the ploughman as his beasts were shod.

Shepherd of the hills and about the last of his kind: John Grant, *far left*, Novar Estate shepherd, with two prize rams and his blanket-plaid over his shoulder. His tall, slightly-stooped figure was instantly recognized round the Northern marts of the 1920s and he could recall storms so severe that the farmtoun's rent could be raised from the skins of smothered sheep. Shearer of the Isles: wool was the prize on the back of a black-faced sheep and the summer shearing was always a convivial (and competitive) task. *Left*, an Arran shearer uses an improvised clipping stool: a bench built up of stones and turf.

right up and into the present century all-women turnip-singling
gangs were a common enough sight. They were drawn not only
from that ready reservoir of farmtoun labour, the cottar-wives,
but also from the nearby villages. Like the men of a later time (and
of lesser farmtouns) their pace was probably highly competitive,
and though their stories may have been less coarse the gossip
must have been ferocious.

The pay for the woman outworker was never worthwhile: the
bondagers of the South-East, harvest apart, got 10d (4½p) a day in
the mid-1800s; at the other end of the country almost, at Haddo
House, in Aberdeenshire, twenty years earlier, for out-women the
pay was 8d (3½p) a day with the women finding their own food at a
time when the price of a pound of sugar was 9d (4p) and tea cost
6d (2½p) an ounce. A later time and different farmtoun needs would
hardly improve the woman-worker's fee. A cottar wife at a North-
East dairytoun in the 1930s, milking morning and night in the
dairy byre, seven days a week, might be adding as little as 5s 3d
(26p) a week to her ploughman husband's wage.

The regular milking of cows was not the only byre work the
farmtoun women did, for up until the late-1800s at least they
might be found working as stockwomen. And even later, of course,
the conditions of war brought them back as bailies to the byres of
the dairy and stock-fattening touns. Gibson's poetic picture of the
mid-eighteenth century in *Under the Cruisie*, mentions "the lass
that mucks the byre", and from the farmtoun ballad, "Sowens for
Sap" comes quite convincing evidence that women were so
employed on equal terms (if not equal pay) with the men of a
toun:

> Likewise we hae an orra woman
> For waiting on oor nowte.
> Ye widna see the like o' her
> The country roon aboot;
> For she does wear her leggin's
> And snap her brose, I troo——
> Sowens for sap at our New Tap,
> Ye'll find it winna do——

The latter two lines recur through the ballad, indicating in the
idiom of the region and the time that the second-rate had no place
about that particular farmtoun, in itself a high testimonial to the

C

woman-bailie concerned. "Nowte," of course, is cattle, and interesting also is the mention of her leggings, presumably the winding of straw-ropes round the ankles and the lower part of the leg, in the days before wellington boots, to keep out the mud of the farmyard.

Nearer our own time, the arrival of the threshing-mill in any district brought its own unique demand for the delicate skill of the "lowsers"—those women with the knack of cutting the binder twine on the sheaf near the knot so that a thrifty farmer could use the string again: to tie the corn sacks at that moment being filled at the end of the thresher. In their voluminous skirts, tight blouses, and with their wide-brimmed hats scarf-tied under their chins against the all-pervasive dust, they stood through the windiest of winter days on the mill's high shelvings, cutting the twine and preparing the sheaves thrown down from the rick, for the man feeding the mill-drum. Only when the mill stopped at "piece-time" or for the dinner hour did they come down from their high perch, giving male hands a chance to guide a dainty ankle on to the ladder rungs, and make off for the concealment of the nearest hedge or building. Any but the men of the farmtouns might have misunderstood their errand, which was simply to shake the mice out of their petticoats. About the big touns of the Borders and Lothians where they built their stackyards high and wide (and at times singularly handsome), the women of the farmtoun as "striddlers" would play a vital rôle in speeding-up the stack-building by "feeding" the sheaves forked up off the harvest carts to the builder on ricks that could be up to twenty feet in diameter.

But if progress around the great Lowlands farmtouns gradually diminished the rôle of the woman outworker, it in no way lessened the chores of the womenfolk about the toun itself, or their influence on its management. From the middle of the 1800s right through to the 1900s and well up to the outbreak of World War II there were farmtouns which were dominated by formidable mistresses; they indeed, were a hardy breed, in the direct line of their ancestors, those tough, leathery-skinned women of the crofts and the earlier farmtouns. They were wives and rough-tongued mothers who took to their marriage beds without great ceremony, child-bed without much wonder—and even then, often not till they had finished the milking or the feeding of the hens. Many of them were sonsily-built, Rubensesque rather than creatures of frailty; they

could stook without strain all day in the harvest field before going
home to supper all their folk; fork sheaves to the cart at the leading-
in with the best of the farmtoun men. Like the croft daughters
they were, about the small touns in the days before the reaper they
would bind the whole yoking in the wake of their man's scythe and
think nothing of it; and more than a few took their drams with the
men at the end of the day—or before they put on their lace-
mutches to set out for the kirk on a cold Sabbath. Mistresses of
bigger touns, they were more than capable of giving any fee'd
man a tongue-lashing when their men were from home on mart-
days, and of putting the fear of Hell into any halflin they found
tampering with their daughters or their kitchen-maids. Between-
times, if necessity demanded, they could push barrowfuls of muck
from the cattle-byre and had the kind of well-disciplined noses
that didn't jib at its strong odours. They excited a kind of admiration, even among the men they were keeping on woefully short
rations.

In marriage, they took off their wellingtons or high-laced boots
when they came in from the evening milking, and undid their
stays. They went to their beds in cotton shifts, letting their waist-
long hair tumble down from the captive plaits or bun of the day to
spill gold or silver across the pillow. Many of them took on weak
men and propped them against all misfortune for the most of a
lifetime, confounding delusion at night by climbing meekly in
behind their menfolk's backs in the recessed dark of the kitchen
box-bed. In the mornings they lit their man's clay pipe with an
ember of glowing peat, kept it puffing till he had finished his
breakfast brose, and stuck it firmly between his teeth as (late
again) he strode out to the stable. It was a kind of Scotch kiss that,
in the weary, word-shy world of the crofts and small farmtouns.
And when he came home from the mart incapable and worsened
with drink, they took the breeks off him and put him to his bed
till he was sober. Out of marriage and in early widowhood, such
women in the soft moments of life lay down with a man on the
sheltered side of a stook or in the dark of the barn. Their bairns
took their mother's name, and were none the worse for it. For all
that they needed dour, work-hardened men, it is doubtful if the
farmtouns could have functioned at all without these hardy women.

Their rule in their own farmhouse kitchens was inviolable.
There the pattern had been set from the start of the big bothy-

touns. The day of the kitchen-maid—fee'd home to the farmtoun from the hiring fair for a six-month, like the rest of the farmtoun crew—was a marathon of the purest drudgery. About any big toun, the "kitchie deem's" day started at five, when she rose to light the kitchen fire and put on the iron kettle to boil water for the bothy-men's breakfast. After that, at many a small or medium-sized toun, there would be the milking to do before she could start her kitchen work: an endless routine of washing, butter- and cheese-making, pot-scouring and scrubbing, always interrupted by the "meating" of men. On washdays, as on every other day, the water would have to be carried if not from the burn from the water-pump in the farmyard, to fill the big washing-pot hung ready on the swee above the fire. While the water heated, the wash-tub would be set up on its trestle, in the middle of the kitchen's cold stone floor. When the water was ready, it would be poured into the tub—and the washing began in a fury of rubbing with fists and washboard, until the mistress was satisfied. Blankets, however, were a job for the feet and hilarity could be allowed. The tub would be set down off its stand on to the floor while the kitchen maid, barefooted, treaded the dirt out of them, her skirts kirtled according to her innocence or her desire to lose it should one of the farmtoun men come in. Hardened cases, nothing ventured, took off their frocks entirely and stood in their petticoats as hope wore thin. Clothes and blankets alike had to be wrung by hand, for few farm kitchens stretched to the labour-saving of a mangle, and emptying the tub might well mean carrying it to the edge of the midden, a task impossible for a kitchen lass by herself. In that case, it would have to be emptied pail by painful pail.

Butter was churned in the middle of that same stone floor, and emerged in unruly lumps to be teased and slapped between butter-pats till it showed the disciplined refinement suitable for the master's table; and was almost untouched by human hand all the way to the chill of the milkhouse's marble shelf. Cheese was made and kebbucked before being veiled like a bride in muslin and chessilled to dry for three weeks or so in the cheesepress which stood (frequently) in the farmyard, exposed to all the activity of the farmtoun. At maturity, it was sometimes difficult to say whether the cheese's flavour owed most to the skill of the kitchen maid or to the texture of the farmtoun's dust. Hens' food was boiled (and reluctantly set aside to boil the men's brose

kettle yet again), eggs gathered and graded for the grocer and the
ben-the-house tea-table and then set aside on the big kitchen
dresser with its serried lines of brose caups and the big dished
soup plates that were taken down for the days of harvest and visits
of the threshing-mill. Interminably, oatcakes were baked, and in
summer the jam-pot hottered through the still afternoons, its
contents all to be later jarred away in the ben-the-house press. In a
corner, sowens "sids"—the inner grain husks left after the oats
had been milled—soaked in their wooden tub like stagnant water
against the night when they could be served up as a supper
luxury and a change from the continual diet of oatmeal.

The kitchen cooking range of later farmtoun days exerted its
own tyranny. Each morning its high binks or hobs, its oven-front
and grate were black-leaded, its clear metal, knobs and swee (with
its links and pot-crooks) brightened by scouring them with
emery paper. The stone floor had to be washed daily against the
encroachment of farmtoun dirt, twice a day even where the
mistress was finicky and set in her ways or where it was a toun
that swam in mud all the months from October to April—which
was most of them. Its plain wooden table and chairs would be
scrubbed regularly, depending on much the same factors. And the
kitchen maid's day didn't end when she had given the bothy men
their supper about seven; after that there might still be the
evening milking.

For her sometimes seventeen-hour day, the pay was pitifully
small, and it seems to have varied little through the years, though it
might have fluctuated with the humanity of the gudeman. Mary
Melvin, going home to Mains of Corsindae in 1876, got £6 15s
(£6.75p) for the half-year while Maggie Thom, that same year
and in the same region, got over £2 less. Some 40 or so years
later, the crofter's lass who fee'd home for the half-year to
Raitshill of Tarves, in that same North-East area of the ballad-
touns, got £6. Her day was from five in the morning until about
ten at night. She got Sunday off one week, the Sunday afternoon
only the next. Truly, the servant lasses of the farmtouns, those
madonnas of the brose caups, could hardly have been worse off
sold into slavery. And some would infinitely have preferred it.

# VIII

## *Nomads in Farm Carts*

THE COTTAR-FOLK of the farmtouns travelled light. Each year,
usually at the Whitsunday Term but sometimes the Martinmas
one as well, they threw their pitifully-few possessions into a farm
cart and took the road to a new toun, like pilgrims to a promised
land. Few, in fact, travelled hopefully for the years had taught
them better, but in time the May "flitting" became an addiction, a
rooted custom of a rootless society. It may even have been a kind
of protest against the tied-cottage tyranny of that time that made
a married farm servant—a skilled grieve, ploughman, bailie or orra
man—give his wife and children as hostages to fortune. In addition
to his "fee" for his year's engagement (paid to him weekly and in
such small doses as barely to keep them all alive, with the balance
half-yearly), he had the use of a house and his perquisites, those
staples of Scottish existence: oatmeal, milk, potatoes, and coal or
peat to keep his fire burning. Charitable though it might seem, it
was an iniquitous system that blemished the name of many a good
farmtoun and gave the unscrupulous farmer an unbeatable
advantage. Where a single, bothy lad with a mother's house to go
home to if it came to it, could tell a miserly or tyrannical farmer
what he thought of him and fare little the worse for it, the cottar,
with his family to think of, could hardly afford to. This fact set
him at a permanent disadvantage in the feeing market, too, and he
was often viciously exploited. Many of today's farming dynasties
were shamefully founded on the wealth that came from
squeezing such men into penury. It was all a sad down-come for
men who would once by their title have enjoyed for their labour
the use of their own small parcel of land and a more settled
position in country society, for that clearly once was the case.
  The cottar's past is as shadowy as that of the early farmtoun
settlements, but he first appears from the mists of monastic
farming history in the mid-1400s, when the Abbey of Coupar
Angus formed a cottars' village at Balgersho in which each man was

given from one to three acres and a house. The abbey may also have been the instigator of another innovation, reflected in the later society of the farmtouns. Besides an apprenticeship scheme that enabled a good cottar to graduate to a tenancy, it had, according to T. Bedford Franklin's *A History of Scottish Farming*, a further option whereby he could choose instead to become a "farming craftsman". Were not such men the forerunners of the cottars of the mid-1700s account book of the laird of Balnespick; men who worked loom and needle and awl? At Monymusk, too, where the great improvement laird Sir Archibald Grant would later drag his reluctant tenantry into the new farming at his coat-tails, the abbey had its cottar settlement—six houses with their gardens for the priory's dependants—the forerunner of today's village.

His later status, too, is still as a land-holder of sorts, beholden to the gudeman (or husbandman), that aristocrat of the peasant classes, and giving his toil in lieu of a hut and kailyard, a portion perhaps of both the infield and the outfield. Burns' sentimentalized Saturday Night cottar may have been just such a man, one not without weight and some voice in any gathering of farming men. In the North-East Lowlands, the set-up has been succinctly described by the Rev. Pratt, chronicler of *Buchan*:

> The Gudeman had, according to the extent of his farm, more or fewer sub-tenants, called Cottars, who had each a pendicle of land attached to his cottage—some as much as would maintain two cows, a horse, and a sheep; others less; in some cases only a kailyard. For this they paid partly in money-rent, but chiefly in the labour they were bound to give to the Gudeman, in seedtime and harvest, at hay-making and peat-cutting, at "kiln and mill", and, in short, on every occasion when their services were required.

The cot-toun was always near the big house or farmtoun so that labour was always, and almost instantly, on call. What Pratt also makes clear is that the cottars' lives were of a settled nature.

> ... once established, they were rarely removed, the farmer looking upon them as his special dependants, and they regarding him as a sort of father or chief, to whose interests and service

they were bound. The children generally succeeded the parents in the service, and thus every large farm had its own peculiar and attached colony.

Then, as later, the cottar was a man without title or deed to his house or his land. And in a Highlands context his position was little different, though before the Forty-five at least, one not without honour.

As a sub-tenant of the tacksman holding farmlands from the clan chief—every man of a clan being then an occupier and cultivator of land—his obligation was to put his sword at his chief's disposal should it be needed, though in addition he might have to pay also in meal, butter and a portion of sheep as well as giving labour to the tacksman on his own lands when this need arose. It was a system, naturally, that gave the ambitious or ill-intentioned clan chief an overwhelming belief in high-density settlement and sharp sub-division, for the more sword arms he could raise to the acre the more powerful his voice in that trouble-some time. But the result in human terms was something else again; such a policy in time reduced plots to a size barely able to support a family: sufficient only to graze a cow or two and as much land as could be sown with a boll of seed oats. And if there was discontent before the Rebellion, there was disaster after it, not to say complete disillusionment, for such bold chiefs had suddenly to leave the stage. Attainted, their territories came savagely under the rule of an alien landlordism, fierce renting and, at times, cynical development. The result was a kind of Highland stag-nation. The Highland cottar though was shaken loose, to become a statistic in the study of population-drift. He went south to the industrially-growing cities, abroad in the belly of some disease-ridden hell of an emigration ship.

Elsewhere, and a little later, enclosure and the turnpike road set his Lowlands counterpart free to become the wandering Bedouin of the ballad-touns. From then his way was all downhill.

Landless, he became the pawn of landed men. Incredibly, as improvement spread, it made his life even more intolerable; it was a time which, while it did not at first dramatically reduce the number of men needed on the land of the Lowlands, did sub-stantially change their standing one to another, sharpening distinctions between crofter and tenant-farmer and between farmer and cottar. The bitterness of change, the way in which it was sometimes achieved, drove a wedge between classes that never quite healed. There was tampering, too, in other ways with the old structure of country society for the cottar ploughman or herd might be additionally the tailor, weaver or shoemaker, and this rôle passed down to the crofter.

With the rise of the big farmtouns the cottar's payment in kind was increasingly commuted to wages in cash and this too set his labour at a loss for while he was being paid in kind he was, arguably, still getting the full value of his portion. Money wages made it possible to withhold even this, and the cottar, however loyal or skilled, was denied his share of farming's growing wealth. As the 1800s advanced his future more than ever was that of the old labourer of the Lowlands cot-touns from which the farmtouns had traditionally drawn much of their work-force. These existed well into the 1800s and their squalor was legendary. Listen to the bitterness of Alexander Somerville, who wrote one of the first working-class autobiographies and a classic of its time; he is describing the cot-toun dwelling, in a row of such sheds in Berwickshire, where he was one of eight children:

> About twelve feet by fourteen, and not so high in the walls as will allow a man to get in without stooping. That place without ceiling or anything beneath the bare tiles of the roof; with no floor save the common clay; without a cupboard or recess of any kind; with no grate but iron bars which the tenants carried to it, built up and took away when they left it; with no partition of any kind save what the beds made; with no windows save four small panes at one side—it was this house . . . which, to obtain leave to live in, my mother sheared the harvest and carried the stacks.

The bitterness is understandable: Somerville's father was in a small way of farming in the Ochils when his laird's programme of amalgamations robbed him of his holding. He ended his days an impoverished labourer on the farms of the Borders, one of the many "dispossessed". And though his condemnation is of the misery of his parents' hovel, Somerville draws attention, in passing, to the special thraldom of the cottar wife. That, too, took long a-changing, and its long echo came down even to the 1930s, when a cottar-wife-to-milk might be a condition of her husband's employment. There was this difference though: she would be paid. Saved, her silver in time would be enough to buy the family's first wireless.

Happily the days of the old cot-touns were soon to end, their *raison d'être* outmoded by the new high farming, the changing face of country society, the new patterns of settlement. They may have housed shoemaker, tailor, weaver and the men of other trades and special skills as well as an ever-ready pool of farmtoun labour, but even the tradesmen among them had "taken a hairst" and been landsmen first and craftsmen afterwards. From the early 1800s they began to meet a diminishing need as the early mechanization of farming advanced with the birth of the reaper and the adoption of the barn-mill and the chain-plough which needed only one man and a pair of horses. In their turn the folk of the cot-touns drifted away to the towns—or to re-settlement in the planned villages that had begun to spring up round the country, promoted by the improving lairds with the best of intentions and sometimes the saddest results.

In the new farmtoun society that emerged—tenants, cottars and bothy-housed men—his special commitments made the cottar's lot the least enviable. The cheapness and ready availability of farmtoun labour were the constants that ever undermined him. There was always a man at his back, behind him in the queue, ready to take a shilling or two less and in more urgent need of the tied cottar house. But it was not lack of intelligence that snared him forever in the fields of some cottar-toun, it was the pinching poverty. It made sure that he had no room for manoeuvre. Often it robbed him of all dignity.

Yet, if his fee fell abysmally behind, his dwelling at least showed improvement. From as early as 1832 the then Highland and Agricultural Society of Scotland was offering prizes for its betterment. Lairds and farmers were encouraged to build two- and three-roomed houses instead of single apartments like the one in which Alexander Somerville had first faced life in the raw. All the same, even in the 1920s it still often took all the cottar wife's ingenuity to turn a cottar-dwelling into a home. New-married, she might work her own economic miracle by trading some of her man's perquisite oatmeal and potatoes with the travelling merchant for needles and thread, or simply in a straight cash exchange for the money to buy curtain material in the nearest town next time she could get to it. There might be a chance to supplement her man's fee, in some areas, with fruit-picking in season, potato-gathering, or even by taking a hairst at some smaller, neighbouring toun if she were not by then heavily-bairned. Such supplements were a way of affording a new frock or a new bed, even—where the lass had come from something better—a ben-the-house suite. But when the children came, as they usually did, all the oatmeal and potatoes would be needed to fill hungry stomachs—there would not be the silver to provide home comforts. Nor, given the lifestyle and the sometimes appalling condition of cottar-houses—left by previous occupants with wallpaper flapping and a window or two broken, and with the mice constantly scurrying behind the wainscoting—was there much incentive. Into the 1930s, in the North-East Lowlands many cottar-homes did not have the decency of an outside privvy, and their occupants were obliged on the coldest of nights to take a pail to the outside coal-shed, or in summer to squat in the protective screen of some nearby wood.

It was little wonder that come Term Day, the roads of every parish rang with the crunch and slither of the iron-ringed wheels of farmcarts as they carried the flittings of the cottar families home to their new touns. It was the custom for a man's new toun to send the two boxcarts that would move him. The loading didn't take that long.

Somerville's folk had carried their firebars with them, and George Hope, when he first took over the running of Fenton Barns about 1860, noted that the people of the cot-touns carried their own locks for fitting to their dwelling doors. The cottar man of the 1920s and early '30s had a few more possessions perhaps but he moved on as easily. On a fine day it was like starting a new life, on a wet one it was a heartbreak. It would take a month to get the soaked bedding dry again and if the journey was a matter of some miles the black iron bedsteads could be rusted by the time they got there. It was a Grapes of Wrath existence that, in the North especially, never really got unionized and it was always cheaper for the farmer to change the cottar than to repair the leaky roof of his dwelling. Such folk did not put down roots; they lived without most of the creature comforts, always on the edge of flight.

# IX

# The Bothy Lads

MORE THAN ANYTHING the rigours of the bothy were what turned a farm boy into a man—almost overnight; when he was sometimes little more than eleven; when he was still so small in stature that he needed to stand on a box to put the collar over a Clydesdale's head; while he still might not have mastered his fear of the dark and was glad of the kitchen lass to put him to his bed and blow out the candle. It was a bigging designed to house labour—the itinerant unmarried men who moved from farmtoun to farmtoun with every feeing fair—as easily and as cheaply as the byre housed the beasts of the field. If there were a difference at all it was only that any stockman who treated his cattle half as callously would have been sent from the farmtoun. The bothy varied in its capacity from area to area, depending on the size of the farmtoun as well as the pattern of its agriculture. In the Lothians it was a kind of agricultural barracks—an unlovely long, pantiled shed in lonely isolation on the otherwise pleasant flatlands of the country-side, Cobbett found, shocked by the encounter in 1832 on one of his rural rides. Only a savage army discipline could have made it habitable. In parts of the West and in the North-East Lowlands it was a bare apartment built above or on to the end of the stable, or above the cartshed, sometimes on the edge of the midden—anywhere where an outcrop of masonry could not interfere with the serious business of the farmtoun.

The Lothians bothy housed a whole crew of men, as did those of Moray, the Mearns and Angus; the smaller North-East version, called the chaumer (presumably from the French *chaumière*, though never can that language have been more misguidedly used to give the cachet of sophistication), usually held only a handful, perhaps four horsemen, a stockman and an orra man at most.

If there were degrees of squalor, then undoubtedly the bothies of the Lothians were the worst. Sheer numbers ensured it. In

1855, the East Lothian farm, with its flat acres and steam-age husbandry, might carry a work-force of up to 90; though some were housed in the cot-touns that equally blotched the landscape, a substantial number were bothy folk whose cooking might be done for them either by an old wife, one of their number specially appointed to the job, or by any or all of them as hunger moved them. But, northwards into Fife, at Dunfermline, Cobbett found conditions almost as bad, if a trifle more intimate. In one bothy he looked into, measuring sixteen foot by eighteen foot but sleeping six men, he found the furnishings basic, to say the least: three beds stood on its earthen floor, there were six brose caups—the wooden bowls from which the farm men traditionally supped— and a large iron pot, for cooking the other main dietary item, potatoes. There was a heap of those, loose, under one of the beds, and ten bushels of coal were piled in a corner of that austere apartment. Coming farther north, Angus acquired a kind of bothy notoriety; here the dependence on the cheapness of the system was such that a young man wanting to marry had to look for a "fee" outside the county in order to get a cottar house for himself and his bride. Nor were the occupants of the bothies always men. For six weeks of the year, at least into the latter half of the 1800s, there were women in the bothies of the Lothians: the girls who went south from the Highlands, Deeside, and other districts where crops ripened later, in all-girl and mixed harvest crews.

That the bothy system could in time have a brutalizing effect on the young men and young women of the farmtouns, there is little doubt; the astonishing thing is that the scars it left were not worse. Many years after the experience, at the turn of the century, an old man from the slopes of Bennachie in the North-East Lowlands was able to look back on the hardships of his youth with little rancour. His written reminiscences were published, long years later, in that area's newspaper, *The Press and Journal*:

My first farm chaumer was a hut resembling a pighouse, the floor of which was 18 inches below the ground level. In rainy weather the water came in at the door and ran out under the wall at the other end of the hovel. There was no fireplace. I had planks to walk on to get to bed with dry feet. . . . And I was a boy of eleven, alone.

That was about the 1850s. His next fee took him to a farmtoun bothy above the stable where the horses had first breathed the air. Rats ran in its roof-thatch, so that he and his bothy companion soon got into the habit of holding their heads downwards over the side of the bed in the morning before opening their eyes. During the night, while they slept, the dust the rats had shaken from the thatch would have covered their faces.

So, though his radicalism might make one inclined to discount some of Cobbett's criticism, there is little doubt that what he reported was substantially true. We have the word of a vastly different man: Hugh Miller, the Cromarty stonemason who took the crofters' part in the Clearances and who became editor of *Witness*. His acquaintance with bothy life was a lot closer than that of the blunt man of Surrey. Travelling round the steadings of the northernly counties of Scotland as an apprentice stonemason, he had to live in the bothies for the single farm men. Recalling his first encounter with the life, in what seems to have been a big bothy for the region, he wrote:

> Some twenty or thirty years before it had been a barn; for it had formed part of an older steading, of which all the other buildings had been pulled down, to make way for the more modern erection. It was a dingy, low, thatched building, bulged in the side-walls in a dozen different places, and green atop with chickweed and stonecrop. One long apartment, without partition or ceiling, occupied the interior from gable to gable. A row of undressed deal-beds ran along the sides. There was a fire at each gable, or rather a place at which fires might be lighted, for there were no chimneys; the narrow slits in the walls were crammed with turf; the roof leaked in a dozen different places; and along the ridge the sky might be seen from end to end of the apartment. We learned to know what o'clock it was, when we awoke in the night-time, by the stars which we saw glimmering through the opening.
>
> It was, in truth, a comfortless habitation for human creatures in a wet and gusty November, and the inmates were as rugged as their dwelling-place was rude.

It was the kind of material that the Free Kirk paper's editor was to rework again and again in his newspaper and in his books such as

*My Schools and Schoolmasters*—and use as ammunition against the cynicism of the Moderate-inclined lairds and larger tenant farmers. Again, he talks of

> . . . twenty-four workmen crowded in a rusty corn-kiln, open from gable to gable and not above thirty feet in length. A row of rude beds, formed of undressed slabs, ran along the sides; and against one of the gables there blazed a line of fires. . . . A few of the soberer workmen were engaged in "baking and firing" oaten cakes, and a few more occupied with equal sobriety in cooking their evening porridge: but in front of the building there was a wild party of apprentices.

Those slab-built beds, by the way, were filled with hay, a soft-enough bed, if a little dusty. But like others before him and since, Miller found the rats a problem. A colleague had his ear bitten as he slept, and to keep them away from their oatmeal they had to string the sack by a rope from the rafters.

Interesting, though here perhaps one should allow for Miller's asceticism as for Cobbett's radicalism, is the stressed contrast between the sobriety of some of the occupants and the "wildness" of the remainder. It would have been surprising indeed if men left so ill-equipped to look after themselves had not found it easier at times to tip the contents of a whisky bottle down their throats than to make a pan of porridge. The belief that the bothy life was highly licentious (as opposed to just immoderately immoral), especially when the hairst and other seasonal work brought the lasses to the big farms of the South, may be a little wide of the reality. John Ord, the Glasgow police superintendent who saved so many fine bothy songs of the 1800s in his *Bothy Songs and Ballads*, refutes the idea of indiscriminate mixing of the sexes in the harvest bothies as the all-girl or mixed crews travelled round from toun to toun with their sickles. He based a part of his judgement at least on the ballad the "Lothian Hairst", written it is thought by one of the Highland lasses of such a squad about the mid-1800s. The grain crops undertaken were cut, gathered and stooked at a pre-arranged price per acre. The words of the song tell of the itinerant life of the band of shearers and of their foreman who led them. He was called Logan, and sometimes gives his name to the song, here in the slightly-Anglicized version of Ord's own book:

On August twelfth from Aberdeen
   We sailed upon the *Prince*,
And landed safe at Clifford's fields,
   Our harvest to commence.

For six lang weeks the country roun'
   Frae toon to toon we went;
We took richt weel wi' the Lothian fare
   And aye was weel content.

Our master, William Mathieson,
   From sweet Deeside he came;
Our foreman came from that same place,
   An' Logan was his name.

I followed Logan on the point,
   Sae weel's he laid it down,
And sae boldly as he's led our squad
   O'er mony's the thistley toon.

My mate and I could get nae chance
   For Logan's watchful eye,
And wi' the lads we got nae sport,
   For Logan was sae sly.

He cleared our bothy every night
   Before he went to sleep,
And never left behind him one,
   But strict his rules did keep.

And when we come to Aberdeen
   He weel deserves a spree,
For the herdin' o' us a' sae weel
   From the Lothian lads we're free.

Farewell Mackenzie, Reid and Rose,
   And all your jovial crew,
An' Logan, Jock and Chapman, Pratt,
   And Royal Stuart too.

We'll fill a glass and drink it round
   Before the boat will start,
And may we safely reach the shore,
   And all in friendship part.

The ballad makes it clear that Logan imposed a curfew for visitors to the girls' bothy; whether other foremen were as strict seems open to doubt. Ord, of course, is entitled to his opinion, but one could feel happier with it were the song not so laced with a slight disappointment. There may well have been some temptation, in bothies that had changed hardly at all from the time of Cobbett's visit 30 years earlier, to find some diversion after a hard day in the hairst field.

The end of the roving harvest bands—superseded by the reaper and the Irishmen with their larger scythe-heuks who cut tangled crops on the same old contract basis—brought an end to such speculation, but the Free Kirk was far from being the kind of body that could let all the iniquities of bothy life lie, especially when they could be used for lambasting the lairds. Its spokesman on such affairs was the Rev. Dr James Begg, a man rarely at a loss for an ill-word against the avarice that had brought the bothy system into being. He lays the blame squarely at the proprietors' door:

> The origin of the system was quite recent, and to be traced to a short-sighted idea of economy arising from the fact that many of the large landed proprietors of Scotland were non-resident and had no personal connection with the country, and their object was simply to get high rents with as little outlay as possible. . . . No man was entitled to use his property to the injury of his neighbours, and when landlords, for the sake of saving the paltry sum necessary to erect ploughmen's cottages, betook themselves to the immoral expedient of accommodating them in filthy hovels called bothies, they outraged every principle of justice or expediency.

But not all the bothies were bad; there were farmtouns—in the North-East especially, with its smaller chaumer system—where young farm lads were smothered with motherliness and fed like turkey cocks by their master's wives; they were given leave to sit at the kitchen fire and, thus tolerated, came to air their views with the familiarity of one of the family; before they went to their cold bothies they were comforted with a cup of cocoa or a bowl of sowens. But that, of course, was in the latter days of the old farmtouns, in the present century, and such touns were few and existed only where the gudeman was maybe an elder of the kirk

and from charity or fear for his soul could not countenance the
stark neglect of another human being. Even so, there was a rub in
feeing home to such farmtouns: the farmer, like as not, would be a
strong advocate of the Presbyterian principle of salvation through
work, and a believer that idle hands soon had a hand in mischief.
He made sure his farm folk did not have the time to be
backsliders.

Where the bothy-housed men looked after themselves without
the help of a bothy-wife (usually an elderly woman who would
make their simple meals, light the fire and give the bothy a per-
functory sweep with the besom) the cattle-bailie would have the
job of cooking the crew's food, since his work kept him usually
in the vicinity of the steading. He would be allowed to stop work
half an hour earlier at night, too, to get the bothy fire lit. Whatever
his skills as a stockman, his culinary talents rarely stretched beyond
the basics of oatmeal and tatties. Elsewhere, and especially about
the smaller touns of the North-East Lowlands, the chaumer men
were fed by the kitchen-maid in the farmhouse kitchen. There they
got their supper at seven with an ungracious suddenty and were
then sent from the farmhouse to their bothy, each giving his face
a spit-wash in the kitchen sink in the by-going and a rub on the
sacking towel hanging on the kitchen door before he stepped into
the night. Here, as in the hoe-rig or the stable, the farmtoun
protocol was as rigid as any palace's. The first horseman washed
first, just as he set the pace in the ploughing and the tone about the
farm steading. He got the best seat by the bothy fire and was first
served with his food at the head of the farm kitchen table; a fourth
horseman neither sat to his supper nor rose from it till the foreman
did so; and if he had any sense at all, he left the kitchen lass alone
till such time as the "first" man had been rebuffed.

It was to avoid such attentions, unwelcome or otherwise, that
the servant lass had orders to light the men's bothy fire while they
were all in the kitchen at their supper. In the cold charity of the
farmtouns, the later "ration" of coal might be just one bucketful
for the entire evening, and the fire could be out and cold by eight
without having dried the day's mist off the chaumer walls. Faced
with such miserliness resourceful bothy-lads leaving the kitchen
after their evening meal would find themselves stumbling against
the peatstack by the door—and a peat apiece under their jackets
as they straightened up to walk away from it. Failing that, there

was always the odd fencepost that could be removed without danger of the fence itself collapsing.

The years added little to the meagre furnishings of the bothy. Even in the 1920s and 1930s, its contents were sparse: besides the beds and the closed-in corner stove or open fire, there might be a form and a chair or two to sit on, a broken mirror on the wall where a man could see to trim his whiskers or moustaches or put on a dicky to go to a dance. The box-beds of later time though were an improvement on the primitive bunks of Miller's day. The mattresses, made of striped ticking, were filled yearly with fresh chaff the corn-husks left after the mill had threshed the grain. If he kept his drawers, vest and socks on (which he usually did) a man could stay warm in them on even the coldest of northern nights. But even if it had, by the grace of some kindly mistress, lace curtains to mask its windows or blinds to pull against the night and the blatter of rain on the window panes, the bothy, like the cottar house, was a place of transience. Compared with the cottar, the single bothy-housed man might have more silver to jingle in his pocket but his stay about a farmtoun was usually shorter. Good "fees", anyway, were as few as drams in a manse. Sooner rather than later he was gripped by that old restlessness, and his itchy feet took him again to the feeing market and ultimately to another farmtoun. They moved on nonchalantly those young men of the farmtouns, carrying their few worldly possessions in their "kists", the strong wooden chests that sat at the ends of their bothy beds and contained their horses' show harness as well as their own Sabbath suits. They "flitted" from one place to the next, half-yearly, almost for the hell of it and it took some lass to make them settle down to life in a cottar house. Then, they might at least stay from one Whitsunday term-time to the next.

Yet, if little good can be said of the farmtoun bothies, one fine thing did come out of them: the bothy ballads—that singing psalmology of the ills of the countryside, a running commentary on the lives of its people. The ballads named names with a fearlessness that latter-day chroniclers would envy; the hard routine of specific farms is forthrightly recorded—that of Drumdelgie and Delgaty for example, both farms still in the North-East —and unscrupulous farmers given their scoundrelly characters. They give advice these ballads on how to keep clear of bad fees on market days, encouragement to lasses but lately forsaken and maids as yet unmolested. That we still have them, in cold print if not on singing lips, is due to the diligence of men like Superintendent Ord and, working at the opposite end of the country in the richest parishes of all, the dedicated Gavin Greig, a New Deer schoolmaster. Enshrined in their untutored lines there is a whole history; now they are almost our only link with the real quality of that life of the farmtouns.

# X

## *Pillars of the Year*

THE WHITSUNDAY AND Martinmas Terms were the twin pillars of the farmtoun year although the whole community was geared to them; not just the farming folk themselves but the smith, the souter (the shoemaker), the saddler, the tailor, millwright and miller and every other country tradesman. They were the times when the men of the farmtouns, servant and master, took stock of their debts and settled their affairs, the culmination of a six-month during which they had lived on a kind of open-hearted tick with hire-purchase as yet unheard of. If the cottared man needed a new pair of boots or another pair of working breeks, the souter or tailor would make them on trust against that time, twice-yearly, when farmers paid their cottars the full balance of their wages. Until then they paid them only enough to meet the travelling merchant's bills and buy an ounce or two of tobacco. At the Term a man had silver in his pocket, even if it was, most of it, usually spoken for.

Even so, it was a time approached with some consternation. Three months beforehand the cottar men and their wives would be quietly scouring the Farm Employment columns of such newspapers as they could lay hands on for some idea of which farmtoun was needing what, and decisions would be made about whether it would be worth applying; whether indeed it would be any better a "fee" than the one they had. But there was even more to it than that; by the "Sits Vac" columns the folk of the farmtouns could trace the whole pattern of movement, the shifts of the rural population. More intimately, a cottar might know from a vacancy advertised precisely who was leaving which farmtoun—and in the case of a former colleague even guess why he was being asked to go. Though few of the cottars themselves bought a daily newspaper, into most cottar houses on a Friday night (or at least over the weekend) there came the *People's Journal*, the Dundee-based weekly that editionized throughout the country. It carried such a choice of farm employment that in time it came to have a second name: *The Ploughman's Bible*. And throughout the length and breadth of the country, there were smaller weekly newspapers, each carrying its quota of local vacancies. They read oddly, those farmtoun Wanteds, like something in a foreign tongue unless you had been born and brought up with that strange language of the touns. Then it was second nature to you. Down the columns of tight unrelenting type the eye today wanders over the lists, like rolls of the dead from the days of the old farmtouns; halts over the outlandish requirements, the strange inducements, that litany of sought-after folk—orra men and kitchie deems, grieves and horse-men (first, second and third), halflins (those teenagers from whom you could get a man's work while paying only a laddie's wages), bailies (without powers magisterial), often with wives to strip (not at all what you thought it)—all with the promise of "cottar house and the usual perquisites", a word, like many another, that had its currency about the farmtouns long before it passed into the patois of the executive suite.

So the papers were carefully scanned. A farmer with a reputation as a fair employer, even if he were also known to be a hard one, would get plenty of replies; he could pick and choose. A farmer who was ill to please would be lucky to be considered and in time might be forced to put his requirements into an up-country paper where neither his temper nor the conditions of work about his farmtoun were known. Yet, important though it was, the reliance on the newspaper was not total. There were the cottar markets, held well in advance of the feeing fairs and usually associated with the weekly mart of the area. Again, likely chances would be canvassed when the cottar men met away from home at inn, kirk or market, or when the wives went visiting old neighbours now at other farmtouns. A man was always willing to tip-off an old neighbour who had been a good one.

There was hard bargaining done in the cottars' markets but they were gentlemanly affairs compared with the big feeing fairs; mainly for the single men, their notoriety was a byword in the bothies of the land. There the men of the farmtouns hired their brawn and their skills to the highest bidder and bound themselves to that bargain for a six-month. They were held, these hiring fairs, in every principal town in the country, a few days to a fortnight before the Terms, 28 May and 28 November, the dates on which a farm servant officially ended his engagement at a farmtoun. The fair names differed but the scene they presented was remarkably similar: a slow-moving mass, a figure detaching itself from a group here, adhering to another there, knots of men sundering with handshakes, all of them farm folk little at ease in a town environment. Besides the ploughmen lads, there were kitchen maids who had pleased their mistresses too little or their masters too well; orra men who had done orra work and stockmen who could not rise in the morning. The occasion had its own protocol. Moves were measured, cautious, circumspect; gambits so veiled as to slip past undetected by the inexperienced, for whom, unknown, the day might turn into a vale of missed opportunities. It was a slow dance, a verbal minuet. Among the milling folk, a servant would wait to be approached with an offer, with a hint perhaps from a former bothy colleague. A champion ploughman might do well enough, or a man known to be a good workman whatever his particular skill. A man who had been third horseman at one place would seek the second pair, and the few pounds extra in the half-year that went with them, at another; a man who had been "second" would be on the lookout for a first horseman's fee. It was a chancy business; a man might stand all day and not have his services sought after for there was a kind of grapevine among grieves that whispered the worth of a man one to another, pinpointing his frailties as a servant and sometimes as a man. They wheedled and dealt but it was the farmer or the grieve he invariably brought with him who had the upper hand for there was always a spectre at the fair: the stark dark dread of unemployment. That was always a possibility that had to be faced by the men of the farmtouns, and for the hard-pressed farmer of the depressed 1920s or '30s any ploughman was better than an expensive one whatever his work was like. At worst a farmer could always hire a halflin. There are men around still who remember with bitterness those days of the hard bargaining on which many of the great farmtouns were built. They are bracketed still, some of those touns' names, with the unscrupulousness of a system that made many a farm servant see the recruiting sergeant as a kind of saviour. For, he too, went to the hiring fair.

The bothy ballads are redolent with advice for the farm lad or young horseman unfamiliar with the hiring market's harsh routine

or the sly behaviour of farmers, and with warnings about the
outcome of taking the whole business of feeing too lightly. There
was one man in particular to avoid in Turriff's Porter Fair:

> Come, all ye jolly ploughman lads,
>     I pray you, have a care,
> Beware o' going to Swaggers,
>     For he'll be in Porter Fair.
>
> He'll be aye lauch-lauchin',
>     He'll aye be lauchin' there;
> And he'll hae on the blithest face
>     In a' Porter Fair.
>
> Wi' his fine horse and harness,
>     Sae well he'll gar ye true,
> But when ye come to Auchterless,
>     Sae sair's he'll gar ye rue.
>
> He'll tell ye o' some plooin' match
>     That isna far awa';
> And gin ye clean your harness richt,
>     Ye're sure to beat them a'.
>
> For the tackle's gained the prize afore
>     At every country show;
> And gin that ye lat it fa' back,
>     Ye'll be thocht little o'.
>
> A pair o' blues that lead the van
>     Sae nimbly as they go;
> A pair o' broons that follow them,
>     That never yet said no.
>
> A wee bit shaltie ca's the neeps,
>     And, oh, but it is sma';
> But Swaggers he'll declare to you
>     It's stronger than them a'.
>
> But he'll aye be fret-frettin',
>     He'll aye be frettin' there;
> And he'll gie ye regulations
>     That are worn a' threadbare.

And Swaggers in the harvest time,
  He's got too much to do
For the twa-three jovial laddies
  That ca's his cairt and ploo.

Sae he'll gang on some twenty miles,
  Faur people disna him ken,
And he'll engage some harvest hands
  And bring them far frae hame.

He'll say unto the foreman chiel,
  "Keep aye the steady grind,
And dinna lat the orra lads
  Fa' idle back behind.

"For I pay ye a' guid wages,
  And sae ye maun get on,
And gin ye are not able,
  There's anither when ye're done."

He'll say unto the girlies,
  As they are comin' back,
"Come on, my girls, and hurry up,
  Gie them nae time to sharp."

But noo the cuttin's ended,
  And we've begun to lead,
And mony's the curious plan he tries
  For to come muckle speed.

And noo the sheaves they are all in,
  And formed in the stack;
And noo the windy days are come
  When we maun hunt the brock.

When we maun hunt the brock, my boys,
  Wi' mony a fret and frown;
And Swaggers cries, "Come on, my boys,
  It's like for to ding on."

And when that we gang to the raips,
  He gets up wi' a bawl,
Says, "Come on, my girls, ply in the twine,
  Ye're sure to beat them all."

Now the harvest's ended,
  And a' thing is made snod;
The harvest hands wi' bundles big
  They now must pad the road.

They now must pad the road, my boys,
  Amang the frost and snaw;
And they hae sworn a solemn oath,
  They'll ne'er come back ava.

But Martinmas it has worn on,
  My fee's into my pouch;
And sae merrily, merrily, I will sing,
  "I'm oot o' the tyrant's clutch."

For he is the worst master
  That ever I did serve;
And gin ye dinna me believe,
  Never mind ye this observe.

Here then is the perfect con-man of the farmtouns, milling with the throng of the feeing market, smiling, joking, letting it be understood that his toun has fine Clydesdales, fine harness that has taken the prize many times at the local ploughing match. But, once home to Swaggers' farmtoun in the North-East district of Auchterless the ploughman finds a different story, the bonhomie of the hiring fair is forgotten; Swaggers at home is a nagging, forcing tyrant who has to go far to hire his harvest labour because his ways are so well known locally. And even when the rain comes on in the middle of the harvest operations and the hairst crew retire under cover to make the ropes that will tie down the thatch on the ricks of the cornyard—a job that traditionally gave folk a breather in the middle of the harvest—he is still harassing and cajoling. The ballad is a prime example of the way farmers and grieves exploited the competitive urge among the folk of their farmtoun crew.

One trick of the rogue farmer was simple enough: it was to bide his time until the end of fair-day, till the drams had done their worst and the gnawing bile of uncertainty had frayed the nerve-endings; he knew that any cottar man then still without a fee would take £10 in the year less than the figure he had been wanting a few hours before. It seems suitably just that the true names of such men often passed into the balladry of the farmtouns with a fine disregard for the laws of libel. In this way at least the men they tricked were revenged.

All the same, sometimes for the better and as often for worse, bargains were struck and sealed with a dram or a drink and the passing of silver, five shillings (25p) or a half-crown (12½p), from the hirer to the hired—arles money. When a farm servant had accepted this, rather in the manner of taking the queen's shilling, he had made a deal that was binding, and the law could be heavy on a servant who broke his contract.

Yet another ballad, from the same area, gives a reminder of the farmer's approach to a youngster whose first feeing fair this may have been, since he engages himself to be the orra loon of the farmtoun:

> 'Twas in the merry month of May
> When flowers had clad the landscape gay,
> To Ellon Fair I bent my way
>      With hopes to find amusement.
>
> A scrankie chiel to me cam' near,
> And quickly he began to speir
> If I would for the neist half-year
>      Engage to be his servant.
>
> "I'll need you as an orra loon;
> Four poun' ten I will lay down
> To you, when Martinmas comes roun'
>      To close out our engagement.
>
> "Five shillings more will be your due,
> If you to me prove just and true;
> But that will be referred to you
>      By my goodwill and pleasure."
>
> An' to a tent he then set sail,
> And bade me follow at his tail;
> And he called for a glass o' ale
>      Therein to keep us sober.
>
> Said he, "A saxpence noo, my loon,
> I freely will to you lay down,
> Thrippence for ale I will pay soon,
>      And thrippence buys my fairin'."

When I went hame to my new place,
And at the table showed my face,
It's to the brose they said nae grace——
    The time was unco precious.

Although our usage was but scant,
Of wark we never kent the want;
And aye to carry on the rant
    The farmer cried, "Come on, lads."

An' when the hairst it did come roun',
It's to a scythe I hid to boun';
Likewise to draw the rake aroun',
    To keep the fields in order.

The arles are smaller than those a horseman would have expected —naturally, for a lad hardly out of school—but the glass of ale and the bite to eat were part of the farmer's feeing-day bond. For the rest, the tale is woefully familiar: the hurry over the meals, the sly pattern of giving the lad a scythe as the harvest came and getting a man's work from him. There was one comfort though for the orra loon: if he behaved himself and his work pleased he would be due at the end of his engagement for a bonus of five shillings (25p).

Only first horsemen could hope to drive a satisfactory bargain in the feeing market. The reason was brutally simple: most farmers were willing enough to pay well a man who would work hard and, even more important, make sure that his underlings did the same. Where the farmer was his own grieve, in fact, the foreman was an exceedingly important figure and conscious of it, not only about the farmtoun itself but when he went from home. And if he were fee'd to a big farm like, say, Milne of Boyndie (pronounced Mullnabeenie) in Banffshire, in the 1860s a place of twenty pairs, he would be far from thinking everybody his equal, as this snatch of ballad makes clear:

When I was young and in my prime,
    Guid-fegs, like me there wisna mony;
I was the best man in the Boyne,
    And foreman lang at Mullnabeeny.

And when he went to the feeing fair it was in some style:

> I had a hat upon my heid,
>   It cost me mair than half-a-guinea,
> Held a' the lasses in Brannan Fair
>   Gazing at the foremost man o' Mullnabeeny.

But the hiring fair was more than just a feeing market; it was a kind of half-yearly festival. With a shrewd eye to trade one market town's bakers would bake very small currant loaves, called "monkey loaves", for sale at a penny apiece. These helped to stay the hunger of the crowd, for folk that day came to town from the far, outlier farmtouns, strange folk some of them who had seen nothing but sheep and black cattle for most of the preceding six-month. A single man, whether he was leaving or staying at his place, would make the fair an excuse for a spree, for hadn't he the balance of his previous fee jingling in his pocket and likely to burn a hole in it? The day indeed got wilder as it went on and fights developed as the drams went down. If there was little dignity about the hiring fair, by late afternoon it had descended into pure débâcle. It was time then for the constables to move in: quarrelsome men were escorted to the peace of a police cell where they could inconvenience nobody and conveniently be ready to appear before the magistrate in the morning; amiable drunks were taken to the town's bus termini to await the next bus and the help, with luck, of a sympathetic acquaintance. But long before that the more sober men had left the market square to look elsewhere in the town. It was not every day that an opportunity came to buy a new bonnet or a pair of ready-made breeks, or simply to wander through the serried wonders of Woolworth's, that remarkable emporium that held all that a sixpence ($2\frac{1}{2}$p) could buy and nearly all that the human heart could yearn for.

## XI

## *Fairs and Trysts*

FAIR DAYS WERE like holidays; they punctuated the rhythm and calm of the country calendar with the brilliance of the chill stars exploding in the northern night. They brought commerce and the countryside together in an atmosphere a little alien to both; farmers came to buy and deal, their wives to sell their homespun and their lint sheets as well as the results of the winter knitting from which their hands were never idle. It was a raucous, roistering occasion of bargaining unwisely blurred by whisky for it was, too, a day of drams taken and of old friendships recemented, new enmities sworn. And stealthily towards night, beyond the shadows of the booths and the gingerbread stalls and the glare of the tarry flares, there was that oldest of all transactions hurriedly undertaken. It was a time when men got a chance to give a nod to their earthier natures, for young women to stand momentarily closer to the Devil yet escape unscathed if they still had a mind to. It was the drink that did the damage and made widows prematurely; though many men may have died from the effects of cold bothies and the severe strains of the work of the farmtouns, not a few slipped suddenly out of the life by the drunken mischance of slipping off the fording-stones in the fairday home-going.

Every country town had its fair, often linked with a saint's day since it was the monks who had started it all by taking advantage of a holy festival to sell their produce. By the 1800s, however, the fair had come far from its saintly origins. Indeed, there were fairs whose notoriety far exceeded their commercial importance: Aikey Brae, for instance, held on the third Wednesday of July in the parish of Old Deer in the North-East Lowlands. Its reputation was such that genteel folk spoke of it only in whispers and after the children had gone to bed and even then with a shake of the head that suggested wickedness beyond all understanding. Originally a three-day event, in time it had come to stretch over the

Sabbath and draw the young folk of the parishes round from their prayer-books to the banks of the Ythan. There by Tangland Ford they gathered to see the livestock driven through on their way South to the trysts—a mêlée of bellowing beasts, cursing drovers and their yapping dogs. The names of these occasions have grown into the folklore of the farmtouns, kept alive as much in some cases by the apt quaintness of their names as their supposed iniquities: Seed Thursday (at Biggar in March), Scythe Fair (at Old Cumnock in July), the Timmer Market (at Aberdeen in August). They were scenes of colour and movement as well as excitement; besides the drovers and their dogs, the horse-copers and the gingerbread stalls there was the persuasive, smiling packman peddling his chapbooks, the ale-wife, the recruiting sergeant be-ribboned and crimson-coated—a temptation to those disillusioned by the farm life, selling adventure and the chance of glory. Probably for this reason fairs have been recorded more authentically than any other aspect of Scotland's rural past and by such accomplished country artists as David Wilkie, whose painting of Pitlessie Fair (held twice-yearly in Fife in May and October) captures all the vivid, thrusting vitality of that occasion. The country fairs drew other painters too, many of near-equal stature. Three works by James Howe preserve just as vividly the markets of Skirling, a small village in Peebles-shire, whose June meeting (the others were in May and September) was one of the biggest horse fairs in the country. The deaf and dumb Walter Geikie put on canvas the scene at Edinburgh's All Hallows Fair (in November) and Alexander Fraser depicted the town of St Andrews' Mercat Cross gathering.

The pulse of such events is perfectly caught: you can almost feel the atmosphere, smell the fresh-made gingerbread and the roasting chestnuts, hear the merry scrape of the beggar-man's fiddle. In the North, Keith's famous three-day affair, The Summer Eve Fair, was claimed by some to be "by much the greatest . . .". In the far South-West, for Galloway's Kelton Hill Fair, held later at Castle Douglas, the roads were crowded with folk for days beforehand and a whole tented village sprang up. Again, there were fairs noted for some particular speciality: Ardersier's Lammas Fair (held yearly on 12 August) was a byword for its gingerbread men, if such they were for they had quite unique "breastplates". One reverend researcher at least took them to represent the knights of the Crusade, though in view of Ardersier's numerous inns and the wildness of the event they may well have symbolized something erotically nearer to nature. Peebles' Beltane Fair (in May), providentially for those with a liking for a wager, coincided with the local horse-racing.

Though Edinburgh's celebrated All Hallows, held sometimes in the Grassmarket and sometimes on the higher ground of Bruntsfield, originally stretched over eight days, most fairs lasted only three or four.

The days had a traditional pattern. The first was for the sale of such home-made articles as table-cloths, blankets and so on from the district's weavers, but it was the second day that was the high-point. It brought to the fair the droves of travelling pack-men, the country shoemakers to hawk for trade, the sweetie-wife with her home-made confectionery, the ale-wife with her barrel. The day started early with the sheep and cattle-dealers doing business briskly so as to be done before the foot-market, the larger general gathering of the afternoon, got under way and the drams began to go round in earnest. They could continue their dealing on the third day again, though this was recognized as being the day of the horse-copers, who came from far regions to trade Clydesdales with the shrewd men of the farmtouns. Even when time shrank the occasion to one of a single day's duration, the ancient order would be maintained with the cloth-market early in the day, the cattle-dealing and the big gathering of folk about noon and the early part of the afternoon, the latter end of the day being given over to the horse-trading. It was a day that many lived to rue: men whose judgement had been blunted by drink bought horses so broken in the wind that they could hardly pull the farmtoun gig let alone a plough; young lasses, their imaginations fevered by what they had been told in the spae-wife's tent, took their chances with dark-haired men and long lived to regret it. For the fairs were occasions that not only replenished the farmtoun tables, stables and implement sheds; they changed human destinies.

For the young kitchen maid of a farmtoun the day could indeed be one to remember, for besides the livestock and the long lines of Clydesdales—Old Rayne's St Lawrence Fair at one time might have 600, with one of the big dealers alone bringing 200—there were also the fiddlers, conjurors perhaps, all the folk who needed an audience before their gifts could flower. Maybe, through the crowd there would be a glimpse of John Milne, the Poet of Livet's Glen, radical shoemaker, smuggler and minstrel champion of the hard-worked ploughman's cause, dressed in his knee breeches, plaid and the old blue bonnet of Scotland and drunk or sober with a song on his lips. Whatever fair it was, if she were bonnie enough she would have the sly glances of ploughboys, the speculative stares of older men, the innuendo-laden banter. That was the way of it; little she would have thought of it. But at Lowrin Fair—the North-East's name for the St Lawrence occasion—she might win a bouquet as the bonniest lass of the fair, and cause brawls among the ploughman gallants anxious to escort her. In the uplands parish of Auchindoir, in the shadow of the same northern mountain, Mary Fair (named after the Virgin) also had a beauty contest for servant lasses though the decorum there seems to have lent the thing more dignity. That may have been because of the panel of judges. It was formed by the local lairds and it awarded a single lily (the Virgin Mary's emblem), with a one-pound note wrapped round the stem of it. With it for a year, in the manner of later and more sophisticated events of the kind, went the coveted title, The Flower of Mary Fair. From the fair, held on the Market Hillock at Newton farmtoun, the lass might go home to her kitchen with a song on her lips, a snatch likely of a local ballad:

> Fare ye weel ye bonnie Newton.
> Happy hae I been at thee;
> Gaithered up the Market Custom,
> And muckle did they think o' me.

There were other amusements that enlivened a fair day; other contests too, and with all the drink taken, never a shortage of competitors however ludicrous the spectacle. At one time the laird of Strichen gave fair-day awards to the man who could catch a sow by the tail (the sow herself) and to the drunkest man (an eight-day clock, though God knows why).

Yet the day too was one for hiring folk as well as buying stock. There was always a "fee" to be sought for at any of the great occasions of that northern ballad country, and a man or a lass looking for a "hairst fee" at the Lowrin Fair, at nearby St Sair's, or the notorious Aikey Brae, would wear a spear of "shot" corn in their bonnets or jackets to show they were for hire. Roadmen

D

came (seeking the seasonal work); tradesmen's apprentices (who had only their keep as they learned their trades); and poor fisher folk (sadly out of their element) from the coastal towns.

Doctors attended the fairs, maybe to have the half of their due fees at least before the ale-wife got them, though most of them were farmers themselves and would have been there anyway. But it was the ale-wife that day who did the best trade, for there were small tenant farmers and many farmtoun men who could not keep clear of her however much, sober, they might lament it:

> The ale-wife an' her barrelies,
>   The ale-wife she grieves me.
> The ale-wife and her barrelies
>   She'll ruin me entirely.
>
> She's ta'en her barrelies on her back,
>   Her pint stoop in her han'
> An' she's awa' to Lowrin Fair
>   Tae haud a rantin' stan'.
>
> But I hae owsen i' the pleuch,
>   An' plenty o' gweed corn;
> Fesh ben to me anither pint,
>   Though I should beg the morn.

It is difficult now to point the actual moment of the fairs' fall into decline, but by the mid-1800s or so their wild heyday at least was over. Some indeed were already remembered only as a date on the calendar, a measurement of the year in the minds of the old folk of the district, while others continued as feeble shadows of their former greatness.

In the mid-1700s East Lothian had fifteen fairs; by the start of the nineteenth century they numbered only six. By 1840, certainly, Lochcarron's New Kelso market, the parish's only organized stock sale (on the first Monday in June) had diminished in the words of one reporter "into an annual term for settling accounts and drinking whisky". This change of pattern from the fair's original purpose would seem to have been general, for at Shiel House, in Wester Ross, where three cattle fairs were held during the year, the local minister noted that "the practice of exposing pedlar's wares at these meetings which has lately been introduced, threatens, by attracting young females to them, to do injury to their morals".

The least days of the country fairs, certainly, were almost over before the farmtouns came into their own, and even Aberdeen's Timmer Market, held once for the sale of wooden implements but later for the purpose of re-stocking the North-East Lowlands kitchens with their ubiquitous brose caups, coggies, luggies, spurtles and potato-mashers as well as the creepie-stools that could bring the bairns in to the fire between the big folk's chairs, was in sad decline by 1890 and an anachronism long, long before its move from that city's historic Castlegate in the 1930s.

For the big livestock events the auction sale and the coming of the railway brought the beginning of the end. Before then, well into the 1860s, the butchers had bought at the fairs, and some, indeed were unwilling to give up the custom for it was a convivial way of doing business, with a dram in your hand. But time and men like the enterprising John Duncan persuaded them. Duncan, a dealer, first separated the cattle-sales from the context of the fair by selling by private bargain on a site on the university side of Aberdeen. His King Street stance, in time, he converted, adding a rostrum and permanent buildings. But he was not the first. The idea had been in operation since 1817, when the son of a Kelso tenant farmer, Andrew Oliver, had first begun auction selling in the Border town of Hawick. The scheme, however, was slow to succeed, probably due to the penal level of taxation. Although Oliver advertised by handbill—there was a tax at the time, too, on newspaper advertising—and doubtless bribed the town bellman to put in a favourable word for him on his rounds, the dealers and butchers were at first unwilling to forsake the great fairs of that Border area, those of Newton St Boswells, Lockerbie and Melrose. It was into the 1860s before the auction mart really got established and again change came from Peel and the Repeal of the Auction Tax—one shilling (5p) in the pound on auctions held anywhere other than on the farm itself. Now centralized selling and the auction mart became a feasible alternative. The revolution that it wrought on the pattern of country life would prove as far-reaching in its way as the invention of the reaper. More so even, for not only did it hurry the end of the fair days, for the first time it distanced the farmer from his buyer.

The cattle trysts of Crieff and Falkirk, with their highpoint in
the latter half of the 1700s, by the nineteenth century were also on
the wane. Their decline too was not without its sadness for in
losing them the countryside also lost some of its characters, the
old drovers, that band of itinerants who worked the cattle fairs
from end to end of the country. They would become, alas, but a
romantic memory on a Landseer canvas. They deserved better:
the realistic brush of a Wilkie, or at least a Geikie, for they were
highly-intelligent, highly-thought-of men who would sup with a
laird whiles at the end of a fair-day. From the North and the West,
on the new roads built to keep the Jacobites in check and through
the wild passes of the mountains—over from Speyside to the
valley of the Dee—Gaelic drovers brought cattle as black and as
lean as themselves to meet the fat purses of the English buyers.
The droving began about the middle of August when the cattle of
the islands came down from the shielings in prime condition and
the beef was sweet. It was an old trade and its origins barely stand
scrutiny, for it was at the Michaelmas moon that the old caterans
who levied blackmail for a living had "lifted" the beasts of those
found to be backsliding in their payments. In time the cattle-
lifters' trade would become so countenanced that they could sell
a man back his own beasts, but in their early days at least, they
had had to drove South to get a market.

It was a trade that grew into better things and passed into the
hands of more respectable men. And it grew: black cattle from the
Highland hills fattened out wonderfully in a gentler landscape
and rolling English pastures. The demand for a time was insatiable.
From one district alone in the North-East Lowlands, in a single
year, one family of dealers would drove up to 6,000 beasts to the
Southern markets. And sometimes their task did not end there,
for from Falkirk they might contract to drove the cattle right down
into East Anglia.

Only the horse fairs, supported by the farmtouns' demand for
the Clydesdale, survived into the present century with anything of
their former glory. Before the first world war 1,000 horses would
change hands in a single night at Aulton Market, on the university
fringe of Aberdeen, county town for a countryside of hard farmtouns and the heartland of the ballads. Yet, like so many more of
the great horse fairs, it died long before the tractor age was truly
with us and became but a husk of what it had been, like Fyvie's

Peter Fair, in the same area. In 1938, in the final years of the old farmtouns, Peter Fair had just one horse forward for sale. It was an unhappy ending for an event that in its heyday had had three rows of stalls. It was all a sad down-come for those great occasions that had added lustre to the calendar of country days. If the memory of the old fairs survived it would be in the lines of farming's balladry—or even in the names of the farmtouns themselves, like Sleepytown, in the upland district of Garioch in the North-East. Its name is the last link now with an old, old fair. Once, it began at dusk and ended with the dawn, till the local laird turned it into a day affair. That was in 1746, and it may well have been that a night fair was a chancy thing in the year of Culloden. Whatever his reasons, the change lost the aptly-named Sleepy Market much of its enchantment and from then its days were numbered. If it is interesting now it is on the strength of a romantic belief, for the occasion was also known as Christ's Fair, from the church that stood near to the spot. It is sometimes claimed that James I (1394–1437) once visited the fair, that it was the inspiration for his famous poem "Christ's Kirk on the Green", in which he wrote:

> Was never in Scotland heard nor seen
> Such dancing nor deray,
> Neither at Falkland on the green
> Or Peebles at the play
> As was—of wowaris as I ween—
> At Christ's Kirk on a day.

If the belief be true, even kings it seems could succumb to all the excitement of the fair.

# XII

## Meal, Milk and Tatties

THAT DIARIST OF Scottish affairs, Elizabeth Grant of Rothiemurchus, in her *Memoirs of a Highland Lady*, has this to say about
whisky: "... a dram was the Highland prayer, it began, accompanied and ended all things". At the time of which she was
writing, the early 1800s, she says: "At every house it was offered,
at every house it must be tasted or offence could be given."
Whisky, she continues, was drunk from early morning till late at
night, and even "decent gentlewomen", it seems, began the day
with a dram. Had she thought of it, she would doubtless have told
us—what she strongly implies all through her delightful memoirs
—that the gaps between times were filled with oatmeal. Indeed
the two combined even in the most genteel circles, where it was the
custom to offer an oat bannock with the social drink.

They were, too, the two commodities that, over a long period,
sustained the farmtouns. The potato-gang worker of the 1930s,
seated in the lee of a potato clamp, was not only often the descen-
dant of the clansman who mixed a little of his black cattle's blood
with oatmeal to make a palatable bannock, but his lunch-time
"piece" of oatcakes and cheese was little different from what
Elizabeth Grant's Speyside woodmen took to accompany their
noon-time goblet of whisky. Another comparison holds for the food
of the shepherds' bothies of the early-1800s and that of the
farmtouns right into the 1930s. In his summer bothy high in the
Grampians, the flockman's only provision might be a bag of oatmeal which he mixed with cold mountain water to make a very
basic dish of brose: in the later kitchens of the farmtouns where
the ploughmen were given their food the only difference was that
the water that made the brose was hot.

Oatmeal indeed was the great sustainer: there was never a time
in Scotland's long history when a little meal in your poke was not
better than coin in your pouch. It was more than a food; it was a
currency that in its time was a unit of rent; the stipends of

ministers; the fees of schoolmasters; and payment for hardy Highland postmen. Gamekeepers sent into the hills for something to fill the chief's pot took oatmeal in their pockets—their only provision on an expedition that might stretch over several nights in the open before they brought home the venison. Like the laird's firlot or two of barley or oats to the tradesmen, oatmeal honourably settled debt and was welcome as dowries. About the farmtouns it was both a scourge and the very substance of life itself. And, as a part of his perquisites, it was an important part of the ploughman's fee.

The men of the farmtouns, in fact, lived on an infinity of brose: brose when they fell out of their beds in the morning, kail brose for their "denner"—the mid-day meal—and oatmeal brose again for their supper, when they had stabled their horses for the night. This endless, unvarying diet, eaten out of wooden caups or bowls, like so much else of the bothy life, is burlesqued in those farmtoun photographs that show the men seated, brose caups in hand, posed in mid-sup, small flagons of accompanying milk a-dangle from their little fingers. The number of brose permutations would hardly have disappointed a football-pools promoter: there was water brose, whey brose, ale brose, cabbage, kail and turnip brose, and knotty-tams—a picaresque variant achieved by mixing the oatmeal with boiling milk instead of water. The standard dish of the bothymen, however, and one just right for the haste of a farmtoun morning, was oatmeal mixed with boiling water, with salt and pepper added, and taken with cream or milk. You could, if you had a mind to, sugar it, lace it with treacle, instead of the milk even have stout or porter. It wasn't haute cuisine, yet generations of farmtoun men marched on it to the very endrigs of life itself and were seemingly none the worse for it except for the occasional outbreak of the euphemistically-named Scotch fiddle, a skin eruption brought on it was thought by the unrelieved diet of oatmeal.

Imagination, certainly, was never stretched. Thus John Ord, preserver of farmtoun balladry, speaking specifically of the North-East knuckle of Scotland, that land of dour farmtouns, in the 1880s:

> . . . supper, as a rule, consisted of oatmeal porridge or brose made with boiling milk, or with boiling ale with a glass of

whisky added by way of seasoning. This was varied at times by
sowens, boiled till they were of the same consistency as porridge
or made like gruel and sweetened with syrup.

Other dishes were served, though less frequently; mashed
turnips when in season; green kail (colewort) boiled in water
and seasoned with pepper and salt and with the addition of a
little cream; rice boiled in skim milk and sweetened with a little
sugar. At some farms, however, the servants were simply
allowed six and a half bolls of oatmeal per annum, and one
Scotch pint of sweet milk per day, and they had to make their
own food in the bothies. In such cases it was brose for breakfast,
dinner and supper.

Moving as he did from place to place at the end almost of every
six-month, the bothy-lad could in time become something of a
connoisseur of brose—an Egon Ronay of the farmtouns—not to
say of the kitchen lasses who made it. The quality of the brose
varied with the age of the oatmeal, according to the mill it came
from, the speed of the servant lass's pouring and the stirrer's own
momentum as he mixed meal and water. It might seem simple
enough to dash a fistful of oatmeal into a bowl, plus pepper and
salt, and then simply to add water to taste. Not so; it was a kind
of morning roulette: the brose could be "drowned" to the vis-
cosity of watery gruel or thickened to such a consistency that it
was unwilling to quit the spoon. Or, as the ballad "The Barnyards
of Delgaty" has it:

> Meg Macpherson mak's my brose,
>   An' her and me we canna gree,
> First a mote and then a knot,
>   And aye the ither jilp o' bree.

It demanded a delicacy of judgement, but at its best, brose was a
blend of perfection, an oatmealy smoothness—especially with
new-milled meal—that the servant lass and the ploughman
achieved between them. And that could well lead on to other
things.

As John Ord suggests, there would be the occasional tasty
morsel or titbit to surprise the bothy men: sowens maybe, thick or
thin depending on whether they were for drinking or supping,

and that depending again on whether they were for the supper or
for taking, stoppered in an old lemonade bottle, as a sustainer to the
harvest field, where the bottle would be thrown into the cool
heart of a stook until it was needed. There were as many kinds of
sowens as there were women who made them. Like the kebbuck
cheese of the farmtouns they were mostly made to a highly original
recipe and were an acquired taste; many a fee'd man who could
not stomach Mains's cheese would find himself in heaven at
Hilly's. There was hangman's cheese, too, or crowdie as it was
often called, the production of which was often a matter of
insanitary simplicity: it was made by strong-wristed farm wives
who squeezed the curds in cheesecloth or double cheesecloth. The
harder the "wringing" the better. Then, in the cheesecloth, it
was hung to drain and dry on a hook on the wall of the barn or
byre, as often as not but a few paces from the farm midden. And,
of course, there was always plenty of milk about the farmtouns of
the late-1800s and early-1900s. Any lack of it was a matter of some
grievance, and such indeed may have been the case in the North-
East during the boom period of the 1870s. At that time John
Strachan, of Cluny's Mains of Corsindae, paid his men 3d (1½p) a
day for forgoing their milk entitlement or 1½d (1p) if they took
only half-measure.

At farmtouns where the men ate in the bothy instead of in the
farm kitchen and the bailie was the cook, it was the foreman's job
to pour on the brose water, and he had no doubt how they should
be made:

> In the mornin' we got brose
>   As mony's we could belly in;
> Willie Buchan made the brose,
>   And faith he did not mak' them thin.

That old man from the slopes of Bennachie, writing of his young
days as a horseman about 1860 or so, remembered:

> The bailie got to stop his work half an hour earlier to get the
> fire going, but we had time only to make brose or boil tatties.
> On Sundays we pooled our resources and bought something
> extra, and the kitchie deem came and helped to cook.

Sometimes, too, there was a rabbit or a hare, covered, fur and all, below the aise of the fireplace and left there until it was cooked, when the skin and entrails all came away as clean as a whistle.

On some farms on Sunday morning we got each one cup of tea, a small pat of butter, and sometimes as a great treat, a red herring. There was no flour bread.

But if the making of brose—an act many of the men and women of the farmtouns never mastered—was the constant subject of song, so too was the matter of farm food generally. The theme of want, lack of variety, hurried meals without grace being said is as insistent a refrain as the hunger pangs the bothy men must sometimes have endured. Listen to the new man at "Newmill":

> I hadna been a week come hame
>     When I could plainly see,
> The tables they were rather bare,
>     They were none suit for me.
>
> The breid was thick, the brose was thin,
>     And the broth they were like bree;
> I chased the barley roon the plate,
>     And a' I got was three.
>
> So unsuccessful was my search,
>     My spoon I then threw doon;
> The knife and fork were seldom seen
>     But in the carpet room.

So we have social comment along with the complaint: the ballad, with its eccentric grammar, draws attention to the fact that the only eating utensil for the bothy men, as for many others of the working class of the time, was the horn spoon.

It was quite a different thing though if the men to be fed were the crew from another farmtoun—coming to help with a late harvest, maybe, or to work at the threshing-mill; a farmer then would not want any taint of meanness to travel home with them to the ears of a social equal. In view of his usual restriction he would have to instruct his kitchen maid accordingly:

You, Annie Scott, ye'll get on the muckle pot,
An' you'll mak' milk porridge a-plenty;
For thae hungry brosers are coming frae Pitgair,
An' they're keepit aye sae bare and sae scanty.

The ballads—and that old man of Bennachie—are talking of the 1860s, '70s and perhaps the 1880s, but things changed little with the years. The single, bothy-housed man's breakfast in the late 1920s was still the inevitable brose, though now that Sunday cup of tea was an everyday thing, accompanied by a slice of flour bread without cover of butter or jam, let alone a smear of civilizing marmalade. There were by then farmtouns where the "denner" menu ran to broth and even beef. But there were as many, if not more, where the ploughmen supped brose again in one of its many disguises. And at supper it would be brose yet again, with another single slice of bread and a single cup of tea.

The cottar, at his own table, was little better off, not always from a lack of ingenuity in his wife's cookery but as often from simple poverty and a dearth of provision where the bad roads discouraged the travelling grocer's cart. The ploughman could marry the cook from the Big House but without the expensive ingredients her greater skill was set at nought. He might bring home a bride from some far part of the country and for a time sit down to powsowdie or clapshot or tattie drottle. For folk not far from the sea there was the chance, from the late-1800s, to salt down a firkin of herring for winter use. Whatever the reason, though, before long the ploughman's diet would come down to the monotony of those farmtoun staples: oatmeal and potatoes. His basic food items were part of a farm man's fee, a constant reminder to him of that time when his status would have been something more—when, as a tenant at will, he would have grown his own food and milked his own cow. The garden that came with his cottar house harked back to that small enclosure of pre-improvement time when it had grown kail to keep scurvy at bay—from a diet so dependent on oatmeal. And that, too, was not without its irony: so dependent had he become on it as a supplementary source that in time "kail" became synonymous with "food"; to "get your kail" was to eat. It took a unique place in the language of the farmtouns: "cauld kail" came to signify a matter much discussed; servants who misbehaved and came under the master's displeasure would get their "kail through the reek". When time and land hunger had ended his land-holding, commutation had given the cottar his fee, house and perquisites agreement that brought him "meal, milk and tatties" as well as his fuel. His potatoes, a farm-cart load, came from the field as they were harvested; his two tons of coal came one in May and the other at Martinmas; and his daily half-gallon of milk he collected from the farm milk-house each evening as he went home for the day.

His cottar's oatmeal, too, usually six or six-and-a-half bolls annually (that magical quantity that had been the allowance of schoolmasters and servants alike down the centuries), came home twice a year, a few days after the Term. Milled from the farm-toun's own corn, it came home from the miller's in the farm carts. The vast sacks were carried in, manoeuvred through the door by a horseman under visible stress, and placed on chairs in the middle of the kitchen floor. And there they perched, like stout and important personages, until the cottars's wife had the time to ladle their contents into the girnal, the oatmeal store-chest that stood in the kitchen corner. A cottar's girnal had a capacity of only three bolls or so but filling it was a long job, since the meal had to be hard-packed to keep it from *winnan*—losing its moistness and flavour. Filling the girnal could be done slowly, pressing down with the big wooden potato-masher, or more quickly by washing the bairns' feet and getting them to trample the meal. Not all the cottars took their full quota of meal in the later days of the farm-touns when the size of country families had diminished; then the farmer would pay a cash settlement for the amount unclaimed.

About the farmhouse itself, where the girnal was bigger and zinc-lined to safeguard against loss of quality—and maybe encroachment by the rats and mice that ran riot about every farmtoun—"taking in the meal" was an even longer task and a harassed kitchen maid might ask the grieve for the loan of the orra loon. His feet washed, he would be set to the "trumpin' " of the meal. Failing that, the kitchen lass herself would take off her stockings, and, feet swilled, climb into the girnal. Her skirt kirtled, she would set determinedly to work, quietly cursing the indignity of it.

# XIII

## *The Social Hour*

HOLIDAYS WERE unheard of about the old farmtouns. A horseman would get a day off to attend a feeing fair, a Term day and
a day at New Year, though a bailie might well get none
if there were no one to look after the byre in his absence. He would
have to wait until later to claim his days. And the tenant farmer
himself might make do with just a day by the sea when he had his
harvest safely won and secure in the cornyard. For all that, the
farmtouns of the mid-1800s and later were far from being places
bereft of the social hour, and when it came, the hard work of the
touns ensured that it was seized with a frenzy that would have
shocked a more sophisticated society. The days of the rockings
were long past of course; those winter occasions of Burns' time—

> At Fastern's e'en we had a rockin',
> To ca' the crack an' weave our stockin'.

—that brought the young women of the countryside to barn or
kitchen fireside with their rocks and their reels (distaffs and
spindles), and with them the young men who had hopes of later
convoying them home across the barley rigs in the moonlight
(and heaven knows what other ambitions), were the *ceilidhs* of the
farmtouns. While the flax and the wool were spun the song and the
tune went round, honing the care of wearying days. It was
probably the coming of the spinning wheel that did most to bring
those lightsome nights so suddenly to an end. It is hard to say
now, but certainly the cumbersome wheel, whatever advance it
brought with it, was less easily transportable even by a love-struck
ploughman.

Yet something of their kind continued when the rockings
ceased, even if in a limited form, and the social hour continued to
be centred for many years after on the farmhouse fireside,
especially on Saturday nights in winter when the early dark in

the fields brought everyone indoors for a time of pause before
the Sabbath. Nor was the formula much different: the round of
story, tune and song held the attention while the womenfolk
shanked (knitted) woollen stockings by the light of peat and
"puirman", that rustic-cottage candelabra that held the rush-
lights, or the flickering flame of the cruisie lamp. The songs, a
fraction less earthy perhaps than in Burns' day, still dealt with the
fundamental things and the feelings of folk who lived close to the
soil. Alexander Gibson, admittedly without Burns' gift for the
phrase, the stanza, that instantly summons up the mood and
atmosphere of such a company, sets the latter-day scene at a
North-East farmtoun in the mid-1800s, in *Under the Cruisie:*

> As round the ingle's friendly glow,
> The cruisie burning faint and low,
> Master and man in converse sweet
> At eveningtide in friendship meet
> And song and music, witching tale,
> With copious draughts of home-brewed ale,
> Go round and round . . .

As the evening wore on, the master himself joined in, reaching
his fiddle down from its shelf and bowing a spring for the young
folk of the toun to dance to. Gibson, a man perhaps inhibited by
his time as well as his own nature, undoubtedly makes it all a lot
more idyllic, more innocent, than it was for it would be surprising
indeed if the fee'd laddie's

> . . . airm aroon the middle
> of the lass that mucks the byre

had not guided her sooner or later into the enfolding dark of the
straw-barn. Two things Gibson's poems do capture though with
conviction: the isolation of the farmtoun folk of that time and
what must have been their last days without class distinction. As
the farmtouns grew into the days of their greatness that countryman's harmony between man and master was to change
dramatically even on the smaller touns, and with it the protective
paternalism of the gudeman and a pattern of social ease that had
come down through centuries.

First there came the bothy system, born of the days of the improved farming; it was necessary to house the larger labour crews of the big new touns. The focus of farmtoun entertainment moved away from the farmhouse fire and into the circle of the bothy stove—encouraged by the tenant himself if he aspired to the genteel life of his better-placed neighbours. It was a move deplored by country churchmen; by it the gudeman lost his chance to show example. Next there came the bicycle; it took the bothy-housed men away from the toun on a Saturday night to other pleasures, and often the uncontrolled drunkenness of the kind of society too ready to judge a man by the number of hard drams he could stomach and still stay on his feet. Both innovations helped to bring a brutalizing element into a life that had once, but a little time before, had a gentler quality.

One traditional entertainment did not die out, however: the meal-and-ale, barn supper or clyack feast that the farmer gave for his "hairst crew" when he had his crop all stacked in the cornyard. The meal-and-ale—in the hard-farming counties of the North-East the supper took its name from its main draw—continued into the 1920s, even the 1930s, a highlight, like the three or four important local dances, of the cottared and fee'd man's year. The ballads clumsily sing of it, leaving no doubt about the determined way the night was squeezed for every joyous instant: it was the triumphal moment of a hard "hairst".

> Come, ye jolly lads and lasses,
>   Ranting round in pleasure's ring,
> Join wi' me, tak' up the chorus,
>   And wi' mirth and glee we'll sing.
> We come nae here for warldly gear,
>   Nae warldly motive did us draw;
> But we came here to flit the fleer,
>   And dance till we were like to fa'.
> Noo, minstrels, screw your fiddles up,
>   And see if they be richt in tune,
> And gie us "Donald Kissed Katie
>   Comin' through the camowine."
> Wha wad see the bonnie lasses,
>   A' sae handsome, trig and braw;
> Them to please wha wad refeese
>   To want their sleep an hour or twa?

The craps, secure frae wind and rain,
    Stand in the stackyard snug and dry;
Boreas' blasts may rage in vain,
    We'll whistle while it's going by.

Now the harvest wark is owre,
    The fields are bare, the yards are fu',
And we unto the ploo repair,
    And for another crap pursue.

He that first does weary here,
    A dozin fleep we will him ca';
But he that's hinmost in the fleer,
    We'll judge him chief among us a'.

Now we're a' here sae happy met,
    Floating around in pleasure's stream,
We winna flit till Phoebus licht
    Be shining out wi' morning beam.

It was not a decorous occasion. In the heat of the dance and under the influence of "hairst" ale men sang songs they shouldn't have and women changed partners in the reels with the leaden grace of sacks of barley—and hugely enjoyed it. Yet men sang also when they were asked to, without trace of self-consciousness, the bothy songs that reflected the life they knew and the simple love songs that gave some kind of tenderness to the basic dealings of men with women. For that night only, circumspect lasses submitted, uncomplaining, to sly indelicacies. The concoction that brought the event to an almost bacchanalian ferment and made sure that any farmer with a very genteel wife or daughter took her home early, was itself traditional. It was handed down in the generations, its formula almost as secret as that of a guarded liqueur. Its potency was something proverbial, entirely different from Gibson's home-brewed ale, its ferocity unquestioned. Though it led to goodness knows what kind of indiscretions and sometimes to open carnality, it too had a poet to extol its virtues. His name was Andrew Sherrifs, a graduate of Marischal College in Aberdeen, and a man who had met Burns when the Bard visited that city; he has left us the basic elements if not the precise ingredients:

A coggie o' yill and a pickle ait meal,
  And a dainty wee drappie o' whisky,
Was our forefathers' dose to swill down their brose,
  And keep them aye cheery and frisky,
Then hey for the whisky and hey for the yill;
  Gin ye steer a' thegither they'll do unco weel,
To keep a cheil cheery and brisk aye.

That it undoubtedly did, and although Sherrifs was writing in the eighteenth century, Gavin Greig, that expert on the North-East farm life, says that "... even in the nineteenth century the dire concoction was a recognized feature of the thorough-going meal-and-ale". In the face of its influence, it is hardly surprising that such stolid, sober-minded men as John Duthie Webster, heir to Collynie's far-famed Shorthorn herd in the 1920s, did not provide ale of any kind when he took the local village hall for the supper. "JD" as he was always called—long before that executive idiosyncrasy permeated the boardrooms of our own time—was a generous man in many ways, but a strong believer in the ale he was not. The men of his famous farmtouns had to walk down the village to the inn—while the tables were being cleared for the dancing—to sloken their thirsts. By JD's time the day of the old ballad-singer was virtually at an end, though the music that livened farmtoun feet still came from that traditional source, the fiddle and melodeon band, maybe with a trump (a jew's harp) thrown in. If there was nothing else that could be said for the drink there was this: the merrier the fiddler the merrier the reel.

The meal-and-ale, except as a social revival, or as a make-shift scene for the television screen, died with the last days of the old farmtouns. There had been other occasions, equally traditional, that offered a break from the unremitting round of farm work and provided their moment of release: the children's picnic, the show day, and the days of the games and the gatherings that brought piper and kilted athlete as well as some out-of-the-way spectacle into the parish for that one day of the year. On such days, farm carts washed in the mill-dam with stable brooms a day or two beforehand were wheeled out to the sunlight; the harvest frames would be fitted and the cart-wells filled with clean, fresh straw. On this the younger children would squat while their older brothers and sisters and the grown-ups sat on the hairst shelvin's.

The cart itself might be decorated, but if not, the docile Clydesdale groomed to a gloss of perfection and yoked into its shafts certainly would be. Ribbon and raffia embroidered both tail and mane, streamers maybe fluttered from the high hames, brasses sparkled on the martingale. A toun's turnout would be talked about for days after, when the daring of the balloonist or the wonder of the tumblers was almost forgotten; he was a poor horseman who would disgrace his toun's name on such an occasion. Not even the children's picnic went past without the adults too having their fling; at the end of the afternoon, when the races had been run and the tea, baps and lemonade consumed, some platform boards would be laid on the grass and a farm cart drawn alongside—as a rostrum for the fiddlers.

Grey winters passed and with them the days of blind-drift that took poor shepherd men out of this world forever, lost in the smoor till their senses numbed. Spring came and brought the cottar wives again to their doors in an evening to watch their menfolk at work delling (delving) the "yard", the plots that came with their tied cottages. Drills of potatoes would be planted (earlies that would keep the family supplied until such time as the farmtoun gathered its main-crop variety and the cottar got his perquisite load); carrots, beetroot and peas would be sown; the planting of cabbage and kail accomplished. For the man going home at the May Term to a new farmtoun it was a time when he strapped his spade to the cross-bar of his bicycle and set off with the seed potatoes to plant out his next garden plot.

Through summer evenings, while the wives sat on their door-steps gossiping and swatting the midges as they knitted or darned their menfolk's socks, the men themselves would be sawing logs (to stack for winter) and axeing the kindling wood (needed to poke sudden life into the fire so that they could all get their brose in the morning). The man with friends was the cottar man with some reputation as a barber; he could hardly get time for such family chores. Before he had his supper finished they were at the door, apologetically and with their bonnets in their hands. Soon they would be sitting straddle-legged across a chair in the kitchen for the kind of short back-and-sides that would have sent any sergeant-major into paroxysms of delight. It was on the days before weddings and funerals that they came in numbers, and sat on, sometimes into the morning, for once "croppit", a man would draw his chair in to the fire and make an evening of it. Family, friends, and distant relatives (in both senses) would be enquired after; "news" was the great solace and the barbering brought in more rumour than the old packman had ever done. It was the children of the house who had the best of it, for though it would have been unthinkable to pay the barber—such services were acknowledged in drams at the inn—it would have been uncharitable to go home without leaving a "penny" for the bairns. Only when winter came might there be nights of respite when the chill frost kept everybody at home behind their own firmly-shut doors. Then, in the long dark of the evening, the dambrods—the draughts—would be taken down from the shelf in the cupboard and spread where the oil lamp threw its yellow glare on the table.

Such was the social life of the cottared man. The single, bothy-housed men made their own kind of entertainment—or devilment. Through the winter, for those without lasses, there was the continuing curse of cards, and before a ploughing match there was harness to clean, ploughs to set. In summer, when they had finished their supper, there was the quoits or football or wrestling, in fun and in earnest, besides the constant discussion of the farmtoun and its affairs. And always, between times, there was the devilry of a feet-washing, that old pre-nuptial rite of the farmtouns, and soon afterwards, when the newly-weds were suspected of still being too early abed, the mischief of the divot on the chimney to smoke them out and put an end to such wickedness. Again, if things were quiet there was an old alternative, a favourite prank. Late on, the bothy men of a neighbouring toun would be awakened by the wild commotion and the direst yells of "Fire! Fire! Fire!" Through the bothy's open door, the hoaxers, doubling with mirth, would watch as its occupants, dazed with sleep, struggled to put unsteady legs into trousers and track down tackety boots under the beds. Late on, too, where the feeder stream for a mill-dam was a minor tributary and when the master was in his bed, there was a little circumspect poaching with lamp and leister; that way, salmon could come suddenly on to the self-catering bothy men's menu. It was, it is true, the time of the mutual improvement society, the debating club and the literary association, but none seems to have enjoyed a following among the folk of the farmtouns; like the temperance movement, these societies drew their membership from the earnest tradesmen and other sober-living folk.

But winter or summer—for Sunday harvesting would not then have been countenanced—there came the Sabbath and its respite; the kirk bell tolled over the silent fields at ten in the morning to tell the folk of the touns it was time to set out if they were coming; at eleven it would toll again to ring them in from the kirkyard to the service. That day, if on no other, grace might be said at the grieve's table and the Bible read round his fire. All the same, it was not a day when the deepest atheist of the farmtoun could lie on in his bed, for a horseman had to feed and groom his pair in the morning as normal, and the bailie tended his beasts as usual. There was only one concession to the Sabbath morn: it started at seven, instead of four or five. For the bailie, it was otherwise almost a normal working day, but the horseman at least had the chance of going from home and freedom for the rest of the day unless he happened to be "tounkeeper" or "catcher"—the duty horseman who would be giving the Clydesdales their noontime feed and their supper at night. For the bothy-housed men, breakfast on a Sunday was at the later hour of eight, and any man who was going to be about the farmtoun that day was then expected to say so, so that meals could be set for him in the kitchen at mid-day and in the evening. Mostly, and especially in the later days of the farmtouns, the single men would set off on their bicycles as soon as they had finished breakfast—home to sample their mother's cooking and leave their bundles of dirty washing. Sooner or later, a bothy-lad would take to visiting the servant lass of some other farmtoun. She would be given leave to feed him from the dinner pot along with the rest of the toun's folk. How long he stayed depended on the lass or on her mistress.

It would be easy to see in such simple courtship an idyll of country ways. But such moments have to be set against a lifetime of the starker side of farmtoun existence: the poor food, the continuous mud, the constant rheumy pains that came finally from wearing clothes that were damp almost from one year's end to the next; they have to be balanced against the squalor of bothy life and the hardships of domestic service; and against the human tragedy that stalked the farmtouns as surely as high spirits. Men were mangled by machinery improperly guarded, gored by bulls inadequately tethered; children drowned unseen in mill-dams.

Illness and contagion struck with terrifying suddenness, scarlatina closed country schools for weeks at a time and the even deadlier scourge of diphtheria swept terror before it: in a single month in 1862, George Marr, the farmer of that far-famed toun of Cairnbrogie, lost all his eight children with the disease. And dark though these times were there was another contagion; it took hold of men's souls: the terrible quality of despair. Drained and disillusioned, men who had once had a vision and dream of farming land well and efficiently, slowly became the slaves about their own farmtouns and too far in at the bank. Nowhere is their dilemma so precisely caught as in the poem, "The Winner of Wars" by David Ogston, the North-East poet and writer:

> Donald, the old farm won in the end,
> Many a time I saw you snared
> In the fields by the restless sun,
> Look back at the old house, cursing
> Its patience as it sifted you slowly,
> Like a valley savouring an echo.
>
> You would not leave it. You remained,
> Spent of feeling, lacking even sense
> Of the great pulse of life, but
> Accepting death as a necessary fact
> Feeding the long roots of your soul
> On the carcase of a dream.
>
> Have you forgotten it? The dream I mean—
> That dream you buried in the ground
> Like an early lamb, many winters since?
> What else could keep you, knowing all
> The odds, but refusing to acknowledge them,
> Thinking that victory was in sight?

Broken men, such victims might finally put an end to it all, taking the shotgun to some quiet wood or lying down, far from the sound of the sea, to drown in their own horse-troughs. Even so, their end would be given a quiet dignity as the men of the neighbour touns put on their best serge suits and uncomfortable collars to convoy an old friend to the peace of the kirkyard.

Yet even death did not end a tenancy; it was the roup, the displenish sale that followed that did that and closed a man's account with the land. The roup, too, was a funeral of sorts and cottar men would leave their delling, coming from far touns in an evening maybe to buy in the bidding but more likely just out of curiosity. One could not be unaffected by the "lots" for auction, the piles of a lifetime's possessions, some of them deeply personal, laid out for critical appraisal in the cornyard or some close-lying field. Like burials, roups gave the folk of the farmtouns a chance to meet others from distant touns and to discuss the state of the work, the lateness of crops. Old bothy cronies took stock of that time long past. There would be a referee, usually a neighbour, to see fair prices for the widow, but the man of the occasion would be the auctioneer, a character in his own right and almost certainly a farmer's son himself. Blustering, cajoling, taking sly advantage of the unwary, he knew, all the same, how much depended on him. Between times there were drams to be taken (such refreshments were usually organized by the local hotelier) and there was trade to be done. You could tell that by the number of implement salesmen moving quietly through the crowd. The young farmer who missed the binder in the bidding would not be long before he felt a discreet tug at his sleeve.

All the same, for all its fair-like atmosphere, it was a sad occasion and nobody liked it; it meant that the hard world of the farmtouns had claimed another victim. But at the end of the day, for his widow at least, there would be a penny or two. All she would need to sit out the last of her days by a daughter's ingle.

# XIV

## *Love and the Servant Lasses*

BASTARDY GAVE THE bothies a bad name. It was remarkably
rife though in no way unusual; it was no more than the expected
outcome of healthy rural courtship. It was only when the first
official statistics about such things began to be published in
Scotland in the mid-1800s that the true extent of the problem
became known. Then, indeed, were genteel eyebrows raised, for
the figure for the ballad counties in particular, from the Mearns
north to the lands of Moray, was about twice the national average.
It was a staggering blow to the forces of morality and to the
men of the Free Kirk, so closely associated with the farmtouns,
in particular. Their wrath was terrible; Free Kirk ministers took
to seeing abomination behind every haystack when all that was
happening was the playful struggle of country lovers coming to
the right true end of love. Its accomplishment was as natural
round a farmtoun as life itself, and there is little doubt that round
the bothy touns especially it sometimes flourished with a fine
abandon. There have been sociologists since who have gone out of
their way and almost to absurd lengths to absolve the bothy from
all blame, pointing out that in the counties of the North-East
Lowlands, the chaumer system was mainly the rule for the housing
of the single farmtoun men whose night-time wanderings gave
rise to so much unauthorized pregnancy. But that, of course, is
hair-splitting of the finest analytical order for the terms, in
everyday usage, were synonymous.

Though the registrar-general's revelations brought shame on the
servant lasses of the farmtouns, they did no more than underline
what the bothy ballads themselves so strongly hinted at: that the
midnight sport of the farmtouns was as close to nature as anything
about the farmyard itself; that the toil of the farmtoun day was as
nothing sometimes against its activities of the night. One would
like to say that the ploughboy's power of seduction was proverbial.
Or that the much-coveted Horseman's Word as the reputed

key to utter and unquestioning compliance was indeed capable
of all the magical things attributed to it, but there is no evidence
that it was so. There is, on the other hand, incontrovertible proof
that the lasses of the farmtouns liked the chase and the midnight
revels and all that they led to. There were genuine casualties, of
course, farmers' daughters, without true knowledge of the game,
who succumbed to the guile of one of their father's own ploughmen and had to be hurriedly married in the parlour dark of a
winter's afternoon to give heavenly countenance to what already
had been consummated in the barn. By such a night's work,
indeed, a slow and stupid halflin on the strength of his good looks
might heir himself in later years into the mastery of a farmtoun.
Equally, there were farmers' sons who crept into the servant
lass's bed and brought the black burning shame of it on their
families, though it was a practice that gave many a generous
cottar's lass a lift up in the world. There were milkmaids who were
at risk in the morning byre:

> Oor dairymaid she is some shy
> At the bailie lad as he gangs by,
> When she gae's oot to milk her kye
> By grey daylicht in the mornin'.

Yet the bulk of the ballads as they come down to us, often in a
modified form that erases all offence, leave little doubt about the
climate of love around the farmtouns—or the ardour of many of
the kitchen maids. Their response was delightfully, un-
complicatedly, on the side of life:

> But the plooman laddie's my delight,
> The plooman laddie loes me;
> When a' the lave gang tae their bed
> The plooman comes and sees me.

That situation, for any strict Kirk man, was almost intolerable.
Thus the Reverend George R. Davidson, of uplands Drumblade
in the North-East where once the Bruce himself had hid, reporting
in 1840 from his rural parish, one far from being behind-hand in
the farming revolution but in the other ways of the countryside,
seemingly still strongly traditional: "The standard of religion

and morality cannot be rated very high. Impurity and intemper-
ance . . . are still not infrequently to be met with. In the class of
farm servants the former vice particularly has been very pre-
vailing." There is a sad mood of resignation almost in Mr
Davidson; not so in the Rev. Dr James Begg, the Free Kirk's great
morals crusader, a man of sterner cloth and not about to let the
ammunition supplied by the registrar-general go past him. Dr
Begg was not a man to mince clerical words. It had long been
known, he claimed, that the bothies were "scenes of obscenity,
drunkenness and Sabbath-breaking"; that the bothy districts
were "hotbeds of profligacy". His phrases had the scorching
fire of a Sunday tabloid journalist. Aberdeenshire in particular
he singled out for comment; there—the very soul-lands of the
ballad—illegitimacy stood at nineteen per cent and nearly every
fifth child born was a bastard—a hard word for what was often a
fine bairn and one who frequently inherited the genius of bastardy.
There may well have been a reason for that area's unenviable
illegitimacy ratio, for though it was indeed a region of fine farmtouns whose names chimed in ballad lines, it was also one of
many small touns where the hired help might number only three
or four and the chaumers sometimes housed as few as two single
men. They were fed in the farm kitchen by the servant maid and
pampered by her even. It would have been surprising if, at the
end of her hard kitchen day and in the isolation of a bleak countryside far from the softer graces of society, she had not found the
attentions of one or other of them (and whiles maybe both) a
little flattering and enjoyed the moments of open flirtation
while well knowing the risks. Their approach to love may have
been simple and uncomplicated, but if it lacked the subtlety and
nuances of city affairs there is nothing to indicate that, for all its
occasional coarseness, it did not have its tender responses. What
is in no doubt is that it was at times alarmingly permissive, openly
and unashamedly sexual. Opportunities were eagerly seized
upon; kitchen maids did not play the doe-eyed maiden. The
servant lass whose eye was taken with the new ploughman,
properly wooed, might soon take to visiting him in the chaumer
when the coast was clear, or on the Sabbath perhaps when his
bothy colleagues were from the toun. But any of the farmtoun's
biggings might be a place of rendezvous, or even, on a summer's
night, a secret corner of the cornyard. Its clandestine arrangement,

the bothy songs make clear, was all part of the excitement of the farmtoun courtship. Circumspect ploughmen laid sly plans, schemes that demanded patience, high skill in the art of deception, as William Alexander, in *Johnny Gibb of Gushetneuk*, that classic of North-East farmtoun life set about the middle-1800s, suggests. Here the small toun's horseman waits the chance to visit the toun's kitchen lass while the master and mistress are from home, spending a few days at the seaside; in the dry humour that is still very much a part of that bare countryside, the author describes what, in those delightfully chauvinistic times, was "the sport of the lasses":

. . . when the cows had been milked, and the calves properly attended to, and the work of the day fully concluded, Johnny Gibb's three servants were to be seen loitering about the kitchen door, and talking over the "countra clatter". Tam, who was seated on the big "beetlin" stone by the door cheek, had spoken once and again of going to bed, and had given "the loon" emphatic warning of the expediency of his immediately seeking repose, as he might depend on it that he, Tam, would pull him out of the blankets by the heels if he were not up by five o'clock next morning. Notwithstanding his urgency with "the loon", Tam himself did not give any distinct indication of hurrying to bed. But as "the loon" failed to "obtemper" his repeated hints, he at last started up to his feet, and went clanking across the causeway and up the trap stair to the chaumer over the stable. And, while "the loon" proceeded to undress, Tam yawned once and again portentously. He then, very deliberately wound up his watch, and, seating himself on his "kist", began, by-and-by, to "sowff" over "My love she's but a lassie yet". When he had got Willie fairly to bed, Tam next rose, and, under the pretence of going to the stable, slipped down the trap and out by the door, which he quietly locked to make sure that Willie M'Aul would not follow him. In somewhat less than two minutes thereafter, Tam Meerison and Jinse Deans were seated side by side on the "Deece" in Johnny Gibb's kitchen.

The "deece" was a kind of farmtoun sofa. It was not, says the author

. . . the first time that Jinse had been wooed in a similar manner, and in that same place. Not by the same wooer, certainly, for until three weeks ago she had been utterly unaware that such a man as Tam Meerison existed.

At any rate, if Jinse saw no harm in receiving a little attention from an additional sweetheart, Tam, evidently, found her company the reverse of disagreeable.

They sat on, the two lovers, past midnight and into the morning, until even the corncrake's cry was stilled—and until another face whispered for admittance at the window.

The outcome of such behaviour was perfectly predictable; only then would Jinse's plurality of lovers prove something of an embarrassment. But even that was nothing new in the life of the farmtouns.

More careful couples laid more careful plans but these too, ent sadly wrong and the bothy songs are full of the mis- , real and apocryphal, that befell country lovers; they were ites at the simple social occasions of the time since all who d to them had at some time or other been in the kind of on they depicted. When the trysting place was the stable e shy suitor had taken a dram to support his courage or his r as he waited for the kitchen lass to sneak out to him, could be the kind of comic misunderstanding that delighted earthy, unsophisticated audience:

> The nicht was fine, 'twas after nine,
>   The frost was biting keenly, O,
> The rising moon owre Mormond's croon
>   Was shinin' on serenely, O.
>
> On sic a nicht the plooman wicht,
>   Wi' whisky fine and cheery, O,
> Has taen the gait we here relate,
>   To visit Kate, his dearie, O.
>
> The road was lang, but Jock aye sang,
>   Oh Kate, ye are my charmer, O,
> Whitsuntide ye'll be my bride,
>   And le'e the weary fairmer, O.

He reached to the trystin' gate,
  And in the stable enters, O,
To wait until his darling Kate
  Wad guide him to the kitchen, O.

He sat and thought, the whisky wrought,
  The whisky fine and cheery, O,
A workin' steer was standin' near,
  Jock thocht he was his dearie, O.

Come gie's a kiss to croon our bliss,
  An then we'll fix the waddin', O,
I'm noo full grown, I've twenty pound,
  And that will buy the beddin', O.

Turn roun' your face, ye're naething less
  Than just a temptin' hizzie, O,
As sure as fate I'll leave ye, Kate,
  And tak' yer sister Lizzie, O.

Come gie's a kiss, ye saucy jaud,
  Altho' I'm fu' I'm cheery, O,
There's nane can gie sic joys to me,
  As cuddlin' you, my dearie, O.

Turn roon your face and gie's a kiss
  And nae be half sae saucy, O,
As sure's a doo, you've turned a coo,
  Ye're unco caul' and hairy, O.

But soon the sport was broken short
  By Jockie's kind companion, O,
A woman ne'er beheld a steer
  Embraced in sic a fashion, O.

The couple they've got married noo,
  And lang may they be able, O,
To lauch at fate, and no forget
  The courtin' in the stable, O.

The lines of "Courtin' in the Stable" have a fine rumbustious ring to them and are, of course, from the days before Clydesdales when oxen pulled the plough, though the song was sung, until a much later time and the same kind of thing was still going on; they also make clear that the lad was waiting for the lass to "guide him to the kitchen, O".

The servant lasses were not saints; when the master and mistress were asleep they slipped the door bolts to admit admirers to their kitchens and, often enough, their beds. There was encouragement, even incitement, for bold lovers, and those who could not darken the door gained entry in other ways. On the evidence of one bothy song alone, "Blow the Candle Out", it becomes clear that a lad who took a lass's fancy was not left to stand by the window all night without consolation. Nor was his leave-taking without its Shakespearean importunities:

'Twas a young apprentice boy
　Came courting his dear.
The moon was shining bright
　And the stars were twinkling clear;
He went to his love's window
　To ease her of her pain;
His darling rose and let him in,
　Then went to bed again.

It's early next morning,
　Before the break of day;
The laddie rose, put on his clothes,
　A' for to go away;
But when that he was going away,
　His love to him called out—
"Come, take me in your arms, love,
　And blow the candle out".

My father and my mother,
　They taunt me very sore
For keeping o' your company, love,
　But I will keep it more,
For a' the taunts that they can gi'e
　They'll never change my heart;
So, come here, my dear, and I'll meet you here,
　Let the night be ever so dark.

Your father and your mother
　In yonder room do lie,
Embracing one another,
　And so may you and I;
Embracing one another
　Without a fear or doubt,
So take me in your arms, love,
　And blow the candle out.

> My bosom is on fire, love,
> The more I gaze on thee,
> And as I wander lower
> I am no longer free;
> And while I gaze your rosy lips
> Do sweetly seem to pout,
> So hasten to my arms, love,
> And blow the candle out.

Thus the unashamed urgency of farmtoun love.

But such nocturnal courtship could be fraught, constantly at hazard if not from a moral guardianship as tight as close arrest, from the wrath and tattle tongue of the farmer's envious daughter, whose own suitors usually had to be more discreet. There was danger for a young ploughman in such a situation, and the song "Rural Courtship" suggests that the objection was not always strictly a moral one:

> As I cam' in by Monymusk,
> And doun by Alford's dale,
> A sad misfortune happened to me,
> And I think nae shame to tell.
>
> As I gaed in by Monymusk
> The moon was shinin' clear;
> As I held on to Lethendy
> To see my Maggie dear.
>
> I did gang, when I did think
> That a' were sleepin' soun';
> But plague upon yon auld wife,
> For she cam' slinkin' doun.
>
> Sae cannily she slipt the lock,
> And set the door agee;
> Then crawled upon her han's and knees
> To see wha it could be.
>
> Then to the bells, wi' a' her micht,
> Sae loud she made them ring,
> Till faith I thocht about my lugs
> The biggin' she wad bring.

And when she saw I wadna slip,
  She ran to the guidman,
Says:—"There's a lad into the house,
  An' that I winna stan' ".

For it is a most disgraceful thing,
  It wad provoke a saunt,
To see a' servant girls wi' lads
  When the gentle anes maun want.

Providence has acted wrang
  Sic pleasures for to gie
To ony servant lad or lass
  Just workin' for a fee.

The auld man cam' ben himsel',
  An' he push'd ben his heid;
Guidfaith I thocht it was a ghost
  Just risen frae the deid.

He'd duddy drawers upon his legs,
  He'd on a cap o' white,
An' he'd a face as lang's my leg,
  An' in his hand a light.

He's ta'en me by the shoulders broad,
  An' push'd me out o' doors;
Thinks I, my auld lad, I'll come back
  When sleepin' gars ye snore.

Summary eviction was the result here. For both the lad and the
lass if they were fee'd home to the same toun the penalty might be
instant dismissal; about other bothy touns perhaps only the
imposition of a fine—say, five shillings (25p) from his half-year's
wages—on the ploughman who preferred the kitchen maid's bed
to his own, but also, likely, a fairly clear directive that when his
engagement was finished it would be time for him to find another
farmtoun. The ballad, like many more, underlines the wisdom of
courting the "maiden", the eldest daughter of a North-East
farmtoun, before turning one's attention to any of the servant
lasses. Here, in another ballad of the North-East region, "Between
Stanehive and Laurencekirk", it seems that the former has given
her father wind of the lovers' stable tryst:

Between Stanehive and Laurencekirk
  Last term I did fee,
'Twas wi' a wealthy farmer,
  His foreman for to be.
To work his twa best horses
  Was what I had to do,
A task that I could manage weel
  Both in the cart and ploo.

I worked my horses carefully,
  And did my master please,
Excepting to some rants o' fun
  That did his temper tease;
Until the month o' January,
  As you may well believe,
For courtin' wi' the servin' girl
  We both did get our leave.

One night into the stable,
  By tryst I met her there,
On purpose for to have some fun,
  And guid advice to gie 'er;
Our master hearing o' the same
  To the stable he cam' o'er;
And he did give us both our leave
  Out o' the stable door.

But it's not upon my master
  That I lay all the blame,
It is the maiden o' the place,
  That high respected dame.
Since no sweetheart to her did come,
  It grieved her sore to see
The happy moments that were spent
  Between my love and me.

Come all ye jolly ploughboys
  That want to mend the fau't;
Be sure it is the maiden first
  That ye maun court and daut;
For if ye court the servant first,
  And gang the maiden by,
Ye may be sure the term for you
  Is quickly drawin' nigh.

> Surely the times are getting hard
>   When courtin's ca'ed a crime;
> For it has been practised noo
>   Guid kens for hoo lang time;
> But yon big toon aboon the road,
>   It is forbidden there;
> And for feein' wi' yon farmer
>   I bid you a' beware.

"Daut" is an old Scottish word with a dubious past covering a multitude of caresses from the mildest to the most passionate—and there is the distinct probability that its dishonourable history doesn't end even there.

There may have been other reasons for the maiden's envy, for away from the toil of their kitchens the servant lasses were by no means drabs; some took to fashion as to the manner born. When they went from home, to kirk, ball or the games, they would invite admiring glances, get attention even above their station and be launched in no time into a heedless, head-long whirl that could have but one ending. The fashion rise and the inevitable fall of a kitchen maid is wittily chronicled in "The Braw Servant Lasses", a fine rollicking tale of a servant lass's social progress as she bounces from one love to the next:

> When schooling is over to service she goes,
> For the greed of high wages as you may suppose;
> And the first of it goes for a white muslin goon,
> And a bonnet wad keep the moonlicht frae a toon.
>
> She curls up her hair like a waterdog's tail,
> Rowed up in a paper as roun' as a snail;
> Wi' that and the veil hangin' down owre her e'en
> There's never ae wrinkle ava to be seen.
>
> And down frae the bonnet there hings a bit silk,
> Like what my auld grannie had for synin' her milk;
> I own it is useful the beauty to grace,
> For it hides a' the wrinkles that is in her face.
>
> And noo she's rigged out like a ship in full sail,
> Wi' sax-seven flounces aboot her goon tail;
> The very first Sunday the buckle goes on,
> Says the ane to the ither, "Jock, wha is she yon?"

E

For Sunday aboot she goes to the church,
But what she hears there she winna mind much,
The text and the psalms she'll no mind  upon,
But she'll mind very weel what her neighbours had on.

At balls and at weddin's she'll rant and she'll rove,
At every new meetin' she'll get a new love;
But wi' her gallivantin', ere three years gae roon,
Her pride that was up it gets a tak' doon.

When some o' her sweethearts kens something is wrang,
Into the same country they'll no tarry lang,
But rin aff to America, oh! sic a trick!
And missie, poor thing, gets the whip-shaft to lick.

And now she's confined like a cow on the grass,
The bonnet's laid by wi' the hail gaudy dress;
The cradle she rocks, while the wee one does roar,
And she greets for the thing that she lauched at afore.

With three years of a fling, the lass of the song may have been luckier than most, but earlier or later a servant lass's predicament would become obvious. There came the moment when the master of a toun, mixing his morning brose in the kitchen along with his fee'd men (which many of them did), would cast an eye on the maid's thickening waist and—in the droll way of such men and with that dryness of humour that could keep a man sane through a disastrous harvest—say kindly: "God lass, there is surely more there than went in with the spoon!" Then indeed would the cat be out, the lass's shame exposed. The mistress would have to be told; there would be tears, as much from relief that the deception was ended as of remorse. Nearer her time if not before the lass would be sent home to her mother's house for her confinement and the bairn would take its mother's name until such time as a father could be found for it. That might take time; fatherhood (to everyone's embarrassment) was sometimes not easily attributed and even where it was certain there might first be the Kirk Session to see and after that, despite its stern encouragement to marriage, a disinclination by both parties. Many a lass left the child with her mother and went back to the world of the farmtouns to repeat her error, often with the same man, before she gave her bairn a father and a home.

It might be thought that the ballads though blatant enough about the midnight courtships of the farmtouns would be less outspoken about their inevitable result, but no, that was but further grist for the ballad-writer. Never though is it the slightest tinge of outrage that shines through, just the simple broad humour of folk who live close to nature and, for all the kirk's preaching, find in bastardy little cause for surprise. Some of the songs of the early farmtoun days, in fact, though sung then in the family circle and to mixed audiences without giving the slightest offence, had a broad humour and a directness that made any editor of the early-1900s hesitate to print them. They contained entreaties of course; mothers shamed who had never suspected; accusation and counter-accusation; and inquisitions into the illicit love-making before the Kirk Session. But to begin at the beginning, as the songs themselves invariably do:

> Frae a butcher laddie that lived in Crieff,
> A bonnie lassie cam' to buy some beef;
> He took her in his arms and down she did fa',
> And the wind blew the bonnie lassie's plaidie awa'.
>
> The plaidie was lost and it couldna be found,
> The devil's in the plaid, it's awa' wi' the win';
> An' what will I say to the auld folks ava?
> I daurna say the win' blew the plaidie awa!
>
> It wasna lang after the plaidie was lost,
> Till the bonnie lassie grew thick about the waist,
> And Rab he was blamed for the hale o' it a',
> And the win' blawin' the bonnie lassie's plaidie awa'.
>
> Then Rab was summoned to answer the Session,
> And they a' cried out ye maun mak' a confession;
> But Rab never answered them ae word ava
> But "the win' blew the bonnie lassie's plaidie awa' ".
>
> The auld wife cam' in poor Rab to accuse,
> The minister an' elders began to abuse
> Poor Rab for trying to mak' ane into twa;
> But Rab said, "The win' blew the plaidie awa' ".
>
> The lassie was sent for to come there hersel',
> She look'd in his face, says, "Ye ken hoo I fell?
> An' ye were the cause o't ye daurna say na',
> For 'twas then that the win' blew my plaidie awa'."

Rab look'd in her face and he gied a bit smile,
He says, "Bonnie lassie, I winna you beguile,
The minister he's here he'll mak' ane o' us twa,
That will pay for the plaid that the win' blew awa'."

The whisky was sent for to mak' a' thing richt,
The minister an' elders they sat a' nicht,
They sat an' they sang till the cock he did craw,
"The win' blew the bonnie lassie's plaidie awa'."

Now Rab and his lassie they are han' in han',
An' they live as contented as ony in the lan';
An' when he gets drunk he minds on the fa',
An' he sings, " 'Twas the win' blew the plaidie awa'."

The song, also set earlier than the great days of the farmtouns
though certainly sung and relished then, could almost be said to
describe the pattern of Scottish rural courtship; the plaid, as much
a part of Scottish history as oatmeal, was a kind of universal
garment worn rather like a shawl over the head and loosely draped
around the body. The resistance it offered to determined suitors
would have been minimal. And even if the joyous conviviality of
the Session is a little unlikely, there is no doubt that they did
earnestly try to persuade backsliders into the soul-saving of
matrimony, often to the continuing happiness of both and face-
saving of all concerned. The Kirk Session records of any Scottish
parish are proof of the fact that a minister and his elders spent
much of their time dealing with just such offenders.

But beyond the rule of Holy Writ, even in the face of it, the
backsliding continued; servant lasses fell victim not only to
farmer's sons but here and there to the charms of a young laird
whose reputation was already well known. A father, whether a
cottar or a tenant farmer, could sometimes profit, it seems, from
such a situation:

On the south-east of Perth there lived a fair maid,
She wandered late and ear' and she never was afraid,
She walked both late and ear' and she never was afraid
    For meeting wi' the young laird o' Kilty, O.

It's out it spake her mother and she spoke wi' a smile,
Says, I wonder very much that you walk so late, my child,
You walk both late and ear' and you never are afraid
    For meeting wi' the young laird o' Kilty, O.

She has fastened up her yellow locks a little above her e'e,
And she's kilted up her petticoats a little below her knee,
And so neatly as she walked by the harrows and the ploughs,
　　And she's down through the bonnie parks o' Kilty, O.

She had not left her father's house I think by scarce a mile,
When she heard a voice behind her say, stay, my pretty child,
She heard a voice behind her say, stay, my pretty child,
　　Don't you know you're in the bonnie parks o' Kilty, O.

She turned her gently round about a sad tear blint her e'e,
Says, I will turn back again if I've offended thee,
Says, I will turn back again if I've offended thee,
　　For I know I'm in the bonnie parks o' Kilty O.

O, stay wi' me, my darling, just stop a little while,
When the harrows and the ploughs are loosed I'll go wi' you a mile,
When the harrows and the ploughs are loosed I'll go wi' you a miel,
　　I'll convoy you from the bonnie parks o' Kilty, O.

He's ta'en her by the middle sma' and gently laid her down,
Where the apples and the cherries were a' hanging down,
The lilies and the green grass were growing all around
　　Where they lay on the bonnie parks o' Kilty, O.

What will you tell your mother, my dear, when you go home?
Who will you say to your mother has done ye a' the wrong?
What will you say to your mother, my dear, when you go home?
　　Will you say it was the young laird o' Kilty, O?

Just as she was going to make him some reply,
It's up it starts her father just from a bush nearby;
Says, You'll wed my daughter quickly or down her tocher pay,
　　Or I'll forfeit your bonnie parks o' Kilty, O.

O, hold your tongue, old man, and do not angry be,
Although that your daughter is of a low degree,
I'll raise her to a higher, a lady for to be,
　　Make her lady o' the bonnie parks o' Kilty, O.

Now, he loved this pretty girlie, as dearly as his life,
He loved this pretty girlie and made her his wedded wife,
And she sits in his house and is happy as a queen,
　　For she's lady o' the bonnie parks o' Kilty, O.


Delightful; though one worries about the young laird—whether,
after all, he did not walk into a tender trap cunningly laid for him

and whether he deserved it. Maybe young lairds were as randy as
young ploughmen and *they* weren't slow to sing of their prowess:

> When I gae tae the kirk on Sunday,
>     Mony's the bonnie lass I see
> Prim, sittin' by her daddy's side,
>     And winkin' owre the pews at me.
>
> I can drink and nae be drunk,
>     I can fight and nae be slain,
> I can court anither's lass,
>     And aye be welcome to my ain.

Such ploughboy casanovas when they came before the Kirk
Session took the matter as lightly:

> The parson then began to scold,
>     Called me a rovin' blade;
> And for the deed that you have done
>     Due penance must be paid.
>
> Pay down your guinea and begone,
>     And never let me know
> That e'er ye do the like again
>     Through a' this life below.

There were obstacles though for such "roving blades" in the
formidable mistresses of the farmtouns where the Word was given
some countenance through the week as well as on the Sabbath.
They kept a strict watch on their servant lasses and did their
best to stem any moral drift where their maids were too easily
inclined to yield to nature; they would even pounce when they
suspected the maid and catch the lovers red-handed (if that be the
appropriate expression) and certainly in all but the most brazen of
cases, red-faced. Their names passed into the world of ballad-lore
as a warning to other ploughman gallants—like that of "Auld
Luckie of Brunties", who forgot to feed her horses properly but
took a strongly Christian outlook in other matters:

> It's a' ye roving young men,
>     Come listen unto me,
> And dinna gang to Brunties toon
>     The lasses for to see:

Auld Luckie she's a wily ane,
    And she does watch the toon,
And ilka lad that she does catch
    She fines him half-a-crown.

'Twas on a Tuesday's evenin',
    As I was told by one,
A laddie went to see the girls,
    Wi' them to hae some fun;
Auld Luckie, growin' restless,
    She jumped out-owre her bed,
And there she found a young man
    Wi' her servant maid.

And there was a Mistress Greig of an unnamed toun on Deveron-side who didn't wait for that kind of situation; she did a kind of captain's rounds of her maids' quarters "to guard them from all carnal danger".

Each night before she went to bed
    Their sleeping-place she searched over,
For fear some fellow there might hide,
    And in among them prove a rover.

There are many more ploughmen's songs which emphasize the common practice of midnight courting about the farmtouns; they are the songs of folk untrammelled by the nicer nuances of polite society, who succumbed easily to that other natural world of joy and the senses. Their simple directness today invites doubt; there need be none. Gavin Greig, that highly-articulate and objective collector, unlike his friend John Ord—who, after all, as a Glasgow policeman may have been totally unastonished by such frailties of human character—is quite specific. Unlike Ord, though, the New Deer schoolmaster was sometimes condescending in his study, and that tone is just detectable here in an extract from his retiring presidential address on Folk-song in Buchan to the Buchan Field Club in December 1905. He is, for his time, admirably unequivocal about what went on around the farmtouns in the 1800s:

If love appears in these Ploughman Songs it represents little more than the natural and inevitable association of Jock and

Meg as lad and lass for the time being. There is in it neither idealism nor chivalry. The roving life which the farm-servant class lead colours their love affairs and gives them a complexion all their own. Thrown together for six months or a year the ploughman and the servant girl adopt each other *pro tem* and without prejudice. People in the better ranks of life are tempted to call this a liaison; but it is hardly fair to use terminology borrowed from a social sphere where conditions are different. Its application is bound to misinterpret the situation to some extent. In any case the parties pay little or no heed to views of what is to them an outer world. Social Ishmaelites throughout the generations, our farm servants have no public opinion to reckon with but are a law unto themselves. They have the courage of their practices, and never seem ashamed even when the results of their amours come to light individually, or afterward in the mass form matter of sinister statistical statement and comment. We are not, however, dealing with the moral aspect of the question. We simply have to recognise that sexual relations in this particular stratum of life are about as nearly natural as the law will allow them to be, and that sexual love appears in their songs pretty much as it would have done in pagan times. But it should in justice be added that however free the relations of young men and women may be about our farms, these persons when once married exhibit as a rule a degree of conjugal fidelity that compares favourably with that found in the higher grades of society.

Which is about as explicit a statement as has ever been made on the subject of farmtoun sex. Not without its significance is the fact that even in 1905 its tense is the present.

By then the popularity of the bicycle was adding a new dimension to farmtoun courtship; a lad could come farther and stay longer. It gave ploughmen a scope they had never dreamed of. It was also a liability; in a countryside where every bicycle was about as individual as the people rumour could start from the sight of two machines leaned casually together in the hedge by the roadside. But soon, too, the granting of favours on the home-road from the harvest dance would become less costly to a servant lass's reputation. With the growing country availability of birth control products the only witness to the course of rural courtship might be the hedge-combing home-going scholar. Mystified, he might ponder the flattened corner of the hayfield and the tributes to Malthus about which grown-up folk, always so garrulous, were so strangely silent.

# XV

# The Kirk and its Shadow

IN THE HEYDAY of the farmtouns the minister was a familiar enough figure, far different from the churchman of the late-1930s. By those final days of the old farmtoun life the kirk's authority had loosened and news of the minister's bicycle turning in at a farm road-end would bring only a quiet oath to the cottar wife's lips as she sent her children outdoors, took the hens' pot off the fire and reached for her best apron. There was an unease now in the relationship, a tension even. But it had not always been so, and its existence may have been as much due to the "new men" of the pulpit as the spiritual disinterest of their congregations. They were a different breed from the old ministers; *they* had been men of rare mettle able to keep one foot in heaven and the other firmly on earth without seeing anything odd in the dichotomy. Such indeed was their affinity with the life of the farmtouns that when one of their number came to write poetry at the start of the 1900s he preached salvation in farmtoun terms without strain or incongruity. His name was George Abel; he had the pulpit at Pitmedden, a small village in the North-East Lowlands. He may not have been a great poet but the striking thing about his lines, in the "braid Scots" of his region, is their one-ness with the farming landscape, mirroring in equal part its endless hope and bitter disillusionment.

That the little United Free Church minister should have written so is less than surprising, for George Abel was just one man out of a multiple mould. Those ministers' link with the farmtouns was strengthened by personal experience in their own glebes and crofts. Many indeed had come off some braeside croft to battle their way to an education before they came to wag their heads in a pulpit; some were to leave their names woven into the pattern of farming progress, their achievements in the fields more frequently remembered than their performances in the pulpit. Patrick Bell of Forfarshire, later minister at Carmyllie, as

a divinity student took the task of harvesting an immeasurable step
forward when he invented the reaper, spurred on by the sight of
the shearers back-breakingly at work on his father's harvest. The
Argyllshire swing plough, designed by the Rev. Alexander
Campbell, was soon copied in every smithy of his surrounding
parishes. And there were others; men of lesser foresight and
genius, but just as persistent, among them the Reverend Mr
Farquharson, an "improver" in his own small way, who seems to
have turned his glebe into a field research unit. Eight years after
Bell had perfected his reaper, Mr Farquharson, long lamenting,
was still bemoaning the non-adoption of the scythe in his upland
parish of Alford. At times, by mischance, such men also took
farming a staggering step forward. The Reverend Gavin Mitchell
was minister at Kinellar, and his year in 1758 must have been a
busy one for Mr Mitchell was pressed for time. He had managed
to broadcast turnip seed in the manse's kitchen garden but then,
occupied doubtless by kirk affairs, next noticed the crop when it
was almost overwhelmed by weeds. The problem seems to have
given Mr Mitchell pause only for a moment: seizing the hoe he
slapped out tangled weed and turnip indiscriminately to leave
individual turnip plants standing in singular isolation, wide spaces
between them. That year the manse garden gave Mr Mitchell the
healthiest crop he had ever grown; he had blundered on to the
value of "singling" turnips. Three years later he was to claim with
an immodesty ill-becoming the incumbent of a pulpit that ". . . the
practice of hoeing . . . was generally adopted by all who sowed
turnips throughout the parish". Clearly, the Rev. Mitchell had
better luck than the Rev. Farquharson. Country ministers even
wrote bothy ballads that reflected their full understanding of the
farmtoun life whatever their other reservations about it. The most
moving, still being sung in the 1920s, was "The Dying
Ploughboy", written by Glenlivet's parish minister, the Rev. R.
H. Calder:

> The gloamin' winds are blawin' saft
> Aroun' my lonely stable laft;
> Amid the skylight's dusky red,
> The sunbeams wander roun' my bed.
>
> The doctor left me in good cheer,
> But something tells me death is near;

My time on earth has nae been lang,
My time has come and I must gang.

Ah, me! 'tis but a week this morn
Since I was weel and hairstin' corn,
As fu' o' health and strength and fun
As ony man amang the throng.

But something in my briest gaed wrang,
A vessel burst and blood it sprang;
And, as the sun sets in the skies,
They'll lay me down nae mair to rise.

Fareweel my horse, my bonnie pair,
I'll yoke and loose wi' you nae mair;
Fareweel my plough, wi' you this han'
Will turn ower nae mair fresh lan'.

Fareweel, my friends, my comrades dear,
My voice ye shall nae langer hear;
Fareweel to yonder setting sun,
My time has come and I must gang.

I've served my master weel and true,
My weel done wark he'll never rue;
And yet, forbye, I micht hae striven
To reach the pearly gates o' heaven.

'Tis weel my Maker knows my name,
Will he gae me a welcome hame?
As I should help in need afford,
Receive me in thy mercy, Lord.

Even more important though, those country ministers wrote the footnotes to the countryside's social history—those invaluable documents, the Statistical Accounts. It is here, says Professor T. C. Smout, in *A History of the Scottish People, 1560–1830*, that one sees them

> . . . come to life, not as pastors but as intelligent gentlemen sowing clover, speculating on ornithology, applauding the new linen work or a new road, agitated over the expense of poor relief, nervous of the effect of rising wages on rural virtue and watchful for any signs of idleness among the labouring classes.

Truly the heavy ecclesiastical hand pinned down the winged hour with a detail that would otherwise have been lost forever and much of that minutiae concerns the farming past.

The link between kirk and farmtoun was strengthened by the Disruption, that cataclysmic sundering of the Church in 1843 that brought the Free Kirk into being and in so doing divided Scotland as completely, if less brutally, than the Rebellion of a century before. This time it was a division almost wholly by class that soured relations between the Big House and the farmtouns, between farmer and farm servant. The folk of the farmtouns largely followed the dissenters; the roots of their disillusionment went deep and stretched back through the years in which they had watched the gentry's influence alter the character of the Established Church—even to the extent at times of making it the mouthpiece of the lairds. In the Clearances, still going on, did it not preach peaceful acceptance of eviction and banishment? That association of manse and landed estate, comparable with that of vicar and squire south of the Border, would have been suspect enough, but the clergy of the Established were, more and more, making God a Moderate and becoming themselves men of letters and other leisurely pursuits. The dissenters were men of sterner stuff; the harder folk of the farmtouns liked their dour God.

When they formed their breakaway kirk it was in the countryside that the dissenting clergy found refuge. Sustained by their evangelical fire, they forsook their kirks and their manses (as they were bound to do) and found shelter sometimes in a cottar house; kirkless, they preached in barns lent generously by farmtouns—often in open defiance of the laird—in stables, granaries, farm lofts, as well as in the unlikely shelter of a distillery (at Campbeltown), an old public house (at Symington in Ayrshire). One farmtoun even built the ricks of its stackyard into a circle so that the worshippers could at least have shelter from the wind. And where no accommodation could be found they met to pray in the fields and on hillsides.

This dislocation of their pattern of worship would have been suffering enough for the people of the countryside but it was compounded by outrageous persecution.

Log bridges leading to any Free Kirk accommodation were burned, the shallow fording places of the river made impassable. On bare hillsides springs that had slaked the thirst of worshippers

who had come far to hear the Word were blocked off. Pressure from
the now denuded Established Church was exerted right down the
social scale: laird threatened tenant, bewildered tenant farmer
warned ploughman and domestic servant. The smaller farmtoun
tenant was particularly vulnerable, threatened with the loss of all
favour if he was—as so many always were—in rent arrears. The
Rev. Thomas Brown's *Annals of the Disruption*, published in the
late 1800s while the memory was still green, describes the kind
of persecution that raged through the divided countryside:

> Factors visited tenants, exhibiting a document called the
> black list, to inform them that they were taking up the names of
> all that would attend the Free Church, to be produced at the
> expiry of their leases. Shopkeepers were told that they would
> forfeit the custom and countenance of the wealthy and in-
> fluential in the country. Servants of every description holding
> situations, from the local manager or grieve down to the herd,
> were threatened with deprivation of office and service. Feuars
> who signified their intention to grant ground for the Free Church
> congregation to worship on, had their charters demanded
> and their rights questioned. Wood merchants were interfered
> with for selling wood for any Free Church purpose.

Cottars, too, paid dearly for their beliefs. In yet another instance
from that same remarkable catalogue of inhumanity in the name
of God, a single parish presents the pattern in a great many more:

> About fifty servants and day-labourers, several of them with
> weak families and destitute of means, were dismissed and thrown
> out of employment, and everything done against them to render
> their adherence bitter. Yesterday, in addition to the servants
> removed at last term, about twenty more, with their families,
> were served with summonses of removal for supporting and
> attending the Free Church; while such as agree to oppose it are
> called from distant parishes to supply their places, and are
> encouraged and protected, whatever character they bear.

Grieves, for once, often behaved gallantly; their situation in the
conflict was an unenviable one. The *Annals* tell the story of one in
particular and his confrontation with the laird. The old grieve had

been in the great man's service for many years and enjoyed the full respect to which his service and judgement over the years had entitled him. But he had swung to the Free Kirk while the laird himself stood staunchly with the Moderates of the Established. The latter's pique, it is likely, was heightened by the fact that the grieve's example had almost certainly helped to empty the Established's pews. There came finally the day when the laird and faithful servant came to grips with their dilemma.

"It will never do," said the laird, "for you and me to be going to different kirks, so come ye back with me to the 'Stablished and we'll continue good friends—just as we have always been."

The grieve may have been surprised, but he was not easily swayed. He had no wish to find a new place, he said, but if that was to be the way of it he would be leaving the laird's service come the Term Day. It was a bold gambit, even for a good grieve, but it worked; his services were too good to part with—and he and his fellow farm-servants were left to worship unmolested.

Generally though, a man's place of worship was no longer a matter for his own conscience. In the circumstances, farmtouns that had promised preaching accommodation sometimes thought better of it.

When rent day came round on one estate tenant-farmers who from duty or conscience had remained within the Established fold were greeted by the laird himself, had their hands warmly shaken and were given ten per cent rebates on their rent. When the Free Kirk tenants appeared, however, the laird left his factor to carry on with the rent-collecting and take every penny-piece that was due to him. Clearly the Established God was a more beneficent God. So were kitchen maids uncharitably dismissed in His name and without adequate reason, and excuses found for putting dissenting cottars from the place.

In Sutherland, the scene earlier of some of the most notorious Clearances, there was a complete refusal to grant sites for the building of Free Kirks or for the erection of manse houses, and the penalty for entertaining a dissenting minister was akin to that for harbouring a felon: instant eviction. It was a kind of justice not new to that particular area.

It was ironical that the Church itself should be the instrument of such hatred and distrust, though that too was not new. The bitterness though would endure down the years, as would the

countryside's abiding link with the Free Kirk forged during those
tumultuous days. Yet, and maybe thankfully, after some summers
of sermons in tents and on windy hillsides there crept in at times
a note of humour in the rivalry of the two kirks. If the Free Kirk
thought little of the Established's moderate men, it is equally
true that the Established flock were inclined to scoff at the bare
religion and the evangelical fire of the Free's preachers—and
especially at the unworthiness of the Free's new quickly-built
wooden churches. There is a story that pins down perfectly the
view of the opposing sects.

One morning a number of Established Church farmers met one
of their Free Kirk neighbours on the Sabbath road.

"And how are ye getting on with your wooden churches?" one
of them asked, maliciously.

"Fine, fine," came the cheery reply. "And how are ye getting on
wi' yer wooden ministers?"

There is no doubt that the Free Kirk ministers could be violent
men in a pulpit. Among the kirk's worshippers in the North-West
was that old chronicler of Highland affairs, Osgood Mackenzie,
and in his *100 Years in the Highlands* he tells the story of a much-
respected visiting minister who worked himself into such a fervour
during the sermon that his clothes were wringing wet with sweat
by the time he had come out at the end of it. However, there was a
problem: so narrow was the minister's own creed that there was
nothing would make him carry on the Sabbath such a secular
luxury as a change of clothes and these had to be sent on beforehand, on a weekday. The Free Kirk's pull was at its strongest
where the Big House had so often put the most unsuitable candidate into the vacant pulpit—even in some cases in the Highlands,
men with hardly a word of the Gaelic who compensated by
roaring at their congregations like demented bulls. To meet the
shortage of preachers the Free Kirk mustered a band of strolling
ministers, all able men and selfless in the service of their kirk.
They took the gospel round to the people of the crofts and
farmtouns like travelling packmen; their arrival in some lonely
glen would bring all other activity to a halt as people gathered to
hear them. Wet or dry, weekday or Sabbath, they came where the
minister was able to preach—and that was sometimes on a windy
beach where the laird took the Established's part and forbade
Free Kirk services on his land. Often these itinerant ministers

would be stopped in their tracks between one destination and the next and sermons demanded; frequently they were cajoled on finishing one service to begin another. It was not unusual for such a preaching to last four or five hours without pause, three ministers preaching one after the other. Sometimes it was even longer, much longer. In the spring of 1848, when Dr Mackay came to give communion in one Highland community he found 6,000 assembled despite the chilly April day and bitter snow showers. He began his service at eleven o'clock in the morning and finally, exhausted, dismissed his congregation about seven o'clock in the evening. Afterwards he learned that the preaching had continued until after midnight.

Those days of the mid-1800s, the early days of the new farmtouns, were the days of the great sacramental event, the less-profane successor to the holy fair of Burns' day. But if the carnal excitements were fewer, the preaching was just as ferocious: "Satan is behind you," some zealous ministers would shout, with such hellfire conviction that folk sprang to their feet in alarm sure that they had felt Auld Nick's breath on their cheek.

But they were solemn and moving occasions. They drew scattered congregations in from the hills, from the outlying farmtouns for five days of almost continuous worship, a kind of spiritual conference. Men came and brought their prejudices with them and probably carried them away again; callow youth sat by hardened sinner. But from the well of some natural amphitheatre loved psalms would rise in the summer air. The surrounding hills flung back the echoing voices of the ministers who followed each other into the makeshift pulpit. Briefly, in that impoverished countryside there was a deep-felt communion of man and earth and heaven. Who knows whether the cottars' flight was from the Established Church itself, seen so often in that time of the Clearances in collusion, or simply from the hopelessness of their own predicament? They came in their thousands over bad roads and from places with no roads, from as far, at times, as 60 miles away. The common folk slept where they could, unwashed, unable to undress, in farmtoun stables and barns, wherever some straw or hay could be spread; the more genteel found beds at the big houses of the local gentry, where the housemaids were run off their feet and the extra work could put a kitchen maid off religion for life.

As many as five ministers might take part, preaching daily in the days before the Sacrament, giving guidance, inviting those intending to take communion to examine their own consciences, their fitness to take it. Their creed was ironclad; young lasses who liked the dancing were considered into Hell and the door shut. They were passionate against pleasure, no leniency was shown; the face of the Free Kirk was as austere and as stern as the bare little kirks it built, its religion so soured against any ostentation that there must have been an imaginative few in its flock who hungered occasionally for just a little of the magnificence of Popery.

But that grip, to all outward appearance, did not slacken for many years. Well after Mr Abel's time the genteel folk of the farmtouns, however backsliding about the weekly Sunday service, kept a kind of faith with their kirk and there would be a heavy gig and bicycle traffic on the roads on the morning of a Sacrament Sunday. Which is not to say that sin did not flourish quietly where a bad road cut off better influences or that even the kirk-going kitchen lass being urgently courted did not occasionally slip from grace. There was—as we have seen—a consternation in many manse studies about the close-to-nature life of the farmtouns and a dark suspicion about the bothy life in particular.

All the same, the ties were strong: the Free Kirk's minister was not the kind of man to be seen only in the eminence of his high pulpit on the Sabbath. Far from it; he was seen about the countryside every day of the week, calling over the fence to the ploughman turning his Clydesdales on an endrig or chatting with the roadman seated with his metalling stones at the turnpike's edge. He was almost a member of the family, consulted constantly about its affairs, officiating solemnly at its christenings, which took place in the home within the family circle, giving them then a greater significance perhaps than today's conveyor-belt baptisms in church in the slack of a Sunday afternoon. In the pulpit he drew his analogies from farming with inspired fluency. In order of season he blessed the seed as well as the sower, at harvest the bounty of Heaven as well as the fecundity of the earth, and the clyack sheaf and the corn dolly in the bygoing, transmuting their pagan past. Truly the line was thin and such men could not have been unaware of it. There were dark regions of the soul and the mind where the kirk was a stranger. In the North-East Lowlands

in particular there was that tight-knit secretive Society of the
Horseman's Word with its strange rituals, a freemasonry of
ploughmen that gave its adherents the bewitchment of the
Horseman's Word. Out of such things tolerance grew; there was
amalgamation of dogma and creed that in any other area of life
would have excited the interest of a Monopolies Commission; in
time there was dialogue between the Free Kirk and the Established.
Even in areas where some men from the West had returned to the
old faith of their fathers, the sight of them early on the Sabbath
road drew no more than sly comment on the early rising demanded
by Rome.

# XVI

## *Folk on the Fringe*

SERVING THE OLD farmtouns there was a peripheral society, its prosperity as closely bound to the soil and the behaviour of the seasons: the smith, the saddler, the souter, miller, carpenter and cartwright, millwright and tailor, as well as the travelling merchant who came round with his horse van bringing sugar and soap and semolina, cans of treacle to sweeten the supper brose and syrup of figs to relieve stomachs constantly constipated by their adherence to that oatmealy dish. A voyager from some distant town, the merchant brought with him, like the post, all the news of the outside world. He was as informative as any newspaper and twice as scandalous. And there were others, of course, the fringe figures of a countryside in which the need for labour was always diminishing and the dole as yet was but a dream in the charitable mind: the itinerants who subsisted by odd skills and the speed of their wits. When charity failed them they poached some of the laird's salmon or took a rabbit or two from his burrows. But because they often brought news from even farther afield than the merchant they would get a meal with the men of a farmtoun and permission to spend the night in the barn. They were not all ignorant men and women by any means. They were the wanderers of their time through no fault of their own: sailors too old to set sail, old soldiers who nightly re-fought their campaigns, blithe fisher-lasses with their heavy creels, old women—once bonnie girls who had followed the drum.

The names of some of them took their place in the folk history of the farmtouns; impudent schoolboys commemorated their legends by passing the name down to a character of later time who, eminently respectable, had succeeded to the same line of business. In the Rhinns of Galloway in the early years of the 1900s, one wandering worthy, Jacob McCulloch, was a well-known figure. He travelled the farmtouns finding work where he could, and with him, always, went his "engine", a three-wheeled "cart" which he pushed where the road was flat or uphill and rode on when the way was all downhill. Yet, it was generally accepted in the region that Jacob was an educated man who had come by some unfortunate accident. One of his peculiarities was to wear his extremely long hair rolled in a bun. He died, in 1925, aged 70, of a sudden unknown illness, in the Poorhouse at Stranraer. Understandably but to the shame of a rural society, he was described on his death certificate as a "pedlar"—an undignified and little-intended demotion for a man, like many another, whose ways enriched the life of the countryside.

Round the farmtouns, too, went other men—with wares to sell. At the opposite end of the farmtoun country, in the flatlands of East Aberdeenshire, about the same time "Besom" Jamie Henderson trailed the country from his hut in the Wood of Tillygreig, selling the heather besoms and pot-scrubbers he made there for farmtoun kitchen and milkhouse. He sallied forth with his wares strung round him—a kind of movable market-stall—and if his arrival about a farmtoun coincided with dinnertime he would get his brose or bowl of broth along with the fee'd men in the farm kitchen; at night he would be given his supper and permission to sleep in the barn though the taste for gossip would usually keep him by the kitchen fire till a late hour. Sometimes, if pressed, Jamie would take a fee at a toun for the duration of harvest, eating with the men and sleeping in the barn. When he left, it would be with a pound or two in his pocket.

Round the district of Dumfries in the late-1800s there roamed Old Keely-bags, his donkey and cart turning in at the road-end as familiar a sight as the merchant's van. His name was Johnnie Morgan and he supplied the keely-bags that reddened the hearthstones of the farmtoun kitchens. Johnnie wore the old blue bonnet that was the traditional pride of Scotland and had the kind of broad, lined face that could have fought at Culloden, and "saft" though he was (to use the kindlier Scots idiom for the slow-witted) his visits were not unwelcome for besides his keely-bags he brought the sand that made the "straiks" for sharpening the harvest scythes. Such men—and there was their like in every parish— filled a special niche in the world of the farmtouns in that far-past time before the sophisticated bristle and the attrition of carborundum.

But if the fringe industry had a key figure, it was surely the smith. Without him, the old farmtouns could hardly have functioned. Like fine bulls, good smiths ran in generations, men of impeccable pedigree and deft skill who could make iron biddable. The few must speak for the many. The Grants' "smiddy" in Craigellachie became famous through the North-East Lowlands as the Standfast Works, taking its title from the name of the good ploughs that were fashioned there. The Johnstons of Hatton of Fintray, that district of pioneering farmtouns where the corn of the North-East was first cut with a scythe in 1810, had manned the forge there since 1803. The old smiths were ingenious implement-makers: the fame of Hugh MacIntyre of Innerwick smithy went so far and wide from Glenlyon that many of the best ploughmen of Strathearn, Strathtay, Foss and lonely Rannoch would send their ploughs to him in the 1870s to get them in trim for the ploughing-matches. A century or so before the same forge had been sending forth the swordsmen of MacGregor suitably armoured. We don't now know the price Hugh MacIntyre put on his labour but it was probably about the same as that of Willie Birnie of Aberchirder, blacksmith and implement-maker. Nobody remembers Birnie now of course, or can speak of him even from the folk memory of their time, but his name lives on in the copperplate of old farmtoun logs, along with his charges for 1866. Then he took two shillings (10p) for making a new plough-sock, one penny for re-sharpening it, and was prepared to re-ring a pair of cart-wheels with their iron rims for twenty-four shillings and sixpence (£1.22½p).

Working early and late, the smith snatched what time he could away from the forge to run the croft that usually went with the smiddy. Time was a nigh-unobtainable commodity. Through the day the bairns of the late-1800s brought him sheeps' heads to singe for the making of powsowdie (sheep's head broth); at night the ploughmen of the farmtouns came after they'd had their supper, bringing their plough-points to be sharpened—slung over their shoulders and strung like shark's teeth on paling wire. Later, in their season, it was the broken blades of reapers and binders that came, strapped to the crossbars of grieves' bicycles, when the day was too valuable to break into. By then, the plough-points were coming in the long winter afternoons, and it was the grieve who brought them in the farmtoun's time when the weather was cold and he had a fancy for the forge's warmth and a farming gossip. The smith's forge hardly dulled from one day to the next, nor was his hammer long stilled. For his implement repair work apart, he would have the regular shoeing, twice yearly or so, of 200 or more work-horses on the neighbouring farmtouns as well as the occasional upkeep of a wooden leg on some Boer War veteran.

There were big smiths, physically speaking, and little smiths who seemed hardly capable of lifting a hoof. They ran the same risks—and the chance of ending up head-first in their own water-bowies when their attentions became an irritant to some bad-tempered Clydesdale. They smelled alike too: of hot iron and hoof-parings and all had that terrible pallor that throve in the smiddy's gloom and gave even their children complexions like their father's apron.

The souter, too, worked late, up to nine o'clock even as recently as the 1920s. Like the smiddy, his shop was a sociable place where men had out their speak and in the evenings the old men of the village would congregate there, stoutly staffed in infirmity, to hear news of the farmtouns of their young days. For it was only after he had had his supper that a bothy lad from some far outlier place could get away to have his boots re-tacketed, re-heeled or patched while he waited. In a good souter's, say, in the prime farming areas of the North-East Lowlands, as many as six shoemakers would work steadily through the evening. And there was a keenness to trade. Not content with shop orders, a souter with ambition would send a man and gig round the farmtouns in the evenings to solicit work. Hand-made, a pair of farming boots in the early-1920s, built to the very peak of indestructibility, cost about £2. Ready-mades cost less, maybe half, but these never got a good name round the farmtouns. They had neither the grip nor the durability of the hand-mades, which had a ruggedness that made it necessary to line them with straw to give more warmth and cushion the flesh a little. It took feet of character to wear them.

For the men of the farmtouns a sound pair of boots was a necessity, for an ill-shod man was about as footless in the fields as an ill-shoed horse. Besides, there were farmers who took the worth of a man from his boots. Yet, if the fashion of the farmtouns started from the feet up, the farm servant's next need was for a pair of trousers that would keep his legs warm. Moleskin was a favourite for many years not only with the farm men but with the masons and other tradesmen whose work took them round the touns, and it was not until well into the 1920s that kersey was considered the

better windcheater. The farm men's trousers were hand-made in
the community, too, by the tailor. Once, the latter had been one of
the countryside's itinerants as he wandered from farmtoun to farmtoun making up the home-spun. Now he was settled in a shop of
sorts. He, too, might now be a man with a croft that he tended
between stitches or when trade was slack; he, too, had that empathy with the farmtouns that made him willingly make breeks and
waistcoats on credit against the likelihood of payment about
Term-time.

Millers, though, were less-loved. Laird's men all, the black
shadow of history lay over them, remembered still in that long
memory of the countryside. Tenancy of a farmtoun had thirled
the occupant to a particular mill, and that mill had been a remarkably fine source of revenue, taking a multure (a thirteenth part
maybe, though this varied) when the farmtoun itself was hard-
pressed.

The meal mill stood away by itself as though it knew it carried
the acrimony of centuries, and the miller, knowing his fate, put the
best face on it he could, a merry if solitary man:

> I am a miller to my trade,
>     I'm miller at Straloch,
> I'm a curious cankered carlie,
>     My name is Willie Stroth.
>
> I'm engaged with Dr Ramsay,
>     He's laird owre all our land,
> And when he does give call to me
>     I am at his command.
>
> I can play upon the bagpipes
>     Wi' muckle mirth and glee,
> And I care for nobody, no not I,
>     And nobody cares for me.

By the 1800s and the days of the farmtouns the meal mills were
usually let by the lairds, like the farmtouns themselves, and the
miller was simply paid a fee for his services. For all that, suspicion
sometimes remained: who knew what happened in the secret dark
of the mill; who could truly say whose oats were in the meal that
came home? By the middle of the century there had begun a
massive decline in the number of mills round the countryside,

though the one-man meal mill existed in many communities right up to the late-1930s and even later. Mainly though, in most parishes, they had by then become a memory, only their location recalled by the name of some farmtoun that had usurped it: the Nethermills, Newmills, Uppermills, Little Mills, Miltons and just plain Mills of this or that. The great wheels stopped as even the farmtoun folk turned to flour bread.

Not that the miller's wheel was the only one in the course of the stream. Far from it. The waters of the countryside drove a variety of machinery. Drumblade parish, near Huntly, in 1840 had two meal mills, one barley mill, one lint-mill, two wool mills; the Water of Cruden, a grand name for a modest-enough stream, in its seven-mile course about the middle of the century was turning as many mills (six of them meal mills) and the same number again of farmtoun threshing mills.

Yet even in the areas of the remote farmtouns, the ripples of industrial change would be felt and the mill-sluices remain un-worked—as the town factories took over competitively from the old wool mills for instance. One example will suffice; its decline prac-tically counter-balances the rise of the great farmtouns. In 1837, as Queen Victoria came to the throne, Garlogie wool mill, on the fringe of her favourite Balmoral countryside, was employing 120 people; in 1904, it was forced to close. There were exceptions of course, those wool mills which had managed to make their name a cachet in connection with, say, the making of blankets. They sur-vived for a time among the small villages and in the quiet uplands, but then in a much-diminished form.

That pattern of decline, alas, was to become appallingly familiar. But it was not unexpected. It was the culmination of something that had begun when the turnpike roads first started to thread through the land, linking the world of the farmtouns with the manufactories of the city. In time it would diminish the farmtouns themselves, drain them of their greatness, but that time was not yet. On the contrary, the great days of the farmtouns grew out of that era. Progress would waken small clachans and enclaves of peasant labour from a life on which the outside hardly impinged. Not least in the development would be the emergence of small townships, because of their site or their occupants' foresight, into the villages that would supply provisions, seed, implements and all the impedimenta of the farmtouns, now needed on a greater scale than ever before. Sleeping hamlets sprang out of the slumber of centuries into their new characters; others grew from the new-towns of the early improvers' creation. Again, one instance suffices for many, chosen only because it became the hub of Buchan, the ballad homeland where farming was an obsession more than a way of life. By 1871, the new-town of Mintlaw had a school, markets for the sale of cattle and farm produce on the second Tuesday of each month, several grocery and haberdashery shops, bakers, butchers and tradesmen of every description, a branch of the Town and County bank and two hotels. Its growth was a natural consequence of sitting where the turnpikes of the countryside crossed: twice a day the Aberdeen–Fraserburgh mail coach passed through, morning and night the Banff–Peterhead mail. And the new-town whose future had once looked so bleak was also on the route of the Buchan Railway, and that did not hinder trade. By 1890 the Station Hotel was doing a fine line of business in horse-hiring to the seed and implement salesmen who came by train to trade round the farmtouns.

Nor were they the only people who benefited from the building of the turnpikes. They were a boon too to the men who serviced the farmtouns, the masons for instance, the hedgers and dykers, for every day was still changing the look of the landscape. Hawthorn, planted for the most prosaic of reasons, softened the bleakness of the countryside; dykes, mile upon mile, were built to march over hill and through haugh, lasting memorials to a hardy race of men who could translate stone in the singular into a plurality that was stock-proof, shock-proof and wind-proof. They would weather, those stone dykes with the farm steadings, till they achieved a great venerability, till you could think they had stood there from the first day of Creation. And besides the tradesmen, the turnpikes at the turn of the century carried those other wandering folk, not gangrel folk, neither ignorant nor unruly but the itinerants like "Besom" Jamie Henderson whose particular expertise could find a morning's employment or a sale at a farmtoun: men who could sharpen scissors, make baskets, mend pots, or put a new rush-seat into a favourite chair.

Those were the years that saw, too, the last of the genuine old packmen, the peripatetics who brought minor plenishings round country doors; thread and ribbon, sugar mice and wooden dolls, bootlaces and collar studs, all the minutiae you never knew you needed until tempted by the sight of it. They were welcomed with some excitement about a farmtoun, unlike the cheap-johns of the later 1920s and 1930s, the turbanned sikhs with their cases of silks and French drawers, who were hardly given leave to set their packs down on the doorstep. Even culture came round the farmtouns, albeit in small doses: right up to the start of World War I and even after it the dancing masters took their fiddles and their dainty steps round the cold halls and cleared barns to teach the old set dances. And the *colporteur* came with his black case, a man of impeccable social refinement, soberly suited, and left behind him the *Strand* magazine, a sophisticated journal for any country bookrack, and the more educationally informative *Chambers's Journal*.

And besides that foot army, there was the wheeled traffic; its speed betokened its greater urgency. In addition to the gigs of the seed salesmen, there was the carter's spring cart (delivering hens' mash, maize or bran, wire or wire-netting from the merchant's to the farms), the postman's pony, the grander carriages of the gentry as well as the ragman's cart and donkey. And gigs of doctors raced through the night and the dark to bring bairns into the world and ease people out of it. The country doctor was no stranger about a farmtoun or to the mud that often encircled it and its cottar dwellings and the general health of the community could be gauged by plotting the course of his trap round the touns as surely as the affairs of love might be assessed by the bicycles thrown hurriedly against a hedgerow. And indeed, the two were often not unrelated.

They earned little these men from their practices—little, that is, beyond the undying gratitude of the farmtoun folk. Many of them charged according to the ability to pay. Some were remarkable even among their own kind and one of these was Dr John Muir of the Selkirk Border country. His life-span (1845–1938) almost exactly parallels the great days of the farmtouns. Coming to the Border town in the late-1860s, he first did his rounds on horseback—50, even 60, miles in the day—an early mount being a four-year-old mare sired by Pathfinder, the Grand National winner. For fifteen years he hunted and hacked her, and drove her single, double or in tandem between the gig shafts. Later, unimpaired by such a hardy life, he did his rounds by bone-shaker bicycle and even in his 80s still cycled vast mileages. He brought 3,344 babies into the world and, for all we know, may have helped as many folk out of it. He was a man as sure of a welcome in the cottar's house as in the mansions of the rich.

Folk did not easily forget his kind.

That bond would remain unchanged, but it would be just about the only one. As baker's bread usurped the kingdom of the oat-cake and the butchers' vans and fish-vans of the 1930s began to bring round to the farmtouns the dietary alternatives to brose and porridge, the souter succumbed to selling factory boots and shut his shop at the same hour as the merchant. The locally-made was no longer good enough.

The tailor was undone by off-the-pegs, those instant suits of the 1920s and '30s; they did not last long enough to hand down but if they held together while their fashion lasted the bothy men of the farmtouns were happy. They could buy a new one between making a "bargain" in the feeing market and catching the bus home. What did it matter? Little, except that men who had had heavy tweeds that could stand by themselves were themselves visibly diminished in the suitings of the flapper society.

Some things though were enduring, among them the veneration of country folk for the virtues of education. It unlocked the gates of opportunity and it was seen as a way—the army excepted—of letting the next generation escape to the fuller life of the world beyond the ringed farmtouns. The headmaster therefore occupied a place in that select triumvirate of minister, doctor, dominie, the three wise men of any rural community, and it was the dominie more than the other two who was consulted in the administrative affairs of life. If his personal character did not always bring him respect, then his learning and the breadth of vision that implied did, and he was a figure of some substance in the countryside long before the Education Act of 1872 brought all the truant herd-lads behind a school desk. By 1840, the parish dominie in Hatton of Fintray was getting a salary of £28 with two rooms in the school-house for his own use and a quarter-acre of garden ground. And that seems to have been about the rate for the job, for the parish dominie at Skene, in the same county, was receiving £30 a year. The dominie of an endowed school at Cults, also in the same county, may or may not have been doing as well: he had a salary of £20 plus (that magical quantity!) six bolls of meal. His name was Mr Reith; he was, they say, a great-uncle of Lord Reith, that equally respected disseminator of knowledge, though in another medium. Mr Reith's position seems to have been by no means as secure as one might suppose, for his work and that of his pupils, in those days before school inspectors, came under the trustees' close scrutiny before the school shut for the "hairst play" holidays.

The words "hairst play" tell their own story of the undermining of the dominie's rôle at times and point up the need in those days before reapers and binders for children's labour in the harvest field, where they would bind and stook. Though subject to regional variation, the holiday would usually last from mid-August to the end of September. And of course it was not only at harvest that the children of the farmtouns were forced to work in the fields. The old school logs are a sad indictment of the life lived on the family farm-touns of the time, a life that hovered constantly around the poverty-line. Even in upland Drumblade, with all its mills, its suspect morals and apparent prosperity, that same year of 1840 the parish school had 72 pupils in the winter, 46 in summer. Time and the Education Act would bring better schoolrooms, perhaps even better tutors, but whatever their shortcomings the country schools of the farmtoun communities had a remarkable sense of equality in that time before it was fashionable: the farmer's son sat with the son of his father's cottar. The schools also had another advantage over the glass-and-girder palaces of centralized education that would one day replace them: they were set in the countryside; they did not wrench a child out of his environment in his tender years. Through the old school's broad lancet windows, if he had a mind to, he could stretch up from his desk when the teacher's back was safely turned and plot the progress of seedtime or hay-making more surely than he could solve the algebra problem confronting him. More important, from his seat in the schoolroom he could absorb the turn of the seasons into the fabric of his soul. Who can say but that the balance and outlook he gained may have been worth a whole string of O-levels.

Not that the farmtoun child grew up ignorant of academic affairs. Those dedicated women teachers who staffed the little schools saw to that. Who knows now with what hopes they nourished and directed the young soul of promise? It is those remarkable ladies with their flowered smocks and their lisle hose and brogues that one should remember most vividly from those long-ago schoolrooms. They opened the doors to another kind of life.

# XVII

## *The Heartbreak Crofts*

FOR THE BOLD cottar man there was a way of escape from the tyranny of the grieve's watch: into a croft, one of those holdings that fretted the landscape between the fields of the big farmtouns and nestled on the high hillsides, in the odd uninhabitable corners and on the inhospitable edge of the moor. They looked, at times, as though they had been thrust there willy-nilly by the land-greed of the bigger places, and that was about what happened. Yet they were coveted by young cottars who could see nothing in front of them but a string of farmtouns; they saw in the croft a chance to put their own foot tentatively on the farming ladder. And when they did so, these men took crofting like a fever in the blood; it gripped them like women or whisky and in spite of the damages of addiction they could see all around them. They believed they had the answer, that they could make sense of that impossible dream: sovereignty over a small patch of land with a self-sufficiency in body and soul. The result eventually was disillusionment. Years of dour crofting endurance honed them to the temper of hard steel and in time, as some solace for their frustration, they turned either to the kirk or the whisky bottle, and whiles to both. In the dark week of crofting despair it is a long time from Sabbath to Sabbath. And besides, for a moment at least the drams could put back into their bellies some of the young fire that had been there when they were ploughmen about a farmtoun. For the stark truth of it was this: there was no independence, only a greater tyranny than the grieve ever imposed, from within and without.

The Scottish crofter existed on the very edge of husbandry; in the North-West Highlands on a barren fringe of some sealoch where the Clearances had forced him, in the North-East Lowlands on the margin of the peat-moss where he had been settled in the late eighteenth and early nineteenth centuries in the new areas the "improving" lairds had created for him. Although it escaped the calumny of history, the latter too was a clearance of a kind: it took the clutter of the cot-toun or the crofter township conveniently from the castle gate at the very time the gentry were growing conscious of their own esteem. It was, to be fair, a clearance in good order, even well-intentioned, and almost gave the word a good name. Where the folk of the West got leave to shift for themselves, the "improving" lairds plotted and feued their new towns with a paternal responsibility.

But even if there were qualified benevolence from the Big House, there was the frown of the big farmer or the flockmaster; the one saw the crofter's pitiful patchwork of fields as a nuisance that bent the long straight of his furrow, the other as a blot on the broad sweep of his pasture. They were well-in with the laird such men, and could quietly blacken a man's character when it suited them and that could be damaging in the extreme for it was to the estate and the big farmtoun that the crofter looked for a day's paid labour now and then—so precariously was his solvency balanced. Again, it was from the big farmtoun that he needed the hire of a pair and horseman to plough his few acres (in the farmtoun's own good time), harrow-in his seed and maybe lead in his corn. He was a man forever dancing on a fine wire and always in double harness; if he could not get a day's labour fairly often at the neighbouring farmtouns he had, as in the North-West, to find his second job at the fishing, as postman, or shoemaker, or helper at the pier when the boat came in. He was strait-jacketed from the outset: whenever his croft needed him, whenever his corn was ripe for the scythe, he was contracted elsewhere. His plight was that he was master and servant both. He lost his own harvest while working other men's fields. In time he lost hope as well.

Yet still in their eagerness men entered upon the life with purpose and determination. That old man from Bennachie again, writing about his own youth in the mid-1800s or maybe a little earlier:

My father was a woodman and crofter earning his living like the other crofters from a double source. He took a lease of a patch of moorland at the foot of Bennachie at a rent of £7 for 24 acres and proceeded to build for himself a dwelling house, with barn, byre and stable. The walls were built of stone and clay, faced with lime mortar inside and out.

His father, he tells us, did his own woodwork for the house, the mason taking £20 for his share of the work. The bigging was the traditional but-and-ben, presumably thatched, with a "closet", a small room between the two ends to house the meal girnal—that storage unit that was such a vital item of furnishing. The floor was of earth and became a morass of mud in wet weather, but at least the beasts were to be separately housed and that shows some progress from the pitiful picture of Skye crofting life painted in the *Statistical Account* of 1841. The hand is that of the Rev. Coll Macdonald, a man, whatever his native sympathies, bound by his conscience to the truth:

> The poor tenants are almost universally under the necessity of having their cattle under the same roof with themselves, without partition, without division and without chimney; their houses therefore are smoky and filthy in the extreme; and having little either of night or day clothing, and their children mostly approaching to absolute nakedness they are fully as much without cleanliness in their persons as they are in their houses.

The comparison, of course, is not entirely a fair one, for there were vast differences in the way of life in the crofting of the East and of the West. But they had this in common: poor ground. And for that the Clearances, whether kindly or cruel, must take much of the blame. They continued unrelentingly in the North-West Highlands for more than 100 years, up until 1882, erasing whole communities. Tragic though they were, there was that even deeper tragedy behind those years of cruelty and bitterness: the tragedy of missed opportunity. Sir John Sinclair of Thurso, founder of the Board of Agriculture and a strong pillar of what is now the Royal Highland and Agricultural Society of Scotland, had seen the potential in bringing the Cheviot ewe north to boost a flagging crofting economy. How he must have recoiled from seeing his idea advanced as a means simply of propping up the ailing fortunes of the gentry.

It is now possible, with hindsight, to see that the Highlands had a problem of a scale and magnitude that only wider, more whole-hearted official intervention could have handled. Instead,

Farmtoun away-day: the date, about 1890; the occasion, the Mintlaw Games, a highlight of the North-East farmtoun year at a time when outings were few. The cottars' coach to the event was a farmtoun cart, cleaned and decorated and drawn by one of the toun's more docile Clydesdales, similarly garlanded. The Games drew crowds of up to 12,000 to see such spectacles of awe as balloon ascents and parachute drops and feats of daring horsemanship—and a fine turnout could give any toun a bit of prestige round the parish.

Sowing: *above*, a heavy note of symbolism perhaps in a deliberately posed picture of the late-1800s but one that draws together the elements of farmtoun existence—man, woman, seed and the soil. Practically, it shows the filling of the seed hopper and how it was worn. *Below*, a little later, about 1900, on a Borders farmtoun in Roxburghshire, the hand-sower strides the fields. Behind him, burying the seed, come the harrows.

Power on the land: *above*, a Clydesdale pair, Sandy and Bud, one of the
four pairs at the North-East toun of Tillyeve of Udny in the 1920s. For
their young horseman it was a day for the Sabbath trousers and waistcoat and the white shirt; for the pair, the full complement of cleaned
harness including the Scottish piked collar and lacy "horse-lugs".
Vital though the Clydesdales were, there were also times when human
muscle and skill were needed: *below*, contract harvesters at work with
the scythe-heuk at Braehead, just outside Edinburgh.

Day of the ploughman: *above*, men of decision—the ploughing match committee at a Lanarkshire event about 1910, men from whom any breach of the rules would bring a frown and whose word for all their seemingly casual air could depose champions. *Below*, a match in progress and nearing its end and the final verdict of the judges. The ploughman with this distinctive pair has his sleeves rolled up, out of the way of the reins curled round his wrist.

Ancient and modern: *above*, a scene that captures the incongruity of change on the farmtouns of the 1930s as an old North-East farmer cuts hay with his modern Fordson tractor hitched to an old horse-drawn implement modified by the smith for attachment to the tow-bar. Hopelessly inefficient, it foreshadows the change to come, change that came often reluctantly. *Below*, even well into the 1900s there were men unwilling to leave the oxen-age—in industrious Orkney especially— though willing enough to harness their beasts to a modern plough.

Women's work: summer and winter about a farmtoun there was the milking and the feeding of hens. *Above*, the milkers (and bailies) of Cairnbrogie, that pioneer dairytoun of the North-East where hygiene and milk health were almost a fetish. Before the milking-machine became commonplace, a "wife to milk" was often a condition of a cottar man's fee. *Below*, three farmtoun generations feeding the hens that strutted round the toun on summer days or stood disconsolate on one leg in the cart-pends when rain wept from the farmtoun roofs.

Casting the peats: after the spring work there were the peats to dig. *Above*, a scene from the turn of the century, possibly even a little earlier, showing the men cutting from the peat-bank on to old-type peat barrows, ready for the womenfolk to trundle away to set out the peats for drying. *Below*, setting the peats to dry about 1900 on Strichen moss in the heart of the ballad country. Later the peats would be carted home to the farmtouns to be stacked by the house-gables.

Fringe figures: when the folk of the farmtouns went from home it was on the turnpike road, maintained by men like Richard Nesbit, pictured *far left*, who sat by their cairns of stones ceaselessly making the "metalling" to keep the road in repair. Nesbit, here pausing to light his clay pipe in Dumfries-shire's Whiteshiels Wood, was pictured on 18 May 1895. The men of the farmtouns marched on heavy tackety boots like the one being repaired, *left*, by a venerable Angus souter of the late-1800s, a figure quite typical of his whiskered time.

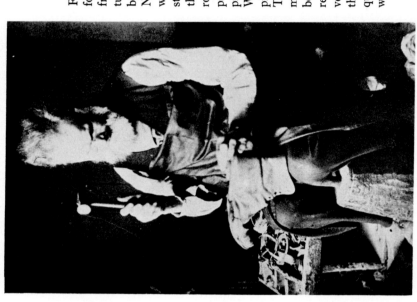

the attempts were paralysingly piecemeal, stifling all chance of working towards a viable crofting agriculture. Real interest came so tardily as to amount almost to gross dereliction of duty by Westminster; it came only in March 1883, when Gladstone set up a royal commission of inquiry into crofting under Lord Napier. It was a month that saw also the conviction in Edinburgh of a handful of Skye crofters. Determined men, they had led a revolt against eviction in the now celebrated Battle of the Braes so effectively as to bring reinforcements of 50 constables from Glasgow, a warship to stand by offshore, and troops to march intimidatingly through her majesty's rebellious crofting townships. Born of the commission's findings, the Crofters' Holdings Act of 1886 lifted the constant threat of eviction from the crofter's shoulders and continued his tenancy beyond the caprice of the estate factor.

The measure may have done some general good, but certainly it was too late for the Highlands. The region's sad story has been related *ad infinitum*; what had been so heartlessly induced went on voluntarily. Emigration continued: south to the growing industrialism of the cities, to the sea, to domestic service in the big houses and into the bothies of the farmtouns. But the exodus was not without its influence on the crofter colonies of the East. Many of the dispossessed drifted to the North-East Lowlands, to Banffshire, Buchan, and even the rich red earth of the Mearns. At New Byth, in the 1830s, the Earl of Fife granted Clearance victims ten-acre plots on the Hills of Fisherie. Over 100 new crofts were taken in from the heather.

It wasn't paradise, of course. The land of the new crofter communities of the East was marginal; the thatched biggings marched with the turnpike road where the moor was at its barest, their but-and-bens forming a wide unswerving main street. Sometimes the ben-ends of the dwellings were elongated to hold a loom, for the founders of these new crofter villages had made an earnest attempt to solve an age-old problem by linking them with a second source of income—usually the linen trade. There in the East the newcomers mingled their Highland names with the unromantic ones of the North-East and maybe softened its guttural speech with their Gaelic cadences. There is no evidence that these exiles were unwelcome; equally there is little indication that they had the slightest impact on the East's crofting, where

F

the pattern of the year followed that of the surrounding farm-touns. And again that is hardly surprising, for the crofter of the West, then and now, is a man out of agricultural time without a place almost in his country's farming development. Conditions forced an allegiance to anachronistic tools, the *caschrom* foot-plough and the *croman*, an equally rustic-looking handmade hoe. Either would bring a blush to the cheek of the most primitive Moroccan tribesman. Again, he was hampered by hostile weather, a winter so unkindly that he was forced to leave his ploughing until late in the spring since the rains and the winds would have hardened it to the point of making a suitable seedbed impossible to achieve. Crops were sown into the ground almost within hours of it being broken by the plough. If the crofter of the West seemed unreasonably unwilling to break from the past, to reshape the pattern of the crofting year that echoed down to him from immemorial time, it may have been simply that he felt himself to be the best judge of his hostile landscape.

Yet there must have been among them men of great guile who brought with them secrets out of the crofting past, who had conjured fine crops of potatoes off their lazy-beds with the help of sea-wrack or, inland, bracken cut at its richest; who by the same magic had taken a good return of oats off them in the second year. Oh, and there were buccaneers among them: men who had managed to run their sheep along with the laird's on the hill pasture, though it was forbidden, by getting a nod from the laird's shepherd when there was to be any in-gathering. It was a service that had to be paid for in generous drams but since such men were oftener to be found at the inn than the kirk, that was no hardship; their frailties were expected of them, and they argued that what the laird only suspected could not be of hurt to him.

Surely, then, there was an agreeable softness about the life that the men of the east-coast crofts might have heeded? Alas, the crofter of the North-East Lowlands, was an entirely different kind of man; his was a date with destiny. The croft, initially anyway, may have satisfied something in his own soul but it did nothing to raise him in his banker's esteem. Definitive fact is a very rare thing in the minefield of crofting statistics, particularly since a croft can be any patch of ground from the size of a large garden to 80 acres or more. All the same, the representative east-coast crofter of the 1930s might be fairly accurately assessed as a man working ten acres, keeping a cow or two maybe, fattening a couple of black stirks and a pig as well. Normally he would make a little hay, grow a patch of turnips and two or three acres of oats. The turnips he barrowed home from their field himself, the sweat streaking his back by the time he got his load to the byre-door; he made his hay in the balmy evenings of mid-summer— after he had done a hard day's work at his alternative occupation maybe. All the same there was an unhurried sweetness, an idyllicism sometimes, about that season as the scent of clover hung in the dusk. But his small harvest was something else: a week or ten days with the scythe, watching the clouds anxiously even as the hot sun blistered the back of his neck, his hardy wife or daughter gathering and binding behind him, lifting the crop almost off the tip of the scythe-blade. And when he had had his supper he took back to the field to stook the day's sheaves. Only the gloaming and the fall of the night dew sent him in to his bed.

The irony of it was this: he was no better off even in the 1930s than if he had still been second horseman at a neighbouring farmtoun. By then, crofting was well into a decline from which it would never recover. The croft-houses would become the homes for the workers of the factory-farmtouns of the future, retreats for weekend men who felt the vague unease of city streets. In the upland glens the heather would again encroach on the fields so sorely won from it nearly 100 years earlier.

It had all of it a rather sad kind of inevitability for the croft was always more of a family unit than a farming one; at hay-making and harvest as the old folk wore on in years sons came home from the sea and from southern police forces and daughters left their men unfettered to come with their bairns, to bind and stook and fork. It was either a Gaelic Eden without a future or a treadmill on which men broke themselves pursuing an impossible dream.

# XVIII

## The Hub of the Farmtoun

THE CLYDESDALES took precedence over every other living thing about a farmtoun, man or beast. They came home to the touns from the horse fairs such as Aikey Brae or Peter Fair in the North-East, Skirling in the South, or were bought from the dealers who travelled round the farmtouns buying and selling. And when the old copers finally faded from the farmtoun scene, in the 1920s, they came from the fortnightly sales at auction marts up and down the country. There was reason enough for the status they enjoyed: at about £80 each, even in the 1870s, they represented a considerable investment, three times and more the yearly wage of the farmtoun's first horseman, in fact. Through to the 1920s and 1930s their prices varied little, though if anything the trend was upward with a good beast then costing the £100, still twice the yearly wage of a cottared horseman.

Before the horseman dared to set his foot in the farm kitchen for his own breakfast his pair had to be combed and given their feed: corn (bruised or crushed so that the beasts could digest it properly and get the utmost nutrition from it) and hay. It was the same at dinner-time and before the men went in for their supper— and if ever there was doubt about a partnership, well, with the cheapness and ready availability of labour the man was easy enough to replace. In any case, there was little sympathy about a farmtoun for a man who ill-used his Clydesdales, for they were usually quiet and docile beasts. Only the odd one or two were vengeful enough to try to trap a man against the travis, the wooden stable partition that separated one horse from its neighbour. Hooves, too, could fly, taking the legs unexpectedly from under a man, sometimes damaging a limb, or even inflicting serious injury as the horseman stooped to hitch the traces to the swingletrees in yoking harrows or plough. "Oh, aye," one old horseman admitted, nodding quietly as he recalled the twelve pairs he had driven about as many farmtouns in as many years before good fortune steered him into an easier, more lucrative life, "they were quiet enough for the most part, though not always. The odd one who was nervous or jittery would use his teeth or his feet to get at you if he got the chance." Worse, the nervous beast could become frightened of his own shadow in the plough, making it impossible for his ploughman to hold his place in the protocol of the plough-rigs; bolt from the muck midden in terror at the sound of the bailie rattling milk-churns and end up with the cart in some ditch, limbs and shafts broken. On the road the sight of a train would put such a beast into a hysteric frenzy that threatened cart, contents (including the horseman himself) and anyone else unfortunate enough to be on the same stretch of turnpike. Even more frightening to the beast, if that were possible, was a traction engine coming into a toun with the contractor's threshing-machine. A scared Clydesdale, beside itself, would try to leap the dyke, cart and all. For such occasions, old grieves had a piece of terse advice for young ploughmen: "Saw the heid, saw the heid!"—that is to say, pull first one rein then the other in rapid succession. It was good enough advice, if the horseman got time to take it.

They had short terse names the Clydesdales of the farmtouns, names a horseman could get his tongue round in a hurry if he had to, such as Nell, Bell, Mick, Prince, Jock, Jamie, Charlie, Clyde (naturally), Star, Dick, Sandy, Bud, Bess, Jean, Tam, Kate, Daisy—to name a few that came readily to that old horseman's mind. Yoked at the age of three—the "clips" they were called in the North-East irrespective of gender—they came into their prime when they were aged about seven and were ready for retirement at the age of fifteen. Some were foals reared by the farmtoun itself, but others were bought in from the dealers. They would be yoked at first, perhaps in the plough, in the company of an older beast, having been "broken in" by being given a log to drag. Breaking the clips was one of the farmtoun's odd jobs—for a slack Saturday afternoon perhaps—but nonetheless an important one for a young beast that had been yoked could fetch a better price in the sale. It was work that took guile, empathy, endless patience. Not every horseman could do it, and some were masters of it. Their voices slowly implanted the pattern of command—the words *Hi*, *Whissh* and *Whoa*, and with them the language and ripple of rein; more importantly they began a dialogue that would be a part of all the beast's working days. Yoked with an older horse, the young Clydesdale would soon settle to its work; there were few instances of antagonism between the beasts themselves.

It did a farmtoun no harm to be known as a place with good Clydesdales; there were subtle ways in which the farmer could use his toun's reputation for good "pairs". In the feeing market, for instance, it could be held out as an inducement to some swithering ploughman—often with a guile that suggested that the man was unreasonable in wanting wages as well. Just as often though, the beasts a horseman inherited when he went home to a new farmtoun turned out to be a poor bargain, as much skin and bone as the pair he was leaving, for in the hard times of the late-1800s and again in the 1920s and 1930s there were farmers who pared the stable feed to the borderline of starvation. Auld Luckie of Brunties, that crone with such a Christian concern for the souls of her kitchen maids, was, as the ballad suggests, singularly neglectful of the well-being of her stable Clydesdales:

> Sax bushels a week amongst the five,
>> It's a' that they do get,
> And sometimes in the evening
>> They got a taste o' bait;
> But it's composed of cauf an strae,
>> And keeps them aye so thin,
> The men they do declare to me
>> The banes will cut the skin.

About many touns, for all the dependence on them, they were no better fed than the men who drove them. The young ploughman who went home to the North-East farmtoun of Darrahill had cause to rue his fee in a Buchan fair:

> When I gaed hame to Darrahill
>> To work the wark I took in han',
> The horse they werena very guid,
>> And the harness werena worth a hang.

> Darras' horse were very poor,
>> They got their corn ance a day,
> And ither twice got neeps and cauf,
>> To gar them nab their pickle strae.

In short, while they might get corn once, the two other feed-times
were provided for by turnips and corn-husks meant to deceive the
beasts into filling their bellies with straw, which was also a part of
the diet.

But the ruse, the false promises, was all part of the quiet
trickery that gave the feeing markets their bad name. Witness the
empty words that took another horseman home to a more famous
farmtoun of the North-East Lowlands, the Barnyards of Delgaty:

> He promised me the ae best pair
> I ever set my e'en upon;
> When I gaed hame to Barnyards
> There was naething there but skin and bone.
>
> The auld black horse sat on his rump,
> The auld white meer lay on her wime,
> And a' that I could hup and crack,
> They wouldna rise at yokin' time.

And if the hard work of the touns took its toll of men, it was as
unrelenting on their work-horses. The tyrant farmer of Bogieside,
near Gartly, inspired one fee'd man to that time-honoured revenge,
the ballad-line:

> Assist me, all ye muses,
> For to compose a song,
> 'Tis of a tyrant farmer
> Near Gartly did belong;
> An' while we were his servants
> Oft times to us he said—
> "Come, drive them on some smarter,
> Ye're noo on Bogieside."
>
> We did drive on his horses
> Till they were out o' breath;
> They were fitter for the tannerie
> Than for to be in graith.
> For want o' corn they did lie hard
> And he with us did chide,
> And he swore we had neglected them
> Upon sweet Bogieside.

Even so, the thing that most strongly shines through in so many ploughmen songs is the horseman's pride in and loyalty to his pair; it points up the closeness of the relationship that could grow between a man and his Clydesdales, a closeness understandable perhaps only to a man who has himself worked horses. That relationship grew from the moment the horseman went home to a new farmtoun. An indication of that harmony which could exist between man and beast, as well as a sidelight on the care the man gave to his pair's appearance, comes from the almost elegiac "Harrowing Time":

> So on we drive until the sun
> Ahint yon hills does hide;
> And syne we loose our horses tired,
> And homewards we do ride.
>
> And homewards we do ride fu' keen
> To get our horses fed;
> We kaim them weel baith back and heel,
> Their tails and manes we redd.

Another of the recurrent ballad themes is the special reverence paid to a "pair of blues", and certainly there was competition among the horsemen themselves to drive a distinctive pair whether they were the highly-prized greys or, equally uncommon, a pair of blacks. There is also some insistence in the ballads that the first horseman always had the best pair about a farmtoun though in practice this seems not to have been invariably the case. What he did have, always, was an *able* pair of Clydesdales; this he had to have in order to set the pace of the work and preserve the in-built discipline of the toun. And there was of course protocol in the stable as well as in the bothy and at meal-times. The first horseman's pair were always nearest the stable door, followed by the second man's, the third's and so on. Though there was usually a second door to the stable, the first horseman "led out" and the other horsemen followed in order of rank, a practice no less rigid in the farms of Southern England at the same time.

The clean-footed Clydesdale was always the predominant breed north of the Border, its pedigree, it is often said, going back to the time when a Duke of Hamilton imported some black stallions from Holland. But if there is some doubt about that, there is no question about the cradle of the breed: the Clydesdale district (later Lanarkshire), an area which had long had a reputation for good horses before evolving the breed that took its name. The Clydesdale, it is thought, may have been founded on the horses the old drovers brought back from English fairs, and, whatever the duke's earlier claim, it is likely that its Lanarkshire origins rest with a black Flemish stallion brought North from England in 1715 by John Paterson of Lochlyoch. The name that shines above all others in the lists of the breed's champions, however, is that of James Kilpatrick; it was he, in the 1880s, who gave the Clydesdale its international standing. His farmtoun of Craigie Mains of Kilmarnock became the shrine of the breed and men who knew good stock the world over made a pilgrimage there.

It is a far cry now from those days, when there was something like 140,000 horses working the Scottish farmtouns, but even now the reason for the Clydesdale's popularity isn't hard to find. Besides its equable temperament, in its later, finer strain it had the kind of stamina needed for the tough soil of so many of the Scottish touns, and a manoeuvrability unique among the heavy horse breeds—ideal for those hill-set fields where the land ran back from the flat coastal belt to take shelter in the glens. Walking, the Clydesdale could average five mph almost forever, and even on some braeside field its stride was steady and unfaltering, the creak of its harness, as it took the strain under a warm summer sun, quietly reassuring.

Besides the plough, the reaper and so on, the Clydesdales powered the barn-mill in times of drought or where water power was not otherwise available, harnessed two, three or four to the outside capstan that gave life to the mill inside the barn. They carted-in the turnips all winter through from the fields to the bailie's byre; they carted meal (from the miller's), milk (to the railhead for the city dairy), potatoes (from the field to the steading and the cottar's yard) and coal and peat (from merchant's sheds and the moss respectively). And of course they carted the farmtoun folk themselves: to the Games or to the seaside picnic; then were they combed and groomed like beauty queens and had their tails and manes primped and beribboned as though for a royal progress. The cart, too, might be decorated to an elaborate degree and there were sociable men who carried in their chaumer kists all the frivolous trimmings for such grand occasions.

About the middle of May each year the farmtoun Clydesdales got a change from their stable diet when they were put out to grass for the summer—for a short time at first, for a week or ten days maybe only while the horsemen had their own mid-day meal. Then they went out to pasture full-time, being brought into the stable in the morning from six o'clock to six-fifteen, to be given a brush-down by the horsemen before they started work. In their freedom, after the winter constriction of the stable, they flung their legs like foals, and thundered round the field with their manes flying. For the horsemen, too, there was a greater freedom with the let-up in stable work. Yet it was a time not without its own acute anxiety, especially in the 1920s and 1930s, as the men watched for any sign of grass-sickness, that plague of the farm-touns, then particularly rife; it could empty a stable of beasts with a terrifying kind of inevitability, for its cause was a mystery and its cure unknown. First signs of it brought a kind of mute misery to a farmtoun as the men watched a beast first go off its feed then slowly pine away till it was no more than a living skeleton. It would have been humane to shoot a beast long before that time and there there were farmers who did so, unable to bear the sight of its suffering. But there were other farmtouns where the sick Clydesdales had to pine out their days to the last. To have killed them might have meant forfeiting the insurance money, and that the depressed down-at-heel farmtouns of the between-the-wars years could not afford to do. The insurance money was needed to replace them, quickly; until that was done the work of the farmtoun came virtually to a standstill. There are men who can still remember those days. For them the grass-sickness was a terrible thing; it broke men in heart and bank account as surely as bad crops.

Usually the Clydesdales were shoed twice a year: in summer with flat shoes that were as lightsome on the horse's feet as the patent shoes of a dancing ploughman when he put them on on a Saturday night. Winter shoes were heavier, built up with a bar at the front to give hooves a grip on wet, muddy or icy ground, and in especially icy conditions, sharps (or "pikes" as they were called in the North-East) would be fixed into the frontal bars and the backs of the shoes in the morning before the pairs went out to work and removed by the horsemen when they finally stabled their beasts for the night.

The stable itself was the focal point as well as the administrative hub of a farmtoun. It could be a friendly place at the end of a winter's day, warmed by the mingled breath of men and horses that rose through the mellow light of paraffin lanterns. There was news, a coarse story or two—even from the grieve who was there to see that there was no scrimping of feed or grooming in the haste to get to supper. Between the droll stories and the back-chat men slipped collars from the Clydesdales' necks and, with saddles and breeching straps, slapped them on to brackets on the stable wall and then set to work with horse brushes and curry combs as though their very lives depended on it. The energy of it all brought some trace of warmth back into their own chilled blood. The stable, morning and dinnertime, was the place where the grieve gave his orders; it was the place where cottar men lingered on in an evening when they had fallen foul of their womenfolk or could not, temporarily, face the clamour of their children; it was where visiting horsemen from other farmtouns were brought on winter Sabbaths, after they had been given their tea, to "news" till it came time to light the gas-lamps of their bicycles and go home; where, sometimes, at some touns, on wet weekdays the men would be allowed to stay with their horses out of the downpour, mending a bridle or a breeching strap.

For harness was always important, even in the workaday world of the farmtouns and far from the glittering parade of the show-ring; it was a means of transmitting live and sometimes unpredictable horse-power to the plough. It was by leaning its shoulders into its collar that a Clydesdale took up the strain, and that collar had to fit as comfortably on its shoulders as the ploughman's Sabbath suit sat on his own. Good touns took notice of that. They had a stock, usually, of different-sized collars—as many fittings whiles as a multiple tailor's. And there were other ways a good horseman could always make sure his pair were able and willing to do their work. In warm weather, for instance, at the end of a yoking, he would wipe the sweat off the insides of their collars so that their shoulders would not become chafed. When they were carting or being used with implements with shafts he would be sure to clean the underside of the saddle, similarly padded under its leather. The pull of the plough was taken up through the traces, the chains hooked to the collar hames and then to the swingletrees, the equalizing yoke arrangement that made sure neither of a Clydesdale pair got away with taking less than its fair share of the strain. But here again even the rascally beast was protected for the swingletrees were almost invariably of wood so that the "kicker" would always be more likely to damage the swingletree (or the ploughman) than himself. But it was in the time just before a ploughing match that the care and cleaning of harness reached a high point. That day when it came, besides the shining splendour of brasses, might well see a grandiose gesture in the harness itself: the high peaked collar of peculiarly Scottish appeal first made by the Lothian saddlers, and the high hames that went with it. Then, too, might the ear-muffs be fitted, a bright dab of colour on a fine turn-out but with a practical usefulness too for they avoided the irritation of flies in the Clydesdales' ears and the unsettling start that could give to such serious work.

Above all, though, the stable about any sizeable toun was the place of dissension and rebuke; where a man whose work fell below the expected would pointedly be taken aside or loudly harangued. It was the fencing ground on which the farmtoun men tested each other for weakness, and where those unwise enough to contradict the grieve were defeated by his contempt. All manner of men trod the stable stones—the merry, the meek, the braggart and dangerous buffoon, farmyard philanderers and some braw fiddlers—and the Term with its feeing ritual was not the only time that brought a certain tension into it. For it was here too at the tiring end of the day, amid the smell of harness and Clydesdales' urine, that quarrels broke and were summarily settled, often injuriously as some hot-tempered ploughman seized a harness chain to emphasize his point. But it had gentler times too; nowadays especially the stable is remembered for its place in the life of the bothy ballads. In the North-East Lowlands where most of them had their origin, the ballads were also called "corn-kisters". Traditionally it was on the cornkists—the stable chests, one to each pair, that stored the Clydesdales' bruised corn—that the seated farm men thumped out their own tacketed, iron-heeled accompaniment to those bothy songs.

# XIX

## The Lure of Good Implements

THREE THINGS contributed to the greatness of a farmtoun: the "heart" of its land and therefore the quality of its crops or livestock; the calibre of its men; and the number and quality of the machines in its implement shed. There were other things of course that could give a toun something of a name: the regular drunkenness of its tenant or the lasciviousness of its servant maids. But that, after all, was merely reputation. That important trio—men/land/machines—were subtly linked, for it was the chance to use good tools that brought good men to a farmtoun, even, wittingly, into the tyranny of a rascally grieve. As readily as they sought touns where the Clydesdales were in their prime and well cared for, men filled the bothies and cottar-houses of places that let them get their hands on a Sellar's or Reid and Ley's plough, or better still, one that was Craigellachie-made. In colours that would have been at home in the circus—deep blues, intense reds and yellows and greens the shade of no grass known—the new implements came home to the touns and were off-loaded from the carts before a ring of attentive faces that established immediately the farm salesman's masterly psychology. Bright, gleaming, every earth-tearing part elaborately silvered with paint, they drew the eye like a rainbow in a lowering sky. Carts made by, say, Jack's of Maybole, Foss of Stirling, Kemp and Nicholson of Stirling, Nicholls of Perth, Mackenzie of Achnagarron, or Simpson's of Peterhead (to cover the country) could be just as powerful a pawn in the grieve's hand on the day of a feeing market; they had the hallmark of the craftsman and a subtlety of balance these maestro-made carts that could give their farmtouns the same kind of cachet as a Rolls-Royce in today's factory yard.

They came out to the touns from the cartwrights' shops of every country town the length and breadth of the country. In the early years of this century Aberdeen, a sales centre for a vast hinterland of farmtouns and the capital of the ballad country, had about ten flourishing cartwrights' businesses, each employing up to a dozen men, painters and blacksmiths as well as the wrights themselves, who took their cue, it almost seemed, from the world they served, for they too started at six each morning. And besides its cartwrights' shops the city had a further seven coach-building firms making the gigs and traps and phaetons for country doctors and genteel farmers as well as the grander coaches of the gentry.

If the farmtoun carts lacked something of the gilded splendour of the latter, they had nonetheless their own vivid and traditional livery: a particularly deep blue, with the inside of the cart, the wheels, shafts and the axletree a deep red. As though to carry some of the elegance of one into the realm of the other the fore-breast of a cart carried the name of the farmer and his toun and a number (1, 2, 3, 4, etc.) signifying the Clydesdale pair the cart was assigned to—all in the grace of the signwriter's script on a black enamelled plate. To be sure he need hardly have bothered, for a cart was barely home to any toun before his fine hand of write would be buried beneath some splatter of mud. Nor would the fine factory sheen of the paint last much longer; soon enough the floor of the cart would be scored by the tackets of the horseman's boots and thoroughly impregnated with the odour of dung. For that was the reality of it. All the same, despite its apparent simplicity of design, the farmtoun box-cart was a highly-functional, highly-engineered piece of equipment. As in so many other things, the horseman was often the best judge of its worthiness. For him, the seal of its class, its perfection of design as well as the skill of the builder was determined by the ease with which—its front lynchpin removed—he could tip it by putting his shoulder under the "stump", the lower projecting bar of the fore-breast. There are old horsemen about the countryside still who will sing a particular cart-maker's skill.

But it was the ploughs that they talked about most in the bothies of the mid-1800s and in the early days of the new farmtouns these were often of local manufacture, made by men who knew the area's soil conditions and from firms that had grown with the reputation of their products. Most of these local implements had their birth in the bellows-blown flame of a country forge whose skilled smith understood innately the principles of a good plough—men like the Grants of Craigellachie, whose later Standfast Works became renowned throughout the North-East

Lowlands; men who could make that cumbersome implement into a thing of grace. Soon, however, they would be rivalled by the implement dealer and the factory plough, imported from as far away as Ipswich in East Anglia, where the name of Ransome was being stamped on an increasing number of ploughs. If the new farm steadings of that time inherited anything of value from the immediate farmtoun past it was the two-horse swing plough and the barn-mill, both, in their way, a tribute to Scottish genius in the rôle of engineering entrepreneur.

By 1800, the Lothians farmtouns had taken to the barn-mill with a haste that contrasted oddly with the later rebellion of the English farm-men. There was neither rick-burning nor riotous assembly, and if there was a sudden and unexpected redundancy of flail-men—and the barn-mill's coming must have reduced barn labour considerably—it seems to have been accepted much more readily, an indication perhaps that the Scottish farm worker, ill-paid and ill-fed though he was, may have been more at one with the farming revolution he now began to see growing around him. Accepted they were, however, so much so that East Lothian by 1807 or so had something like 350 mills. The area, certainly, was one in the forefront of the farmtouns revolution, but even the parish of Dyke, on the fringe of the Moray Firth, with only 125 farm servants, by 1840 had 16.

Not that such change was universal; and tempting though it sometimes is to measure farming's advance by marking the milestones of the reaper's, the binder's, the tractor's development, such a picture would be far from accurate. The pattern of progress was uneven; there could be—there frequently was—half a century of difference between the methods of one area and the next, even between one farmtoun and its neighbour. Uplands Ardclach, by the Moray Firth, close to the parish of Dyke where the threshing mill had been so eagerly accepted, was still in the early 1800s clinging stubbornly to the old Scots plough drawn by a team of black cattle and a couple of garrons.

Yet by then it must have been evident that another group of men would influence the life of the Scottish farmtouns: the engineers would be the "improvers" of the new-style farming; their contribution had already brought unparalleled progress and with it the seeds of irrevocable change. The strides made by the invention of the threshing mill in 1787 were far-reaching. Andrew

Meikle's machine, powered by two or four horses where no water-power was available and selling at £80, could thresh out 40 bushels an hour and needed only the farmtoun's normal complement of labour. Suddenly the whole business of flail-threshing and hand-winnowing seemed farcical. Over much the same period the old wooden ploughs, made in a forenoon for a shilling and drawn by a team of oxen, were almost universally replaced by the two-horse swing—or chain—plough, made by James Small of Blackadder Mount and an advance of such importance that a Clackmannan ploughing champion was taken to the Royal Windsor farm to demonstrate it before King George III. Such indeed was the fame of Scottish implements and the skill of the Scottish engineer, though in this case, the Windsor farm servants, jealous of the ploughing work, made it impossible for the champion to stay there. His name was Alexander Virtue; he returned home, naturally not unrewarded.

The swing plough certainly was in wide general use by the mid-1800s. T. Bedford Franklin, in *A History of Scottish Farming* says that in 1791 all 40 entrants at a Clackmannan match used the kind of plough perfected by James Small; that ten years later in Dumfries-shire, all match-winners were favouring it. The spread was northwards, and at such a pace that as early as 1813 out of 36 contestants at a match in Banffshire only four clung to the old Scots plough, a long, heavy, twin-stilted implement with a flat wooden mouldboard and iron only in the share, the coulter and the hook for animal draught at the front of the beam.

To Small, beyond question, must go the credit for clarifying the muddle of other men's thinking and enunciating the principles of the swing plough. There were others before him, of course, and their contributions were not inconsiderable even in a purely Scottish context: among them was Lady Stewart of Goodtrees, who invented the Rutherglen plough—quite widely used in the West of Scotland—and went on, unladylike, to produce other implements. If there is some unease about the outright acknowledgment of Small's achievement it is because he seems, before being brought home to his native Borders by his patron, John Renton of Lammerton, to have been for a time an "operative mechanic" in Britain's first plough factory in Rotherham, making an implement that took the town's name.

The English plough, patented as early as 1730, was also a swing plough, made almost entirely of wood, as were the Small ploughs. It was about 1780 that the Scottish innovator took the mouldboard of his implement to be cast in metal by the famous Carron iron company. Although earlier wooden mouldboards had been plated with iron sometimes, it was a positive step forward. The all-iron plough followed, going into manufacture in the early years of the 1800s. It was quickly accepted. The general design was diversified into regional variants. The James Wilkie plough was considered among the best in the South of Scotland and the Small plough's main competitor, though other regional products were by no means eclipsed.

Three things we can be quite sure about however: Small's skill as a ploughwright, the wise guide-lines he laid down for plough design and the fact that in doing so he effectively banished forever from the farmtoun scene that graceless implement of an antiquarian agriculture and the plodding progress of the oxteam. Perhaps there is something else: by his achievements, Small also opened the door for that truly competitive event of the farmtoun calendar, the ploughing match. His chain or swing plough needed only one man against the team of the former wooden implement, and only one pair of horses which the ploughman himself guided. It was an edge quietly exploited by the canny farmers who saw in it a chance to get better work. Individually and with the new agricultural improvement societies, they sponsored matches that set one ploughman against another. It was a shrewd move indeed: after all, was it not likely that a man who wanted to lift the cup at his local ploughing match would be practising, perfecting his skill through the entire winter's ploughing? And while they were at it: why not inculcate a similar care for the more costly harness now needed to yoke Clydesdale power in the furrow.

But the plough controversy was still far from over. Small himself was extremely conscious of the need for good mouldboard design, and even though the basic design might change little with the years, as late as the 1930s the properties of a particular mouldboard and its suitability for a specific soil were still being debated round the last of the bothy fires.

Small, all the same, may have done better for himself than Andrew Meikle, who gave Britain the barn-mill but profited little by it. The thresher's origin too and the hard outline of its development is unhappily blurred by time and the conjecture of historians.

Arguably, Meikle's achievement was greater than Small's since he was dealing with an entirely new concept, an attempt at putting the flail on to a power crank, simply to beat against the threshing floor, having failed. Meikle, however, was the son of a skilled and ingenious father, and that cannot have been a handicap. James Meikle had been the man chosen by that farmer-improver and pioneer of pot barley Andrew Fletcher of Saltoun to go to Holland to study that country's corn-fanners. The machines made in Scotland as a result of the elder Meikle's trip were very soon being copied in every carpenter's shop in the country and were in common use on the farmtouns from 1800 onwards—to the eternal gratitude of every farmtoun man or girl who had ever stood the day long riddling corn in the draught between two barn doors or on the exposed hillock of a shilling-law.

Though the younger Meikle's mill is something less than adequately documented, Fussell, in his interesting and sometimes revelatory *The Farmer's Tools*, traces the story from its beginnings in Alnwick, just south of the Border, where a man named Alderton (or perhaps Elderton) had built a thresher on the drum principle. This was seen by Sir Francis Kinloch, of Gilmerton, who had a model made and sent to Meikle's Houston Mill, near Haddington in East Lothian, for test. Meikle's water wheel, alas, smashed the machine to pieces. But that was enough to start Meikle off first by mechanizing the flail, an idea he quickly discarded, then on to the track of passing the sheaves between revolving drums. Thus the thresher was born. One of the first went to a Mr Stein of Kilbagie, in Clackmannan, that shire of champion ploughmen, and worked well enough for a further ten or twelve soon to be in operation in that same area which had given Small's plough such strong support. The Kilbagie thresher was water-powered but two- and four-horse machines were also being built. Quickly Meikle's machine became known in the Carse of Gowrie, introduced into the district by a Mr George Patterson of Castle Huntly; within seven years half-a-dozen mills, either water or horse-powered, were in use in the area. Soon the Haddington man's thresher was in general use in Midlothian, on all the large farmtouns of West Lothian, popular in Perthshire as well as Stirling, and was filtering into Clydesdale, Galloway, Berwick and Dumfries-shire, where it was mainly horse-driven. A millwright in Stonehaven, in the North-East, was selling it at the rate of half-a-dozen in as many months. By the mid-1800s or so, only the old woman at a tenant son's fireside would remember the days that had been and the morning thump-thump of the flail on the barn floor, as she sat spinning nothing but time.

Yet, as always, the road to perfection had been littered with the ruins of past invention, not the least of them the mechanized flail machines that were being built in Meikle's own county as early as the 1730s. For all we know—neglect is the price of failure—they may have lain in the barns of the East Lothians gathering dust until Meikle's mill arrived to kick them out into the sunlight. For the flail men that was the start of the end and perhaps a develop-ment not entirely unwelcome for they had had to leave their beds at the early hour of four. For the rest of the men of the farmtoun, however, it was the start of a new pattern that continued well into the days of the present century, when the barn-mills were still driven either by horses harnessed to the capstan or, when the mill-dam was full, by the bucket water-wheel. Grieves always found the barn-mill a great convenience: it filled those odd moments of the day when a ploughman might have time to light his pipe.

The mills were installed by the millwright's men, who travelled round the farmtouns as itinerant almost as the old-time tailors. They were quartered with the bothy men when there was room for them, or when there was not, lodged with a cottar or even in the farmhouse itself. The mills themselves were finely engineered, tributes to a craft skill every bit as magical as the cartwright's; their days were eclipsed by the increasing use of the contractor's mill for a "big thrash" and, finally, by the factory age and the coming of the combine-harvester. A few mills may linger on in the dark of old barns, gathering dust, having long outlasted the men who installed them and the men who worked them till their shirts were wet with sweat. Now they are among the last of the monuments to the great days of the farmtouns.

# XX

# The New Sound of Harvest

AS THE GREAT era of the farmtouns began, about 1840, the sound of harvest was still the clean sweet swish of the scythe rather than the mechanical click of the cutter-bar. In some of the uplands areas, indeed, the former had barely replaced the sickle after its long centuries of use, and in the Lothians of course the days of the itinerant shearing gangs were not yet at an end. The sickle had, after all, been a symbol, potent in the religion of the land and in the folk memory, and besides some said, viewing progress with horror, the scythe "shook the grain". There was even a quite convincing and practical argument why the time had not yet come to discard the heuk, as it was called in many areas of the country: in those tight uplands fields the smaller blade of the sickle could circumnavigate the boulders and rock outcrops with greater ease. It was a point not without some validity. All the same, for ten years and more, Patrick Bell's reaper, built with clandestine furtiveness and tested by moonlight, had been a reality, and a greater achievement by far than the evolution of Small's chain plough. One was already being used each harvest-time at Inch Michael in the Carse of Gowrie by a Mr A. J. Bell, who must surely have been a relative. And after being exhibited, early on in 1829, at the farmtoun of Greystone in the parish of Monikie, a handful of machines had been built and, before 1832, three sent to the Continent. Before another two years were out a further four had gone to America, according to one reliable source, and in the interim the machine had been demonstrated south of the Border. Yet—and this according to Bell himself, for as befitted a Scottish minister, he was a thorough chronicler— little interest was shown in his machine until 1840. And even in the following decade it made little headway.

There were probably several impediments to its use, quite apart from embattled tradition and a reluctance as yet among the farmtouns to face a future that entailed increasing investment in machines, something quite new in the countryside. One may have arisen from the Forfar clergyman's own magnanimity: he steadfastly refused to patent his invention with the result that very soon a number of smithy-made replicas were being produced. Their crudity and their often defective construction by men whose enthusiasm may have exceeded their craft skills, could have done little to reassure the men of the farmtouns on the future of mechanization—even at a time when wheat and barley were increasingly being grown as well as the traditional oats.

Yet Bell's machine was not the only one waiting in the wings for the new agricultural dawn. One Perthshire small farmer, James Smith, had also designed a reaper—on a different principle from Bell's but one of almost equal promise. His machine, too, appears to have been worth copying, but like the Carmyllie minister he seems to have become discouraged. Enclosure, new crops, and new patterns of cultivation were one thing, farming by machine quite another; the time was not yet when a farmtoun's stock of implements would provide a rough index to its prosperity. Apart from the stone-clearing that still had to be done in some areas, there was one very cogent reason for the lack of practical interest in those early reaping machines: inefficient field drainage. Significantly perhaps, it was Smith, whose name appears seldom on any Scottish roll of farming honour, who in time made possible the age of mechanical crop-handling. His farmtoun, Deanston, by his own account, was a place of 189 wet, boulder-strewn acres; much more than the large touns of the Lothians, it must have been the typical toun of its time. Its farmer himself though was far from typical. First, he seems to have been an intelligent amateur, perhaps from the merchant classes at that time beginning to take an interest in the countryside; second, if that were so, he would have a flexibility of mind uncluttered by a farming past. Smith went back to Palladius and his parallel hollow-drain system and persisted until he had evolved a drainage satisfactory for the farmtouns. He then went on to invent a sub-soil plough that broke the hard-pan of the soil without bringing "dead earth" to the surface, and his work combined with that of an English agricultural engineer, Josiah Parkes, recently returned from France, whose interest was in bogs and the reclamation of them. Parkes perfected the pipe-tile and, with Smith, ushered in the new farming age. Without them, progress must have been long delayed; the

machines that would take the farmtouns into the twentieth
century would have sunk without hope—up to their axle-beams.
Now, instead, the touns stood on the threshold of a new era of
invention and innovation. Already the implement factories were
in operation, their concentration, not surprisingly, in Scotland
and East Anglia. James Slight and Company of Leith Walk, in
Edinburgh, by 1844 was making swing ploughs, sub-soil ploughs,
double-mouldboard ploughs, harrows and grubbers (heavy
cultivators). It is likely that only the most prestigious of the big
touns of the time had anything like all of these implements; the
remainder might have the swing ploughs and the harrows but
little else, perhaps not even the wood, stone or iron rollers now
available to replace that most ponderous of farmtoun handtools,
the clodding-mell.

Most were, however, the implements of primary tillage, and the
conquest of the harvest fields—despite Bell's efforts—had to wait
for the energy of the Americans, one in particular, and the show-
case of the Great Exhibition of 1851 for the spark in the inventive
stubble. It is the saddest of ironies that it came with reapers that
carried the heavy influence of the early Bell machines. Slight,
reporting from the Great Fair in New York that same year, said
all six of the reapers on show there had cutting mechanisms
resembling that of the Bell machines. He even went so far as to
say that he considered the Hussey a cheap imitation. Yet it was
the name McCormick that was to be linked with the popularizing
of the reaper; not that that proved that the Virginia farmer's son
was a better engineer than the Scottish divine, only that he was a
more pushing salesman with a clearer care for patents.

During Exhibition year both the McCormick and Hussey
machines were tried out at harvest-time south of the Border.
Further trials followed in subsequent years—reaper trials were
the great feature of that farming decade—without exciting the
immediate interest their manufacturers evidently hoped for,
though one observer did offer the opinion that while it might
never be an implement to rely on, the reaper might be a useful
addition to the scythe. It was a comment not without justification
for besides being complicated, the Hussey for instance had been
known not to work at all when brought out for trial. In a confrontation at King's Park, Stirling, in 1853, between it, the McCormick
and the Bell reaper—now brought out to meet the American

challenge though it had not apparently been at the Great Exhibition—the Hussey was considered to be useless and none of those on show were thought at all suitable for the small Scottish farmtoun. The need was for a small, efficient *cheap* reaper, and one was not yet available.

Of the three types at work that day, only the Hussey had comparative cheapness on its side, and this seems to have had something to do with the machine's later success in a country where the boom years had as yet barely begun. Against the odds, however, and against all expert forecasts of the years before, by 1860 6,000 acres a year were being harvested in the East Lothians by 119 of these machines, by then being made in an improved form by the firms of Brown and Young of Stirling, and Jack and Sons of Maybole among others. One of the remarkable features of early reaper history is the amount of modification that went on, the innovations that agents for the American machines attempted and the hybrids that came of much indiscriminate amalgamation. The Bell reaper for instance was considered to have the better of the Crosskill-Hussey in trials at that famous Aberdeen-Angus farmtoun, Keillor. In what the minister himself might well have considered an unholy alliance, Lord Kinnaird, of Rossie Priory, Inchture, working with Patrick's brother, George Bell, combined it with a McCormick and established a factory to make the reaper that resulted, which was good enough to win the Highland Society's prize for the best reaper in 1858. From those first three types of machines, indeed, a whole industry was born; on toolbox lids, fretted on driver's seats that cupped the buttocks and left the imprint of the maker's name on them by the end of the day, a whole platoon of implement-manufacturing names marched into the currency of bothy talk for the first time.

By 1869, the Royal, England's premier farming show, that year at Manchester, selected no fewer than 84 reapers for field trials; not surprisingly, the judges felt "that as the flail had of late disappeared from the barns of the country and been replaced by machinery, so after this successful exhibition will the scythe and the sickle gradually cease to be used in our fields". Their estimate was accurate enough; change did not happen overnight and the old pattern of harvest lingered on. In 1881, the three horsemen of the farmtoun of Easter Beltie, in the Torphins district of the North-East Lowlands, scythed the entire harvest crop—as they had done in years past and might yet do in years to come; the folk of the crofts on the Perkhill of Lumphanan in the same area sheared, as usual, with the heuk. It would be the last decade of the century before the reaper came into general use, and by then it had begat the binder that would harvest America's prairie gold and hasten the depression of Britain's farmtouns. The first sheaf-binder, still at that stage a separate implement, was shown at the English Royal of 1876; three years later the Royal's Gold Medal went to a single-unit string-tying machine that carried an old familiar name. The binder had finally evolved; and that name was McCormick. Again there was a flurry of field trials; at Glasgow in 1883, though a machine by Hornsby won the £100 prize, the judges found that all the binders worked well and cut close and clean and tied securely and evenly. Names that had ridden on the earlier reapers and on mowers leapt the gulf of technology to appear on the gear casings and castings of the string-binding machines. There was none of the traumas that had accompanied the introduction of the reaper, and in the 1890s the machines were lightened and their prices reduced. By the turn of the century, or very early in the 1900s at the latest, there were few big touns without a binder or two. The five-foot cut, three-horse machine quickly established itself and took the farmtouns through to the 1930s, when a number of larger six-foot cut models began to appear in the harvest fields. But there were, too, areas where the poverty of the times clung hard and with an insistence that made the march of farmtoun mechanization something of a slow, limping progress. In the up-country round the hill of Bennachie, though most of the big touns had binders in their harvest fields by the 1930s, there were still reapers to be seen on the neighbouring one-pair touns. The reason for their popularity was not far to seek: they could be used with a pair while the binders needed three Clydesdales on the drag-pole; and how could the third beast be borrowed from a neighbour at the very time he was in most urgent need of it himself? Besides, the old back-delivery reaper was a simpler machine altogether; there was neither twine nor binding mechanism that could snorl—go wrong—to halt the onslaught of "hairst" in a district where the crops could sometimes be late.

If it was a major triumph for early farm technology—and it was—the reaper also wrought a deeper, more significant revolution. It broke not only with the days of the former farmtouns and an almost-pagan past, with immemorial harvests and that happy world of shearers, gatherers and bandsters, but even with the gangs of scythemen and their assistants that superseded them— though the scythe would continue for many years the harvest implement round many modest touns and would be stored, always, as a standby when wet weather laid and tangled the crops far beyond all machine intervention. The days of the heuk had taken sometimes 70—maybe up to 100 harvesters on the farms of the South—into the same cornfield, a vast battalion of folk. Harvest then was almost as much a festival as a farming operation; it is likely young bandsters had their manhood suddenly tested as shearer lasses, fevered with hairst ale, became unexpectedly compliant. For love had its place on the hairst rigs as at no other time of the farmtoun year. At least one young man, working on his father's rigs, has left a record, albeit ambiguously clouded, of those days:

> But a' the pleasures e're I saw,
>   Tho' three times doubled fairly,
> That happy night was worth them a',
>   Amang the rigs o' barley.

Writing to a medical friend in later life he admitted:

You know our country custom of coupling a man and woman together as partners in the labours of harvest. In my fifteenth autumn my partner was a bewitching creature, a year younger than myself. My scarcity of English denies me the power of doing her justice in that language; but you know the Scottish idiom—she was a *bonnie, sweet, sonsie lass.* In short, she, altogether unwittingly to herself, initiated me in that delicious passion, which, in spite of acid disappointment, gin-horse prudence, and book-worm philosophy, I hold to be the first of human joys, our dearest blessing here below! How she caught the contagion, I cannot tell: you medical people talk much of infection from breathing the same air, the touch, etc.; but I never expressly said I loved her. Indeed, I did not know myself why I liked so much to loiter behind with her when returning in the evening from our labours; why the tones of her voice made my heart-strings thrill like an Aeolian harp; and

particularly why my pulse beat such a furious ratan, when I
looked and fingered over her little hand, to pick out the cruel
nettle-stings and thistles.

Later, too, the poet would recall those times, setting the scene of
shearers' days:

> I mind it weel in early date,
>     When I was beardless, young and blate,
> And first could thrash the barn
>     Or haud a yokin' o' the pleugh,
> And tho' forfoughten sair eneugh,
>     Yet unco proud to learn——
> When first amang the yellow corn
>     A man I reckoned was,
> And wi' the lave ilk merry morn
>     Could rank my rig and lass—
> Still shearing and clearing
>     The tither stookit raw,
> Wi' claivers and haivers
>     Wearing the days awa——

The young harvester's name was Burns; he would be some heard
of as time wore on.

The days of the shearers, indeed, seem to have presented the
ideal opportunity for young lovers to slip the bounds of parental
authority, for the shearer-songs with their folk-record are laced
inextricably with the theme of rural love. The "Band o' Shearers"
is probably the prime example. A little over-sweet perhaps after
the sure hand of Burns, it is as much a love song as a hairst ballad.
What it does do is give some idea of the gathering-up of the
shearing band as harvest time draws on.

> 'Twas on an August afternoon,
> When folk could spy the harvest moon,
> The lads and lasses gathered roun'
>     To talk about the shearing.
> I whisper'd Jean if she wad gang,
> And shear wi' me the hale day lang,
> And join wi' me a merry thrang——
>     A jolly band o' shearers.

And should the weather be ower hot
I'll cast my gravat and my coat,
An' help my lass to shear her lot,
   Amang the band o' shearers.
So, bonnie lassie, will ye gang
And shear wi' me the hale day lang,
I'll cheer ye wi' a hearty sang,
   Amang the band o' shearers.

And should the thistles be ower strong,
Thy bonnie feet or hands to wrong,
I'll swear they'll no be standing long
   To hurt the lassie shearing.
And when our daily task is done,
We'll wander by the rising moon,
And string our hearts to love's sweet tune,
   When comin' frae the shearing.

So that, in the old days, was the way of it.

Yet even when the scythe took over, with its more forcing pace, the mood of harvest little changed; it was still gang work and just as fiercely competitive. Though there were, sadly, only lesser men to sing of it, that time too bonded men and lasses in a close working (and sometimes loving) relationship on the corn-rigs; many went home to a toun just for the weeks of hairst, taking a fee at some summer fair. In the days of the shearing bands the girls had wielded the sickle, covering about one-third of an acre in a ten-hour day; the scythe cut two acres in that time but it took a strong man to swing it. Gathering to him would be a young girl or woman, who also made the bands; behind her, a young lad tying the bands of the sheaves. "Johnnie Sangster" is a bothy song of those times when the scythers led out their teams each morning. It is a song of the hard lands of Buchan but like the shearing songs it ends on a more tender note and with the suggestion at least that the hairst could sometimes be a kind of country courtship.

O a' the seasons o' the year
   When we maun work the sairest
The harvest is the foremost time,
   And yet it is the rarest.
We rise as seen as mornin' licht,
   Nae craters can be blither;

We buckle on oor finger steels,
  And follow oot the scyther.

A mornin' piece to line oor cheek,
  Afore that we gae forder,
Wi' clouds o' blue tobacco reek
  We then set oot in order.
The sheaves are risin' thick and fast,
  And Johnnie he maun bind them.
The busy group, for fear they stick,
  Can scarcely look behind them.

I'll gie ye bands that winna slip,
  I'll pleat them weel and thraw them.
I'm sure they winna tine the grip,
  Hooever weel ye draw them.
I'll bang my knee against the sheaf,
  And draw the band sae handy.
Wi' ilka strae as straucht's a rash,
  And that'll be the dandy.

Oh some complain on hacks and thraws,
  And some on brods and bruises.
And some complain on grippit hips
  And stiffness in their troosers;
But as soon as they lay doon the scythe
  And the pipers yoke their blawvin',
They ane and a' forget their dools
  Wi' daffin an' wi' tyawvin.

If e'er it chance to be my lot
  To get a gallant bandster,
I'll gar him wear a gentle coat,
  And bring him gowd in handfu's.
But Johnnie he can please himsel'
  I wadna wish him blinkit;
Sae, after he has bred his ale,
  He can sit doon and drink it.

A dainty cowie in the byre,
  For butter and for cheeses;
A grumphie feedin' in the sty
  Wad keep the hoose in greases.

A bonnie ewie in the bucht
   Wad help to creesh the ladle;
An we'll get tufts o' cannie woo'
   Wad help to theek the cradle.

"Rarest" is used here to mean "grand" and the singer, though
the ballad itself was written by a man, sees clearly the way she
wishes her relationship with the "gallant bandster" to go—into a
kind of crofting Nirvana with a cow, a pig and perhaps a sheep or
two. The bandster Johnnie she would allow a life of indolence.
Hard though the work is, "lowsing time" and the piper's rant will
bring everyone on the hairst rig into high spirits and make them
forget their sorrows. The mood, still, is one of festival.

This was the kind of harvest that brought fisher folk, apprentices, cottar wives and even passing tinks into the fields of the
farmtouns. The folklorist Gavin Greig, nearer that time by almost
70 years, recalled:

> In those days the hairst rig was the scene of some of the happiest
> experiences of the rural year. Scythers, gatherers, bandsters
> and rakers were associated in the work. Besides the regular
> farm hands there were others—mostly local tradesmen and cottar
> wives engaged for the season. An eager happy spirit was abroad;
> everybody was in high good humour. Moving over the field
> in a body, the busy workers had many opportunities for friendly
> word and merry sally. Acquaintances then formed often
> ripened into life-long partnerships.

The songs of such folk, not surprisingly, lingered on the lips of
rural minstrels well into the reaper and binder age, and even the
machine-reaper itself inspired a ballad:

I hae seen the Hairst o' Rettie,
   Ay, and twa three on the throne;
I've heard for sax or seven weeks
   The hairsters' girn and groan.
But a covey Willie Rae,
   Wi' a monthie and a day,
Mak's a' the jolly hairst lads
   Gae singin' doon the brae.

A monthie and a day, my lads,
   The like was never seen;
It beats to sticks the fastest strips
   O' Victory's best machine.
A Speedwell now brings up the rear,
   A Victory clears the way;
And twenty acres daily yields
   Nor stands to Willie Rae.

He drives roon and roon the fields
   At sic an awfu' rate;
He steers them canny oot and in
   At mony's the kittle gate;
And wiles them safely o'er the clods
   To mony's the hidden hole;
But he comes by no mishanter,
   If you leave him with the pole.

He sharps their teeth to gar them bite.
   Then taps them on the jaws;
And when he finds them dully like,
   He brawly kens the cause.
A boltie here, a pinnie there,
   A little oot o' tune;
He shortly stops that wild career
   And brings the slushet doon.

He whittles at the corners,
   Mak's crookit bitties straught;
And sees that man and beast alike
   Are equal in the draught.
And a' the shavies lying' straught,
   And nane o' them agley;
For he'll count wi' ony dominie
   Fae the Deveron to the Spey.

He's no made up o' mony words
   Nor kent to puff and lee;
But just as keen a little chap
   As ever you did see.
If you be in search o' harvest work
   Upon a market day,
Tak' my advice, be there in time
   And look for Willie Rae.

Here then is a song of the new farmtoun age, not of love but of labour-saving, a song of praise for the reaping-machine for the shortened season of harvest it brought in and the twenty acres a day it could cut. Not least there is the charm of some of that early wonder at such machines shining through the mundane considerations, the tribute to Willie Rae, a modest man apparently and not one to boast about his achievements, neither his expertise with the machine nor his knack of guiding the Clydesdales round the clods that could bring disaster. Willie must have been the first of that rare breed, the mechanically-minded farmtoun man.

If it had taken long enough to alter the old pattern of harvest, the men who had initiated that change were not soon forgotten. On his last journey a single sheaf of wheat lay on McCormick's coffin, a fitting farming tribute to the man who had revived interest in the machine-harvester when it had flagged. It is unlikely that Bell, the Scots minister, would have grudged him that final, most moving, recognition.

# XXI

## *Steam, the Unfulfilled Dream*

So, IN TIME, the binder eclipsed the reaper. And the portable
thresher, with the encroachment of steam, came to diminish the
rôle of the barn-mill. Both altered the old patterns of farmtoun
labour, though the barn-mill was still used: for a modest weekly
"thrash"; at the end of harvest to get a sample of the oats and an
estimate of the yield; or to get cottars' corn, that sent yearly to the
miller to make the farm workers' oatmeal. Both, binder and
thresher, in the final days of the old farmtoun life merged in the
combine-harvester, one of the many engineering achievements that
would turn the farmtoun into a thing of the factory age.

The development of steam, agriculturally, ran almost in parallel
with the advance of the reaper in the mid-1800s. But despite Watt
and the carriage-maker Murdoch, farm steam was English; there
were few traction engines made in Scotland and its source of
enthusiasm was always south of the Border, where it was pioneered
by family firms in or on the fringe of the farm-equipment market.
Their names rode proudly under tall smoke-stacks, even now a
kind of poetry to the past and to the steam enthusiast: Burrell,
Garrett, Clayton and Shuttleworth, Ransome, Fowler, Marshall,
Aveling and Porter, and (even) McLaren. But north of the
Border, where its application was always a little less practicable
than in the pastoral English counties, there was an air of expectation. Steam ploughing was being demonstrated near Dumfries as
early as the 1830s, with tackle devised by a Tiverton lace-maker
—the unlikeliest of pioneers one might think, until one knows that
John Heathcote was also a Member of Parliament and therefore a
member of that greatest of all farming clubs and that hot-house
of so many agricultural ideas (as well as one or two measures that
would do it indescribable harm). The Devon man's steam tackle
worked a plough made by a familiar name, Josiah Parkes. The
outfit seems to have been highly successful though there is another
report of the time: of the first ploughing engine demonstrated

near Dumfries sinking into the bog of Lochar Moss and disappearing from view overnight.

There was a more definite interest though in the autumn of 1851 and the spring of the following year about the farmtoun of Niddry Mains, not far from Edinburgh, when rotary cultivation by steam was demonstrated with a machine made by Mr Slight of the capital's Leith Walk (a busy man indeed, since he is almost certainly the same who had been reporting shortly before on reaper design from New York's fair). The patentee though was a man named Usher, and this preoccupation with the rotary principle, existing side by side with the evolution of what was to become the standard method of steam-ploughing—two engines with cable-pulled implement—was to continue into the 1880s. What is so very interesting now is that the Edinburgh-made machine seems to have presaged the one-unit approach of today's mechanized farming. Rotary cultivation, too, had its followers, without gaining any convincing ground as an alternative to the plough. In all probability, however, this one-unit application sprang from an early, astute realization that steam power, clumsy and weighty as it was, could never provide the kind of direct-draught in the field that was possible with a team of horses or oxen.

Yet elsewhere there were men who saw things differently, following the pioneering work of John Fowler with steam and the rope-hauled tillage implement; they were selling their horses with a frenzy that suggested there was no tomorrow, convinced that unless they got them to the horse fair at once they would be worth nothing. Certainly one of Fowler's sets was operating in Scotland in 1859.

But the hysteria for steam was unfounded. In all the misplaced enthusiasm that accompanied so much of the new machine-farming, nothing ever exceeded the muddle-headedness of the farmtouns over steam. There was, initially, a kind of euphoria that robbed thinking men of their reason. Why their judgement should have been so blinkered it is now hard to say, for the price of a steam-ploughing set in 1870 was anything between £800 and £1,500, a capital investment that put it far beyond the scope of the average farmtoun, and must surely have made it plain that the future of steam-ploughing, drainage-work and threshing by steam —except possibly on the largest estates and farms—was in the

G

contractor's hands. The ploughman and his pair drawing their solitary furrow across the face of the countryside would continue, a part of the traditional pattern as yet undisturbed.

There was, though, a further strand in the story of steam and the farmtouns: the traction engine, following the formative years of its design, from about 1870 began to arrive increasingly at the farmtouns, dragging its portable thresher behind it. The growth of the portable threshing set had been just as remarkable as the spread of Meikle's machine. Following the showing at the English Royal in the early 1840s, by Ransomes, of a portable thresher that used its own steam operating power as a means of moving it from place to place, there came rapid development. Within ten years, it is estimated, there were no fewer than 8,000 traction-engine threshing sets at work in Britain; the task was to be the traction engine's predominant job throughout its long history despite all the hauling, drainage, ploughing and showman's work it also did. Just the sight of the traction engine with its train of threshing-machine and tender or housevan turning in at the road-end was enough to set a grieve dancing round a toun like a cat on hot bricks. The threshing mill—or "mull" as it was always called in the North-East Lowlands—passed into the folklore of the farmtouns. Its arrival brought a breath of interest to the drab backend of the year. Small boys left their home lessons to stand in the dusk of a winter's afternoon and watch the great leviathan nudge the mill into the cornyard. Besides the wonder of it all there was the chance to witness the frenzy of men and to hear expletives as yet unfamiliar as posts were dragged up by the root and fences flattened to make way for it. Shouts and curses usually cut long through the gathering gloam before the mill was set to everyone's liking, ready for the following day's threshing.

The steam mill was a kind of endurance test: it sapped a man's virility and called his manliness seriously into doubt if he proved unable to carry two-hundredweight sacks of barley without sign of distress—and that over an "obstacle course" that began with dodging the darting figures of the mill's attendants, involved the tortuous negotiation of a cornyard seemingly full of demented dogs, and ended all too frequently with the back-breaking ascent of rickety stairs to the corn-loft. Men, in mental weakness, broke their bodies rather than admit to not being physically strong enough for the work. And once the mill started, it went without cease; men and women became its slaves: forking, loosing, feeding, carrying the corn from one end, straw from the other, chaff from its under-belly. Men who came smilingly in the morning from all compass-points of the countryside with barn forks strapped to the crossbars of their bicycles went home at night spent of life and wet with sweat.

It took a turnout of fourteen to sixteen folk to man the "mull" for a "good thrash", two men at least forking from the rick and two—usually those women with a special skill for it—to "lowse" on the high mill shelvings for the man feeding the drum. The mill-men themselves, sooty-faced from the dust of the mill and the smoke of the steam engine, took it in turns to "feed", one spreading the loosed sheaves into the drum while his partner stalked the cornyard in his grease-caked dungaree jacket, an oilcan in one hand and oily shoddy in the other. Their travelling life was like a tinker's, here today another toun tomorrow; between places their bicycles were hung on the back of the mill against the home-going of a weekend or the time when the weather broke, for the "thrash" was a fine-day affair and there could be weeks on end when the mill was marooned under its big tarpaulin in some cornyard. They ate and slept where they could, in the bothies with the single men of the farmtouns where there was the room for them or, in the farming uplands of the North-East where the touns were small, in their caravan. Exciting though the mill's appearance was, there were few touns sorry to see it go. Even the farm-loon in his first fee, for whom its bustle and bawdy camaraderie was a new experience, had soon had enough of it. His job that day was to carry water from the nearest stream for the engine—on his shoulders in pails on a yoke, or with the orra-beast yoked into the water-cart.

For the women of the farmtouns having the steam-mill about the place was like having a party, except that it was far from being a picnic. The day before great collops of beef were fetched from the butcher and thrown bodily into a brew to boil in the biggest available pot, whatever its previous contents. It was in a way a day of reunion: round the table at the dinner hour there were faces unseen since the last wedding or christening or funeral, or the turn of the year. Above the ringing of plates and the scrape of ladles, there was good humour and laughter and sometimes the kind of banter that would bring a blush to the cheek of the kitchen maid—as well as the unwelcome attentions of young horsemen from neighbour touns. But if it was a good "thrash", and a good corn yield, the small antagonisms of the day were easily blurred by the bottle or two broached at the end of it before all the folk went home. Next day, or the day after, it would be the turn of another farmtoun to play host to the "mull" and its throng of hungry, thirsty men. Even the dogs had their day when the mill came, for as the ricks of the stackyard were levelled down to their stone foundations this refuge of the farm rats was creived round with small-mesh wire and they would be trapped. And there were mice, too, in those stack-foundations, enough to keep all the farmtoun cats at play. The slaughter went on almost unnoticed amid the heavy *brumm-brumm* of the mill and its satanic dust. It was just part of the "thrash".

# XXII

## *Setting the Milkmaids Free*

SUCH THEN WAS the main thread of early mechanization and the engineering developments that dramatically altered farmtoun life. There were also secondary areas that drew in the genius of engineers and where, though their work might have less impact, it was not without its own interesting sociological significance. The invention of the milking machine, for instance, meant that small boys went off to school well-scrubbed and with their bootlaces tied neatly by their mothers instead of having their clothes thrown hurriedly on to them by an elder sister (or brother) while she was busy milking in the dairy byre. The old Scotch horse rake was certainly around as the farmtouns came into their own about 1840 and was capable of doing the work of a dozen or more women. Whether it was allowed to is another matter: in principle haymaking was more or less mechanized by the mid-1870s but in practice there was little change; the farmtouns turned a blind eye. Besides the rake, there were tedders available and the mower—a development on the skirts of the reaper—had first been included in the Royal Agricultural Society of England (RASE) trials south of the Border in 1857. Yet, as Queen Victoria's long reign came to an end—a reign that had seen the traditional harvest scene at any sizeable toun transformed completely from the laborious task of hand-shearing and hand-binding to the mechanized perfection of the binder, which stippled the harvest field with ready-made sheaves—the scythe was often still the implement of the hayfield.

Even in the 1930s most of the farmtouns were still making hay —mower-cut admittedly, but then raked from the swath into windrows and tossed into haycocks or coles—in a manner that the farm-methods chronicler of the mid-1800s, Henry Stephens, would instantly have recognized and which stretched back in tradition to the days of the run-rig and the farmtoun cluster. Even the ballads seem to fall sadly silent about the hayfield. Yet there was almost as much urgency to the winning of hay as to securing the corn harvest and it is quite probable that this unevenness of progress comes down finally to a very fundamental explanation: the lack of available farming capital, even in the boom years up to the 1880s, to advance on all the frontiers of farmtoun development.

Seed-sowing lagged less than haymaking, yet up to the late-1800s, and sometimes even beyond it, many sizeable farmtouns were hand-broadcasting seed corn from the shoulder-slung hopper, though the seed-drill had long been available: by 1810 there had been a combination machine handling manure as well as seed, and from 1840 drills were a regular feature of the agricultural shows. There were pioneers, of course: the advanced farmtouns of East Lothian, for instance, where, with horse-hoes, drills had been absorbed into the work-routine by 1829. They were also being used in the North-East in the Mearns and probably in the Border counties. By 1860, Fussell says, writing of course of Britain as a whole, "there were many manufacturers of corn drills, but all their products were different modifications of the same principle". Their common source, he believes, the earlier Tull not excluded, was the Rev. James Cooke's patent of 1782, another example of pulpit-power over the land. Certainly the drill had reached a very acceptable standard of work by 1870, and proof of this is the fact that the design of those days was practically identical with that of the 1920s.

But it was an area where Scottish entrepreneurs too made their skills felt, if not with the degree that was the case with the swing plough or the reaper. Drummond's Agricultural Museum in Stirling about 1840 was showing drills and early examples of the broadcast-sower drawn by one horse and capable of covering 24 acres a day—a big difference from the acreage that fell daily to the solitary sower and his seed hopper. Come the mid-point of the century and the Great Exhibition, and a further, very practical development could be written down to the Biggar manufacturer James Watt: he "jointed" the machine's long seed chests so that they could be swung lengthwise for travel to the field and to pass through its gate. The broadcaster as still seen on the farmtouns of the 1930s had arrived.

Of turnip-sowers there was no shortage. Again, East Lothian justifies its reputation as the then front-runner of farming progress in the country. There, a John Wightman, of Upper Keith, was using one in 1827, probably of local manufacture. Whatever its make, it seems to have been highly satisfactory in its work for 30 years later similar models were being "very generally used". In Roxburghshire even more sophisticated machines may have been at work, all of them locally-made by wrights whose skill spread from one farmtoun to another on the strength of the horsemen's opinion rather than on the sometimes dubious claims of the show-stand. Although in England one-, two- and three-row seed barrows were used, Scotland seems quickly to have settled for the double-drill version. By the 1890s, such a model, horse-drawn, was coming home to the farmtouns from William Elder of Berwick-upon-Tweed at a price of £6. It is unlikely that the local wright long survived the competition.

In two further areas of invention, Scottish engineers resumed their former pre-eminence, though the impetus in one case came first from America. Reporting on a US "milking machine" of 1862, *The Illustrated London News* foresaw the end of "the ruddy milkmaid". If the humour was unintentional, the correspondent at least showed a high awareness of the machine's social importance. Not surprisingly, the next known development came in Scotland's South-West, spurred by that most critical of farmtoun considerations: the quality of labour. Among the women of the farmtouns there was nearly always a shortage of *good* milkers.

Yet it was nearly 30 years later before Mr Stewart Nicholson, of Bombie, Kirkcudbright, and a Mr John Gray between them won a RASE medal with their invention, and before a Kilmarnock sanitary engineer, William Murchland, patented the apparatus he installed at David Shaw's farmtoun of Haining Mains. Murchland's machine at least must have had some success since the farmtoun's milkmaids rose against it. Both inventions, however, relied on continuous suction and were not really satisfactory. It was not until Dr Alexander Shields of Glasgow hit upon the pulsation principle (which simulated the intermittent sucking of a calf) that the milking machine became a feasible farmtoun aid. Among the early manufacturers was the firm of J. and R. Wallace of Castle Douglas, but it was joined and overtaken by others whose machines in time would break one of the last tyrannies of the farmtouns: that condition of cottar's employment that so often demanded a "wife to milk". There is no evidence, as has sometimes been said, that cottar wives came to include an insuratory clause in their prayers ("God Bless Alfa-Laval") but certainly if the price of such progress was a loss of income it was also a release from a routine that meant treadmill attendance in the dairy byre, early morning and night, seven days a week.

The potato-digger, too, was a mechanical labour-saver; indeed it is doubtful whether Scotland would have reached her dominance of the potato-seed market without it. The digger had its birth in that frenetic burst of farm engineering in the mid-1800s, but it then seems to have been submerged by the weight of so much other, and sometimes more acute, development. It did not seriously surface again until the 1870s, when the Highland and Agricultural Society held trials near Perth. The venue reflected the potato interest of that central Scottish region, as did the firms whose machines were on display. Entries came from Bissett's of Blairgowrie—soon the firm would also be making binders; William Dewar of Kellas, Dundee; James Mollison of Ruthven; James Robertson of Coupar Angus; R. Stewart of Buttergask, Coupar Angus. All their diggers, "spinners", were drawn by a pair of Clydesdales and each was awarded a Silver Medal, an indication that all had reached a fair level of work. Though it did do some skin damage to the crop, the "spinner" prevailed on the farmtouns until the 1920s, when the seedmen, seeking better handling, turned at last to the gentler elevator type of machine.

There were many other machines, too, in the long march towards mechanized "improvement"—barn, byre and dairy equipment all of which at first lightened the load on the farmtoun men and women and later hastened the coming of the factory-farming age. There were areas in which advance was at such a pace that one improvement was rendered almost obsolete by another before it had reached the field; in other spheres there was virtual failure or at least such bitter disappointment on expectation that the farmtouns were left dangling tantalizingly between tradition and competitive farming. Again, many of the "inventions" of the time were but ephemera tossed off by ingenious minds and never lifted off the drawing-board for unaccountable reasons: perhaps because the engineering techniques they demanded were as yet imperfect; or because the mind that conceived the idea lacked the application and stubborn insistence to see it through the duller stages of construction and prolonged trial in the field. What emerges most strongly from any study of the machines of the farmtouns and their impact on the work routine is the fact that the history of mechanization is not measurable by the award of a Gold Medal here, a Silver Medal there, but only in the old account books of the farmtouns and countryside firms. These now are few and far between and in the context of our farming history undervalued; they underpin the belief that the date of a machine's public trial had little to do with its final acceptance on the farmtouns.

# XIII

## *Inklings of the Factory Age*

BY 1910 THERE was an inkling for thinking men of the way things would go, if no hint as yet of how cataclysmic the change might be. Steam was in its prime still, but down in Bedfordshire, eight years earlier, the farm tractor had been born and was already exposing the weakness of the traction engine as an agricultural machine while, paradoxically, following a parallel line in design. By 1906, Dan Albone, the son of a Biggleswade market-gardener, was demonstrating his machine's adaptability by harvesting at night, his Ivel tractor drawing two binders and cutting seventeen acres in a matter of only six hours. And he was by no means alone in demonstrating how the internal combustion engine could be applied to farming. In 1903, Ransomes, Sims and Jeffries, the East Anglian implement firm whose name is intertwined with farming history, built a petrol-fuelled four-cylinder machine intended to sell at £450, though it finally dropped the tractor through lack of market support. The firm was only one of the many well-known names that saw the tractor's potential if the farming community itself did not. Blackstone and Company was another. So was the traction-engine firm of Marshall, and the American Case company. Sharp's of York produced a machine which had a mid-mounted cutterbar for mowing and launched it with the advertising promise that it would "mow 35 acres of grass in 10 hours" at a cost of 2d (1p) an acre. It did all the usual tractor jobs besides and weighed only fifteen cwt. With hindsight it is easy to say that this may have been the very moment that tractor-design took a wrong turning, for the idea implicit in the Sharp machine was overlooked and tractor layout reverted to the example before it: the traction engine.

For that the engineering industry itself was not entirely to blame, for the Royal Agricultural Society of England, in conducting trials in 1910, came down heavily on the side of the steam engine, while side-stepping outright endorsement. It considered that the future must lie with a machine that would allow the farmer to dispense with the hiring of a traction engine for farmtoun tasks—but one also capable of undertaking a substantial amount of field work. Among the machines on view at the trials was the Saunderson and Mills' "Universal", the "S" model of which, when demonstrated four years later as war was about to break out, hauled five binders—in Albone's home county of Bedfordshire. Such was the competition in an industry that has always needed more than its quota of showmen-salesmen as well as its skilled engineers.

But if the men of the Scottish farmtouns heard anything at all of tractor trials and so on, it was in an abstract way, dissociated from the real world of the touns which they knew, something for the future, maybe, and for the few. War, however, lent an urgency and the commandeering of Clydesdales gave savage point to such developments. Tractor design got a fillip when the Ministry of Munitions built the MOM tractor intended for hire to the hard-pressed farmtouns, though this seems never to have been produced in numbers. Instead, Lloyd George, as prime minister, asked Henry Ford to ship 7,000 of his Fordson machines to Britain, thus strengthening an "invasion" already begun by the International Harvester Company's Mogul tractor, a sixteen hp chain-driven, single-cylinder machine, already being hired out by the government. Between 1914 and 1920, International were also to send some 3,500 models of their twenty-five hp Titan. In Scotland itself, John Wallace and Company of Glasgow produced a quite indomitable little machine and with a notably bad lapse of taste called it the Clydesdale. That didn't go down well round the farmtouns.

War or no war, Scotland's Highland and Agricultural Society found time to stage its own trials in 1917, and its committee concluded that "to suit conditions in Scotland an efficient land tractor need not exceed 30 cwt in weight", an interesting and early recognition that brute power alone was not the answer.

It was the Fordson—despite International Harvester's early lead—that was destined to carry the American banner strongly into Britain and certainly into the life of the Scottish farmtouns, where the make had a dominance that turned the salesmen of other models into a race of gloomy alcoholics. In 1917, 5,000 of the promised total were shipped from America, followed by a further

1,000 a little later. These war-wanted Fordsons had all the basic features of a design that would remain almost constant until after the end of World War II, including one-unit construction and worm-drive. Later, through the 1920s and 1930s, the Fordson would be joined by other makes with sleeker lines, more finesse in the controls. They were fine machines that guaranteed any tractor-driver an interested audience of small boys every time he stopped at the village shop for his black twist tobacco, but they never offered serious competition to Henry Ford's machine. Their names though had that cachet of glamour that the Fordson lacked and reflected in many cases a long and honourable association with agriculture: besides International Harvester, there was Case (the Wisconsin company which had made traction engines for the American market made its first tractor in 1892), John Deere, Massey Harris, and nearer home, the Marshall and Fowler (both converts from the traction engine). By 1920, the United States had no fewer than 166 tractor manufacturers.

There was a remarkably forward-looking Austin seen on Scottish farmtouns, too, in the 1920s. A Scottish-made machine called the Glasgow, from the D. L. Motor Company of Motherwell, and selling at £450, was entered in RASE trials in 1919. But mainly the farmtouns bowed to Detroit right through to the end of the 1930s: that early twenty-two hp Fordson—later made in Cork— went on sale at £280, £20 cheaper than any of its rivals. Its weight was 20½ cwts, vindicating those early trial judges. They might almost have written the formula for Ford's success.

Though its numbers grew substantially through the 1930s, the tractor was never constructively integrated into the farmtoun routine. It was treated as an extra and faster horse in an emergency and proved useful for pulling milk lorries and country buses out of ditches they invariably slid into on icy winter mornings on their way to town; for carting hay and turnips to the sheep in stormy weather; and for bringing in the doctor to a toun cut off by snowdrifts when it was a case of life or death. But if lack of vision put a curb on tractor sales, there were other, more potent reasons: the depressed state of the farmtouns and the dread most farming men had of fire. Though most tractors of the time ran on paraffin, their engines had to be started and warmed-up on petrol, a dangerous commodity to store about any farmtoun far from a telephone and even farther from a spare-time fire brigade.

Nonetheless there were grieves who enjoyed the status a tractor bestowed on a toun, as well as the chance it gave to work sitting down, and in that time before the term "tractorman" was part of the farmtoun language, they took on the task of tractor-driving along with their supervisory duties. In any case, a horseman could hardly be trusted to handle the thing, and the job was most jealously guarded. There were let-downs, of course, and loss of face. One of the big advantages of the tractor over the traction engine—supposedly, and the salesmen were never slow to point it out—was that it started at once, needing none of the prolonged preparation that had traction-engine men out of their beds by 4.30 to raise steam. That claim was, at its mildest, something of a fallacy, for the age of Instant Starting was not yet. Whole regiments of farmtoun men were required to hazard their lives in crank-starting machines whose magneto timing had been tampered with—and had their wrists broken when the handle lashed back at them faster than any Clydesdale's hoof had ever done. Maintenance, to many grieves, remained one of life's great mysteries: some indeed—good men in many ways—were unable to read the instruction book (which in any case they kept safely on a shelf at home where no one else could absorb its wisdom). Icy mornings brought the kind of cursing the stable beasts rarely inspired. Men ran from the farmhouse kitchen juggling scalding oven-ready spark-plugs in their hands (or ignited petrol-soaked rags in the middle of the farm close to heat them), rushing to insert them again in the cylinder-head while some semblance of warmth remained on them. In the 1930s there grew up a race of grieves with hands as calloused as a fakir's feet, whose response to any trouble that came of maladjusted magnetoes, inconsistent carburettors, valve, piston or air-intake disturbance was an unhesitating "Heat the plugs!"

Looking back, the marvel is that the tractor survived. Yet it did, and though it would have been hard at the time to see exactly where design was leading there was a kind of progress in the adoption of the pneumatic tyre, fitted first to an Allis-Chalmers machine in 1932. The step was one regarded with more than a little scepticism about the farmtouns, where tractor rear wheels, taking a cue from the traction engine, had been traditionally straked or spade-lugged to prevent wheel-slip in the fields. In time, however, there was a consensus that the pneumatic tyre was a move in the right direction, that its versatility in allowing a machine to come straight out of the field to haul a bogey-load of potatoes or corn to the railhead was not negligible. Even so, from the visionary's standpoint it was pedestrian progress without anything revolutionary in the way of ideas until Harry Ferguson's hydraulic lift and three-point linkage system appeared, in the mid-1930s, to make the implement a part of the tractor unit. The implement could be wielded as a claw—entirely different from the separate unit cumbersomely dragged. Now at last could the future be clearly seen. Though the Harry Ferguson system would not be generally adopted until after World War II, like the wireless and the motor bus it hastened the end of the old farmtoun days and the era of the Clydesdales.

# XXIV

## *Day of the Ploughman*

BUT FOR ALL the pace of advance, the refinement and multiplicity of machines, the farming year began still with the plough. The old ploughman, with his Clydesdale pair, was the craftsman of the old farmtouns. The rick-builder might give symmetry to the gold of the stackyard in the autumn sunlight and draw admiring comment from old farmers on the kirk road but it was the ploughman's art that gave a farmtoun its reputation. His work on some hillside, set up for the country round to see, was a testimonial to his skill between the plough-stilts, or his lack of it. There was a kind of magic about ploughing, a mysticism even; it was the start of a new cycle, the first tentative step in the new farming year. The ploughman's work went forward with a kind of hope, and even well into the nineteenth century in some of the upland areas of the North-East with a kind of high ritual that for all their kirk-going seemed remarkably like the propitiation of pagan gods. The cutting of the first furrow would be marked by the appearance of the gudewife of the farmtoun with a trencher of food and refreshment for the ploughman and her solemn salutation of "Guid speed the wark". "Guid speed it," would come the ploughman's reply, as he sat down, traditionally on the plough's beam, to eat the fare that had been brought to him. That night there would be a supper feast at the farmer's table. But then, in those upland glens one was near to dark gods, and to have started the new pattern of the year without some sacrament, or the customary dram, would have been a chancy thing.

Elsewhere, too, that first furrow and that moment of "renewal" scarred young minds with its heavy portent, among them that of the poet Edwin Muir. Later, remembering his sad youth, the Orkney landscape and the plough horses, he recalled

> Their conquering hooves which trod the stubble down
> Were ritual that turned the field to brown.

Of all the farmtoun men, only the ploughman himself stood in that special, direct relationship with the soil—for all the development of steam-ploughing, a link still with the ancient past, a symbolic figure in the landscape almost as much as the sower. All the bothy balladry sings his art and his importance; he is cast as the gay gallant of the farmtouns and could not have been unaware of it.

If there are songs that testify his popularity as a bit of a "roving blade" and make it abundantly clear that his attentions were shamelessly sought-after, there are further ballads that burnish his image as the generous, good-looking, laughter-loving lad of the farmtouns. Bailies, grieves, strappers, orra men—none, anywhere in the whole range of the ballads, enjoys the same bohemian glamour:

> Where first I saw my Jockie
>   Was at Huntly feeing fair,
> Wi' his rosy cheeks and dimpled chin,
>   And bonnie curly hair.
> When he looked at me so slyly
>   Wi' his bonnie e'en o' blue,
> I found my heart from me depart
>   To the lad that hauds the plough.
>
> The ploughman lad's a jolly lad,
>   He spends his money free,
> And when he meets a bonnie lass
>   He tak's her on his knee.
> He puts his arms around her neck,
>   And prees her bonnie mou',
> Wi' kisses sweet he does her treat.
>   The lad that hauds the plough.

Such praise could go, at times, to extravagant lengths. The ploughman's skills were constantly being set against the contributions of other trades to the quality of rural life. One, "The Praise of Ploughmen", displays a bias as strong as any but at least has the excuse of reflecting traces of a minor talent. Not unexpectedly, the writer was himself a man of the farmtouns, the farmer, in fact, of Upper Boyndlie in the North-East. It was written about the mid-1800s, just at the dawn of the new farmtoun era.

Ye lads and lasses a' draw near,
I'm sure it will delight your ear,
And as for me I'll no be sweir
   To sing the praise o' ploughmen.
The very King that wears the crown,
The brethren of the sacred gown,
The Dukes and Lords of high renown,
   Depend upon the ploughmen.

The gardener he cries out wi' speed,
I'm sure I was the first man made,
And I was learned the gardener trade
   Before there was a ploughman.
Oh gardener, lad, it's true you say;
But how long gardener did you stay?
I'm sure it was just scarce a day
   Ere ye became a ploughman.

The blacksmith he says, I hear news,
Do I not make your iron ploughs,
And fit the coulter for its use,
   Or there would be nae ploughmen?
Oh, blacksmith, we must all allow
That you can make an iron plough,
But you would ne'er got that to do
   If it were not for the ploughmen.

The mason he cries, Ho, ho, fie,
Do I not build your castles high
The wind and rain for to defy,
   Far better than the ploughman?
Oh, mason, ye may build a house,
And fit it for its proper use,
But from the King unto the mouse
   Depends upon the ploughmen.

The miller he speaks out wi' glee——
Do I not sit at the mill e'e,
And grind the corn food for thee
   Far better than the ploughman?
Oh, miller, ye maun haud yer jaw,
And sit and look at your mill wa',
And see if dust frae it would fa'
   If it were not for the ploughmen.

The souter he cries out, Hurrah,
Do I not make boots and shoes richt braw
For to defend baith frost and snaw.
    That's worn by the ploughmen?
You may mak' boots and shoes wi' speed,
Wi' last and leather, birse and thread,
But where's the meal for to mak' breid,
    If it were not for the ploughmen?

The tailor he cries out wi' haste——
I pray of this don't make a jest;
Oh, I can make coat, trews, and vest
    Far better than a ploughman.
Oh, tailor, ye may mak' braw clothes,
But where's the meal for to be brose?
Ye might close up baith mouth and nose,
    If it were not for the ploughmen.

Success the ploughmen's wages crown;
Let ploughmen's wages ne'er come down,
And plenty in Scotland aye abound,
    By labour of the ploughmen.
For the very King that wears the crown,
The brethren o' the sacred gown,
The Dukes and Lords of high renown,
    Depend upon the ploughmen.

Written by John Anderson, a man said to be "the best dancer in the district", the song was put to a tune by another hand. It argues the ploughman's case in the strongest terms. Without him, where is society? Needless to say the song quickly travelled round the country from one bothy fireside to the next and soon bred almost as many variants. If it has a saving grace it is that it is a bit above the average in bothy songs; it was one of several written by Anderson, a tall, distinguished-looking man and an amateur actor as well as a farmer. He lived to be an old man and long after his active farmtoun days were over must have heard his song sung at country gatherings.

Yet if time and birth denied the farmtoun "braw gallant" a chivalric rôle, it did leave him a field of prowess: the ploughing match. There he got a chance to show his mettle and his craft; it was his field of contest.

They came to it in the heyday of their skills and, like all champions, faded from it only, reluctantly, as their hands lost their touch on the plough-stilts. Then they came as spectators, grey-whiskered and stooped, to stand on the endrigs and speak among themselves, remembering the old days. The young men would parade before their critical gaze, taking a quick glance round at their rivals as they unloaded their ploughs from the farm carts—men they had beaten the last time, new faces among the young challengers, grinning nervously, cloth bonnets set jauntily defiant on close-cropped hair. The longboard men watched it all with dark smiles and a quiet superiority. Raiders from far parishes, their reputations had travelled ahead of them; they had had to show their worth with the shortboard plough to qualify for the longboard class. They were the virtuosos; when they entered the field it was like knights coming into the arena. Clydesdales were caparisoned like regal chargers and preened for the occasion, their fetlocks bleached and combed, their tails beribboned and braided. Though docile beasts, they champed and cavorted like circus ponies, their eyes glittering as they caught some of the excitement of the field. Brass, polished for nights under the pale glow of the bothy lamp took the glints of weak-wintry sunshine; harness warmed by back and flank and belly gleamed darkly.

In the 1920s, the latter years of its long history, there might be as many as 60 competitors still at a local ploughing match, which took place at the turn of the year and was organized by the bigger farmers and the agricultural societies, which had first made it one of the events of the farming calendar in the late-1700s. For a likely candidate who might bring honour to it (or at least not outright disgrace) a toun would allow a cart, his plough, and the help of a farmtoun companion to assist in lifting the plough down from the cart and so on—though the helper could take no part in the contest. No "tampering with the work" was allowed. The ploughman had it all to win or lose by himself—and might even be beaten before he ever put a plough-point into the ground if the competition rig he drew from the hat was a particularly stony one. That could be a disappointment, for however good the ploughman, his chances of doing good work on such a rig were slight indeed.

As the match ploughing went on, the attention of all but the most loyally committed would turn on the men in the longboard class and their rakish ploughs. Low and long-stilted, the long-

boards had the fleet look of greyhounds; they streaked through the
ley ground of the field with the grace of old clipper-ships, turning
earth with effortless ease, setting one unbroken furrow faultlessly
against its neighbour—almost, at times, putting a bloom on the
work. There was a kind of wonder whiles in the perfect affinity
between man and beast and implement that made the watchers
forget their cold feet and their frozen fingers. The old men on the
endrigs would nod one to the other, well-enough pleased and
anxious to be home: there would be a worthy champion. But the
ploughing went on for up to six hours, the contestants stopping
only briefly on the headland to take a bowl of soup and a mouthful
or two of oatcake brought to the field by the farmer's wife and her
kitchen lass (and maybe her daughter, too, if the ploughmen were
thought handsome enough). The judges stumped the field,
nodding, comfirming, quarrelling quietly among themselves,
dismissing without words the man whose skill that day had
unaccountably left him.

The day with all its dramas, as so much else, is firmly entrenched
in the farmtoun balladry, with humour and pathos if not with
consummate skill. All the same, the excitement, the partisanship,
the frequent rancour as well as the matters of detail and organiza-
tion are vividly caught, as in "The Dalmuir Ploughing Match",
an account of a spirited contest one 21 January at the West
Barns of Clyde, a toun of the South-West. The champion that
day was to be a "good ploughman", Will Aikenhead, a man from
Campsie. His big day started early:

> Aikenhead he got up for to get a' things right,
> Put his plough in his cart and tied it down tight.
> Awa' he did gang wi' his master's gude will,
> Some wad rather nae seen him, I'll wad ye a gill.

At the match field . . .

> The rules were read out just before they began——
> A guide to go after the plough or ploughman;
> While the police was there wi' his stick in his hand,
> Cryin', "Keep aff the grun', can ye no keep the land?"

Soon there was to be some commonplace commotion, which
doubtless shook concentration.

Now the ploughers got on, but the first kick-up was,
Young Jamie Park's mear she got intil a fuss,
The men started it as down the field they did rin,
And frightened the poor beast out o' its skin.

It kickit and flung, ay, and jumpit aboot,
Till at last they were forced for to lowse the beast oot,
He sent down to the Brocks, the milk pony he got,
To make out the day and to finish his lot.

Because of its size—there were classes for junior and senior
ploughmen as well—this particular occasion had its spectator
comforts:

The tents were set up for to serve out the drink,
It paid them gey weel, as ye may a' think;
The day it went round as fast as it could slide,
And some got half-drunk at the West Barns o' Clyde.

But for Will Aikenhead the day was going well, his mood one of
sober satisfaction—until one of his fellow-contestants, perhaps
envious of Will's superior skill, became awkward.

Aikenhead was near finished, and a' things gaun right,
When an ass of a fellow tried him for to fight;
He said his time was up and five minutes gane,
He might lowse oot his horses and gang awa' hame.

But his watch like himsel' it was tellin' a lee,
For twa or three pu'ed oot their tickers to see,
And said he'd a quarter to finish his bout,
If he managed the time then he would be ploughed out.

Such trickery was calculated to rattle the nerves, to harass the
competitor into "poor work". Aikenhead, however, got finished in
time and may well have begun to relax. But that ploy having
failed another plot was quickly hatched. This time there was a plea
for Aikenhead's disqualification on the grounds that he had
ploughed the wrong bout—the rigs for which the ploughmen had
drawn lots at the start.

Now Will he got finished, his time was not out,
When among the ploughmen there fell out a dispute;
Some said he was wrong and had ploughed the wrong bout,
Some said he was right, and they argued it out.

They argued and argued, they cursed and they swore,
Some tried on poor Will their vengeance to pour;
But the judges were there the case to decide,
At that great ploughing match at the West Barns o' Clyde.

But Willie Aikenhead's work that day was not to be denied.

They got tired and at last down to Sandy Reid's went,
And there at the dinner a wee while they spent,
Till auld Jamie Taylor the prizes did read,
Some thrawd their faces, and some shook their heid.

The first, Aikenhead—that was Willie Park's man;
The second, the fellow that tried him to wrang

It was not a popular decision, but then the result of a ploughing match never was, and though this particular ballad does not give the judges their character another one, from the North-East, has no hesitation:

The judges cam' fae far and near,
Tae pit them right they had nae fear,
But some wad say their sicht was peer
That day amon' the ploomen.

What the judges would be looking for that day were furrows as neat and as regularly set together as the pages of a book. For the man whose work pleased them best there was—in the 1920s and 1930s—the Champion's Cup and the £1 note that usually went with it. The title might bring the chance of a better "engagement" next Term-time, almost certainly the chance of a better lass. The cup was his to keep, to set if he so wished on the bothy shelf; the money—it was a week's wages—soon went. And so, usually, did the lass.

There were prizes too for the ploughmen who ran close, money sums down to five shillings (25p). At matches where the competitive spirit verged on the ferocious there would be awards for the best first furrow, the levellest ploughing, for the straightest furrow, and for finish. In the harness section prizes might run from £2 for "first" to ten shillings (50p) for a fourth place. And grooming, too, was rewarded: there would be a cup or medal valued about two guineas for the best-grooming combined with the best-cleaned harness. Naturally there were drams to be taken on the way home, though when the farmtoun men got round the bothy fires that night the speak would be of the sleekit longboard ploughs and the smiths who made them. Their names were a byword; they, too, were craftsmen with an extraordinary fine instinct for line and balance. It was their skill, too, that could make a common ploughman a king—for a day.

XXV

## *All the Laird's Men*

SHIELDED BY ITS thickly-planted policies, its corbelled turrets
and crow-stepped gables rising tentatively above the treetops, the
Big House stood nonetheless at the centre of the world of the
farmtouns—and indeed at the centre of the fabric of country society.
Its fortunes were closely linked with the land. Whatever its past in
feud and turbulent foray, its lead during the days of improvement
through the early 1800s and even before had re-established it in
that new landscape. If there was not always harmony between the
farmtouns and the Big House, there was at least an acknowledged
inter-dependence. Strict lairds who knew nothing of the hardships
of tenanting a small toun were quietly cursed without real malice;
tolerant lairds, on the other hand, would turn a blind eye to
inadequate farming. There was, in that east-coast region of the
farmtouns, no bitter backlog of memory of brutal clearances,
little guilt or calumny to constantly regenerate hate or suspicion.
And where harmony existed leases would lie unsigned for their
nineteen-year renewal, maybe for years, such was the trust
between parties. All the same, he was a bold tenant, estate worker
or farmtoun ploughman who would dare to let the laird's coach go
past him without raising his bonnet. Such insolence could lead to
dismissal, and that habit of courtesy lingered on into the last days
of the old-style farmlife when respect in some cases had worn thin
and the furious pace of the mansion-house car made the gesture a
little superfluous anyway.

By the 1800s, the day was getting past when the laird took his
payments in kind; it was a far cry from the time when his tenants
would have been expected to winter his stock (regardless of the
fact that their own might well die of hunger), cast and carry his
peats and stack them beside the kitchen gable, fill *his* girnal with
the best of *their* corn—after first having sheared his crops before
getting the chance to look to their own. What the Big House of
the mid-1800s did take from the farmtouns was the cream of their

young women, both grieves' and cottars' daughters of good appearance and reasonable virtue, as kitchen and housemaids. From their lowly station they were thus drawn into a sphere of social existence that could fill them with a vague discontent for the rest of their days. Such acquaintance brought the oddest of anomalies: the cottar's kitchen where a former tablemaid, now a wife with a trail of children at her skirts, would serve afternoon tea with teapot, sugar bowl and cream-jug on a tray and betray a more elevated past by her passion for fine bed-linen. Not all of the Big House maids went back to the farmtouns though; after a taste of the social graces, for many only a good tradesman would do.

Even so, class in the farming counties mattered less than it did south of the Border. The clan system had fostered its own kind of equality even while recognizing rank, and the society that grew out of it did the same. There were lairds who took their estate duties very seriously. Glimpses of this are seen in the life of the fourth Earl of Aberdeen, that peace-loving man who, after a brilliant early political career, foundered as prime minister in the Crimean War. Latterly the earl, whose circle included the Prince Consort and Sir Robert Peel (dethroned for preferring cheap bread for the masses to the protectionist politics of the land-owning classes), would see the gardener and forester daily at noon when he was at Haddo House, and each Saturday would receive tenants with problems they wished to discuss. He was, it is said, one of the last of the old Scots lairds to hold court in this way. It must have been a strange come-down from the elevated world of high-statesmanship, in which he had formerly moved, to the stumbling speak about leaking steading roofs and it is fitting that his most striking memorial is that standing in his own Aberdeenshire, the hilltop Prop of Ythsie, a landmark seen for miles around by the men working the North-East's farmtouns. His kindly paternalism passed down to the fifth earl, a man of similar mind, for in the three short years of his succession he built no fewer than 56 dwelling-houses, almost every detail of the work supervised by himself. That kind of concern for the less-comfortable in life continued on that particular estate, for in the 1880s, the Haddo House Association was organizing Saturday classes for the district's farm servants.

Tenants on the estates of the extensive land-owners expected and were without question included in the Big House celebrations, sharing in the jubilation of marriages, births (in the case of the gentry, arranged in that order) and the deep solemnity of death; heirs came to their majorities with bonfires ringing the mansion house from the hillsides of the surrounding farmtouns and the tenantry would automatically be represented at the balls and receptions that followed. It is one of the sadder ironies of history that the tenantry of Balmoral danced away the night of 9 February 1859 in wild conviviality. They would have been surprised had they been able to see into the future; the bairn they hanseled that night was the son of Victoria's favourite daughter: the Kaiser whose war some 50 or so years later would decimate the young manhood of the country's farmtouns. Weddings certainly were not allowed to pass unmarked, and the young Countess of Airlie's homecoming to Cortachy Castle in Angus on a bitter January day in 1866, a few days after her marriage to the laird in fashionable St George's in London's Hanover Square, is described in the book of her memoirs, *Thatched with Gold*:

> On the vast Airlie estates there were great rejoicings. The streets of Kirriemuir, the nearest town to Cortachy, were decorated with flags and evergreen arches, and cheering crowds greeted the arrival of the bride and bridegroom at the station. They drove the three and a half miles to Cortachy in a carriage drawn by four horses with postillions and outriders, escorted by sixty mounted tenant farmers and followed by a procession of carts and vehicles of every description, headed by the local band in a wagonette. At the castle gates the horses were unhitched, ropes plaited with Ogilvy tartan were attached to the carriage, and it was drawn the remainder of the way by the tenants while the escort of farmers fired sporting guns and pistols into the air and a couple of ancient cannon mounted in the grounds thundered a salute.

It was a Cortachy bride's traditional welcome from the tenantry and at the Big House, where it took one man just to clean the 100 oil lamps daily, there was free hospitality for hundreds of people. On lesser occasions, too, the gentry's carriage was drawn by the tenantry or estate workers as a gesture of respect that also marked their difference in station. Elizabeth Grant, in her *Memoirs*, describes the yearly harvest home at the largest of the Rothiemurchus estate's farms:

The Doune harvest home was very like that at the Dell, only that the dinner was at the farm kitchen and the ball in the barn, and the two fiddlers stuck up on tubs formed the orchestra. A sheep was killed, and nearly a boll of meal baked, and a large company invited, for our servants were numerous and they had leave to invite relations. We went down to the farm in the carriage drawn by some of the men, who got glasses of whisky apiece for the labour, and we all joined in the reels for the hour or two we stayed, and drank punch made with brown sugar, and enjoyed the fun, and felt as little annoyed as the humbler guests by the state of the atmosphere.

While they stayed, the young lady of Rothiemurchus makes it clear: "We were accustomed to dance with all the company, as if they had been our equals; it was always done. There was no fear of undue assumption on the one side, or low familiarity on the other . . ." A hundred years later that happy mixing of the laird's family with its servants and retainers was still a tradition of estate life. At Haddo, at the ball held for the estate workers at the New Year, the then laird, a former Governor-General of Canada, danced with the servant-maids and the cottar-wives while his lady circled the floor in the arms of one of the Mains's ploughmen. For the Haddo festive season, too, a fat beast was killed. Chosen months earlier by the butcher, it was in the meanwhile, one may be sure, well-tended by the cow-bailie. Each estate family got a portion and with it, a plum pudding. It was not charity though some of them no doubt were glad of it; it was the Big House's way of acknowledging service given willingly and often at inconvenient hours through the rest of the year— from the Big House gardens and the home farm's dairy, for instance. To the Cortachy Castle dinner table in their season came

. . . Hanoverian black grapes, muscatels, peaches and nectarines. The dairy house, built on the lines of Marie Antoinette's cottages at Versailles, sent up to the castle every day bowls of thick cream—to be made into the rich puddings beloved of the Edwardians—and pats of golden butter which were served up in the form of swans, pine trees or anything else the dairymaid's imagination could devise. The side tables were loaded with game pies, grouse and venison.

At Haddo each morning summer and winter at seven the dairy
loon set out from the Mains's dairy to walk the mile to the Big
House with the milk, carried in flagons on a yoke that bore hard
on his shoulders: five gallons and a small pail of cream when the
laird was at home. By the time he got there he was ready for the
piece of cake that was waiting for him.

The running and provisioning of the Big House occupied a large
number of folk. Elizabeth Grant catalogues the staff at Rothiemurchus in the early part of the 1800s: an upper housemaid and
plain needlewoman (the coachman's wife); her under-maid (the
gardener's youngest daughter); a schoolroom maid (the shoemaker's daughter); a laundrymaid (a soldier's widow, who had
followed the 92nd); cook and housekeeper; a plain under-cook (presumably for plain dishes); a butler (the gardener's eldest son);
a footman; the coachman; a groom (yet another of the gardener's
sons); and old John Mackintosh who "brought in all the wood
and peats for the fire, pumped the water, turned the mangle, lit the
oven, brewed the beer, bottled the whisky, kept the yard tidy, and
stood enraptured listening to us playing the harp 'Like Daavid'".

And that was only the tight nucleus of family servants. Beyond
the house's windows there was a wider world with which it was
closely linked: its farmtoun, where the farm lads slept in the
loft over the stable and got their food in the farm kitchen. The
farmtoun had its "shop" for a man who was "turner, joiner,
butcher, lint-dresser, woolcomber, dyer and what not"; his wife
was obliged to spin a given number of hanks of wool through the
winter. Staffing the farm kitchen was an old woman who also managed cows, calves, milk, stores and spinning, with some assistance
from a younger girl whom "I never recollect seeing do anything
but bake the oaten bread over the fire, and scour the wooden
vessels used for every purpose . . .".

And the estate had a further circle of outfolk: the bowman
(in charge of the cattle); the gardener (he of so many off-spring);
the gamekeeper; the foxhunter; the shepherd; the under-
shepherd; a carpenter; masons; woodmen; and saw-millers.

The smith and the souter called twice in the week and there were
frequent visits, too, from some other of the Big House's servitors:
Tom Mathieson the carrier; Tam McTavish the smuggler; and
Mary Loosach and the Nairn fishwives, with their creels on their

backs. Shortly before, Elizabeth Grant had been living in the south of England; an indication of how different was the life of the Big House there is her confession that on returning to Speyside '. . . we had to learn our Highland life again. The language, the ways, the style of the house, the visitors, the interests, all so entirely different from what had been latterly affecting us."

The years would change little. In the early-1900s, Haddo House, a grander seat by far, besides the usual complement of maids and cooks, had about eight keepers and no fewer than sixteen gardeners, counting the greenhouses' staff. The gardeners were housed in bothies, two or three to a room, where a bothy-wife and a young girl helper looked after them, cleaning, kindling fires at the end of the day, and cooking their food. The number of keepers reflects the importance of the shooting on such an estate: though the tenant farmers might be invited with their guns on a summer evening to keep down the number of crows, the shooting proper was the preserve of the gentry, reserved for moneyed men from the South. Though their accents might give mirth in private to the estate staff, their arrival was welcomed at least by the small boys of the estate and the sons of the Mains's cottars. Acting as beaters, they could earn one shilling and sixpence ($7\frac{1}{2}$p) a day crawling through the dark, tight plantations to raise the game-birds for the guns. So close was the woodland that the head keeper counted the boys before they went into it, and again when they emerged at the other side, just to make sure they were all present, for in parts they had to go down on hands and knees to get through the under-brush—and that in a light so dim that they sometimes lost sight of each other. Besides the chance to turn a penny or two, there was the prospect of a fine dinner, brought out to them in the head-keeper's gig and eaten by the sheltered side of the wood. Like most estates of its size, Haddo had its carpenters still and its saw-millers. Wood was constantly needed for the building and repair of steadings and fencing. The estate was one that took to "improving" later than some, so that even in the early years of this century, it kept its architect so busy that he needed his own strapper and gig and two shelts, which he changed-over at mid-day. The factor, too, had his own gig, shelt and strapper. It took a host of grooms to look after the stables and the coachman's status was such that he never had to dirty his hands. When the laird and his lady went from home, the coach and its team was made ready for him. White-gloved and splendidly liveried, he mounted its driving seat just round the corner from the front entrance. It was a braw turnout.

Twice a year the estate drew in its revenues. At Haddo, the rent-collecting was spread over three days and the ploughmen of the Mains got steady work holding the shelts and gigs of the tenants who came to pay their money at the office specially opened for the occasion. Each tenant was given a bottle of beer to regenerate goodwill for a further six-months and there is no doubt that some would have toasted the laird's health more earnestly in something a little stronger. Still, there was this to be thankful for: it was an improvement on 100 years earlier, when two-thirds of the estate's rents still had to be paid in kind. What the "siller" sustained was a gracious splendour, a foothold of some elegance amid the down-to-earth countryside of the farmtouns. One man, his Clydesdale's hooves "muffed" specially so that its weight could not cause unsightly indentations, ceaselessly mowed the summer lawns; four men constantly groomed the walks, picking straws off the bushes where they had blown from some passing farm cart. For the Mains's grieve the laird's obsession with tidiness could be something of a handicap in the running of a farmtoun. Not only could he not abide a temporary "midden" within sight (or smell) of the walks, there was another idiosyncrasy his grieves had to get used to: an insistence on having the stackyard about a quarter of a mile away from the Mains toun—so that the steading itself would not be made untidy by the odd straw borne on the wind.

It was a splendid lifestyle to be sure, but by the 1920s it was almost at an end. Like the farmtouns themselves the Big House settled into a slow decay in the long agricultural depression years. Indeed there is a belief, still, that by selling up its farmtouns as they fell vacant instead of re-leasing them, an estate helped to drain farming's resources. Capital tied into farmtoun buildings could not be invested in the land itself. The criticism may be valid. If it is, it was a policy that availed the Big House little. Like many a proud farmtoun, it has had its own sad come-down—to a time when the curious grandchildren of its once-respectful tenantry can wander its gracious corridors just by paying at the door.

# XXVI

## *The Voice of the Land*

THE BOTHY BALLAD was the ploughman's song; but it was
more than that: at times it was the vehicle of record. It picked up
the echoes of earlier folk songs—not only those of Scottish origin
—and the lilt of the wandering beggar's melody. Of all the strands
in the story of the old farmtouns it is probably the finest and
richest. Though largely limited to the harsh landscape of the
North-East Lowlands the ballads are indeed almost a history in
themselves, a minstrelsy sung to the melodeon. It would be unwise
in any study of the routine and quality of the farmtoun life to
ignore them. The ragged tail though they undoubtedly are of a
traditional balladry, that balladry according to Dr David Buchan
in *A Scottish Ballad Book* is "unmatched in quality and
quantity by any other regional culture in Britain". Simplistic,
sometimes nonsensical, often over-sentimental; the bothy ballads
certainly are all these things, yet there need be no doubt about the
*facts* they contain, the dietary details, the farmtoun routine, even
the parsimony and the peculiarities of particular farmers. Again,
Dr Buchan, speaking of the specimen songs he gives:

> The bothy ballads . . . represent the main concerns of their kind.
> They deal with the work at specific farms, aspects of labour and
> the leisure, and humorous incidents of farm life. . . . Artistically
> these songs do not stand comparison with the older ballads, but
> their great virtue is that they tell honestly and accurately what
> the hard but frequently humoursome bothy life was like.

We have corroboration of that from an earlier time: that of Gavin
Greig, the North-East schoolmaster whose personal odyssey
through the world of folk-song saved so many of the bothy ballads
from extinction. Though a man in some ways outside the farmtoun
society from which he made his collection, there is no doubt
about his authority—neither in the long series of articles he

published in the regional *Buchan Observer* nor in his address on the
subject to the Buchan Field Club (both published in America
under *Folk-song in Buchan*). He was writing and speaking at a
time when the farm-servant class was still "least affected by the
changes in taste and practice which modern days have brought, and
the ploughman song can still be heard sung by lusty lungs in the
field or by the fireside". Not only that. Excusing such country
folk-song of all self-consciousness, he sees the Ploughman Song
(as he styled it) as "the most characteristic kind of folk-song which
we have, and [it] . . . retains a certain measure of vitality. Its
record, indeed is not yet closed." The ballad he recognizes as the
medium of country record; it always had been. He believes
" . . . for the most genuine and convincing pictures of rural life
we must leave the highways of literature and get among the
pathways of folk-song . . .". And he adds the very cogent reason
why: ". . . rustic muse by the very simplicity of its method can
compass an effect which the poetry of culture only labours to
miss."

It is a view he constantly reiterates; he has no qualms about
authenticity being lost in an oral tradition that passed a song from
the lips of one bothy lad to the ear of another, that spread in time
from one farmtoun to the next for maybe 50 years before it was
written down. On the contrary, he sees this as a guarantee of the
ballad's essential truth in a society he designated "the ultimate
stratum in our rural districts" and among the people he believed
to be the last custodians of traditional minstrelsy. Only sincerity
and conviction, he feels, could have given "vogue and life" under
the circumstances to a humble composition. He concludes that
"no kind of minstrelsy . . . is more loyal to fact and truth than the
ploughman song". Greig, like any true collector, went back to the
people. His net was spread through the editorial columns of the
*Buchan Observer*, based then as now in the oil-town of Peterhead,
into the wide ballad country of that North-East corner of Scotland.
Fragments came from farmtoun folk as well as others whose education in the countryside and its traditions had been at their
grandmothers' knees. Thus was memory stretched into the early
days of the 1800s and back to the birth of the farmtouns. Pictur-
esquely, he saw the task he and his correspondents were about as
raising a cairn "to the honour of old Scotland". Everyone, he
thought, should add at least one small stone, and like his friend

and fellow-collector John Ord he travelled to pluck the words from many an old singer's lips at meal-and-ales and other country gatherings. Ord, in his published collection, may have Anglicized more the broad dialect of the ballad region but, like Greig, he never strayed from the essence of his song.

But if further guarantee were needed it would surely be found in the fact that the farmtoun ballads were written largely by the men who lived them. "The Boghead Crew"—to take one almost at random, no better or worse than a whole host of others equally interesting—was written by James Trail, who actually "took a hairst" at the farmtoun of Boghead in the Pitsligo area of the North-East. He woke one night and composed the entire song before going back to sleep. It details the complement of the farmtoun at harvest-time but is valuable for the student of farming history on another count as well: like many another bothy poet, Trail pins down the time of which he writes:

> Twas in the year eighteen-seventy
> On August the sixteenth day.

The song about the harvest, the scythers and bandsters, is a useful confirmation of the fact that the reaper at that time had not reached the Buchan farmtoun despite its invention nearly 50 years before.

"Ellon Fair" with its feeing-market ritual was by a man called John Ker, a regional rhymster. That derogatory ballad about Sleepytoun, the farm standing near to the site of the once-famous fair, was the work of William Clark, a man who strutted the stable cobbles of that up-country farmtoun about the mid-1880s. The writer of the well-known harvest song, "Johnny Sangster" was a man of farther parts though. The ballad is usually credited to William Scott of Fetterangus, in the Aberdeenshire parish of Old Deer. Scott, born in 1785, was first a herd-lad, later went to Aberdeen to learn tailoring and from there went south to London and subsequently to America before he returned home to settle in his native parish. His collection of dialect poems was published in 1832. Even farmers' and workers' names were often correct in the originals; they got changed only when the bothy-song travelled out of its own region—being "localized" to heighten interest for another district's gathering—or were distorted by cautious sub-

H

editing at a later stage before being committed to the immortality of hard, libellous print. Rettie's Willie Rae was real in name and in all probability in the character the ballad bestowed upon him: a virtuoso in the use of the new machine-harvester of his time and as modest a man as we are led to believe. Delgaty, Drumdelgie, South Ythsie, the Guise o' Tough, Lescraigie and Cameloun and all the other oddly-named touns of the bothy songs were a raw reality to the farmtoun folk who worked their acres and drove their teams of Clydesdales; who would have thought then that their names would linger on to become a kind of nostalgic poetry in the mind?

The ploughboy's song is not portentous; it deals mainly with everyday things: the farmtoun's food, its work, its master and gudewife, its implements and its servant-maids. It does not dwell reflectively on life and its theme is often repetitive: when a farmtoun lad sat down with his pencil to make a slight mark for posterity he was far from selective: he covered the field, all was grist to his country muse. If much of it seems trivial, then that is in the nature of folksong; it deals with the everyday things, the feelings of simple folk. But that is not to say that the songs and ballads of the bothies did not concern themselves at times with a larger canvas or that the bothy minstrel never sang of other things. He did. Other ballads encompass the whole of life: hopes, sorrows, heartbreaks. Away from the immediate field or farmstead scene they have, occasionally, a kind of cloying sweetness that the life itself certainly had not. Sentimentality often surrounds the themes of marriage and friendship, whereas the relationships of the men and women of the farmtouns were almost embarrassingly direct. There is a preoccupation with the choosing of a good wife, laments on being saddled with a bad one. There are odes to Peggys and Margarets and Marys: a cataloguing of charms without a great deal of discrimination, not to say judgement; there are plaints for Prince Charlie and for his ill-fated rebellion; ballads telling of mishanters with fast women in the city; tales of lasses who took away willingly with the beggar man; of men taken protestingly by the pressgang; visitations (of the devil); abductions; farewells and parting songs and songs of emigration; and, maybe not surprisingly, and most suitably, a welcome to Deeside for Queen Victoria.

There are glimpses into the lives of the countryside's itinerants.

The wandering masons, for instance—some went regularly to America from the North-East—are recalled:

> Simmer's gaun awa',
>     The winter's comin' on,
> And the bonnie mason laddies
>     They'll be comin' home
> Wi' their pockets fu' o' siller,
>     And their lasses for to see;
> And the bonnie mason laddie
>     He will marry me.

Wars and the men who fought them were the subject of song also, in that time when war had gallantry of a kind. Even in the 1880s the minstrels of the North-East's feeing markets were still celebrating the victory of Waterloo with a song that managed to link Queen Victoria to that occasion:

> Here's a health to Queen Victoria,
>     In peace lang may she reign;
> Likewise the Duke of Wellington,
>     That noble son of Erin.
> For though he was a Tory knave,
>     His courage aye was true,
> He displayed both skill and valour too
>     That day at Waterloo.

Irish songs filtered into the native minstrelsy, brought over by the shearing bands—and strange songs of the sea, of the whalers that up to the 1860s sailed out on their six-month voyages from the east-coast ports of Fraserburgh, Peterhead, Aberdeen and Dundee, among then that Bonnie Ship the *Diamond*. Men even made songs on the making of the turnpike road, taking the ballad back somewhere close to its beginnings—as a thing of record:

> 'Twas in the year auchteen hun'er and aucht
> A road through Buchan was made straught,
> When mony a hielan' lad o' maught
>     Cam' owre the Buchan border.
>
> 'Twixt Peterhead and Banff's auld toon
> It twines the knowes and hollows roon,

Ye scarce can tell its ups frae doon,
  It's levelled in sic order.

The hielan' and the lowlan' chiels
Cut doon the knowes wi' spads and sheels,
And bored the stanes wi' jumpin' dreels,
  To get the road in order.

There was some in tartan, some in blue,
Wi' weskits o' a warlike hue,
And werena they a strappin' crew
  To put the road in order?

And mony a hup and mony a ban
Got cartin' horse and lazy man,
For fou and teem and aye they ran
  To push't a bittie forder.

Chiel Chalmers he frae Strichen cam',
Wi' ae black horse as bold's a ram,
Nae ane could match him in the tram,
  He made a braw recorder.

The Meerisons, the Wichts and Giels,
Were swack and willin' workin' chiels,
Sae weel's they banged the barrow steels
  To gar the road gae ford'er.

The road's as smooth's a harrowed rig,
Wi' stankies on ilk side fu' trig,
And ilk bit burn has noo a brig,
  Where ance we had to ford'er.

The turnpike it will be a boon
To a' the quintra roon and roon,
And lat folk gae and come frae toon
  Wi' easedom and wi' order.

On fit ye're owre it free to stray,
But if a beast ye chance tae hae
At ilka sax miles ye maun pay
  For gaun a bittie forder.

The writer's name gin ye should spier,
I'm Jamie Shirran frae New Deer,
A name weel kent baith far and near,
  I dwell near the road's border.

Ballad-writers had a strong tendency to include their own names somewhere in a song, sometimes when its quality might have been thought to be an embarrassment to them, but here at least Jamie Shirran has little to be ashamed of. His ditty sets a fine skelping pace and conjures up a vivid picture of the road-making gang of 1808, shifting hills with its spades and shovels, all man-powered.

Nobody, of course, would compare the bothy ballads with the old traditional ballads, for the bothy-songs were intended only for the ephemeral hour of farmtoun ease or rural celebration, to be sung if not to the accompanying notes of a button melodeon then to the scraich and poor fingering of a cheap fiddle. Still, it is sad that nowadays they are so little known or cherished even in their own region of the North-East Lowlands, let alone beyond it. The fault, however, may be in themselves for most are in the broad Doric of the area, a tongue so insular that it is only with difficulty that it travels beyond its southernmost limit of Laurencekirk. Given that barrier, it is hardly surprising that the South should know so little of the life of the farmtouns or the men who lived it. The result, alas, is that the region of the hard farmtouns has been, and largely remains, culturally closed country. Its language is without the soft guile of the Gaelic or the genteeler modulation of the Central Lowlands, yet oddly, it is tellingly fitted for dealing with the practicalities of farmtoun life, always, despite its heavy insistence on diminutives, on the edge of grim reality and totally devoid of the silken songs of romance. Given the unending struggle with the soil, so different from the story of the gentler Lothians, that is hardly to be wondered at.

Yet it is also a language that has produced poetry holding more than the commonplace, that projects through it a wider vision, distils from its own bitterness an attar that touches the knowledge-able heart and, in a more translatable tongue, would have capti-vated a larger audience. One thinks here of Peter Still, whose work has its own poignancy and encapsulates dreams in the things of everyday life though his own life was far from being one of reverie in which he could observe affairs from some leisured coign. His own story indeed is at one with the tale of the farmtouns as well as a reminder of the remarkable men they could produce. He took his first fee to a farmtoun at the age of eleven, later took up hedging and ditching—it was the heyday of enclosure—and also went out stone-breaking for pay of 4d (2p) a ton. His working day stretched from five in the morning (the time at which the horsemen rose in the bothies) until seven at night. He died at 34, broken by work. There are those who see Still as the premier poet of that North-East region. But there are other claimants, notable among them the late John C. Milne, who speaks more directly for the farm servant of the old farmtouns. Where Still refines the experience, Milne's is the reporter's eye: he describes the life close-up, as it was. The voice is authentic, unsynthetized, the impact of recorded fact— the back-breaking work, the chaumer rats—a stark indictment. And maybe with those names one should couple that of Flora Garry, a farmer's daughter. Later still, she catches the farmtouns of the ballad country in the last days of their old lifestyle and, her remarkable ear for the speak of the region apart, this alone would give her work a special interest. And there are others, of course, never more but sometimes hardly less in stature, all not only adding to that indefinable thing that is the soul of a land but filling in, parenthetically, the details of its daily existence. Among them is Alexander Gibson, whose *Under the Cruisie* provides an invaluable picture of country society in the mid-1800s and introduces us to the folk whose lives centred on the farmtouns of well over a century ago: the millwright, blacksmith, shoemaker, dominie, fishergirl, tinker and chapman as well as the horsemen, shepherd, the cow-bailie, orra man and kitchen maids. Though his work may be a little cloying for today's taste—unlike the ballads, there is not a single note of roguery or rudery in it—it is impossible not to feel beholden to the poet, a man so modest and self-effacing that he apologizes in advance for his muse, which

> . . . but stammering at the best,
> May fail to please a cultured taste.

If one notices the occasional clumsiness, one is grateful, nonetheless, for the record.

It is doubtful if a land so bare and dour, so pitilessly scoured by wind as the North-East Lowlands could have produced songs other than the bothy ballads, or a people any different from the folk the farmtouns bred: sparing with words, with emotion, making masterly use of droll understatement. Indeed almost the whole of their humour was based on the dry comment abetted by the sly dig. Their favourite comedians reflected that astringency; their jokes were neither convoluted nor richly adorned. They came quickly to the point. There was a reliance on verbal wit and the word, perfectly demonstrated in the "presentations" of Dufton Scott, an Inverurie newsagent and an entertainer of the 1920s and 1930s who used the authentic Doric in his sketches and monologues. This son of a Forgue drystone dyker drawing his material from the farmtouns significantly—perhaps intuitively from the taproots of his past—eschewed the scarecrow figure, the straw in the mouth, and always appeared on stage in evening dress.

Writers as well as poets have added to the collective farmtoun folk memory. The Mearns, southernmost of the ballad counties, with its red earth and its small, rock-clinging fisher towns, has been immortalized by Lewis Grassic Gibbon. Though born in an Aberdeenshire croft, Hillhead of Seggat, in Auchterless, Gibbon's writing is rooted in the farming land of Kincardine with its softer nuances. Yet it speaks for all that North-East area of the farmtouns, masterly in its understanding of the relationship between men and the soil. In his *Sunset Song*, John Guthrie, the man who so purposefully strides through the farmtoun close of Blawearie, is an archetypal figure, never more convincingly drawn. His kind gave the farmtouns their greatness; they stood in the last spark of the day at byre-doors up and down that country, gazing out on their fields, tamping tobacco into the bowls of their Stonehaven pipes with calloused thumbs before setting light to it and going indoors to their supper. *Sunset Song* has another great value. It stands (whatever date Gibbon himself put on it) at the great divide of the farmtoun generations: those, like Guthrie, who never dreamed of any other life and those who dreamed of nothing but leaving it. Together they stand by the hinge of farming history, Guthrie's landscape already almost in the past.

Gibbon's own understanding of the farmtouns though is never in doubt. As a baby in the Howe of Auchterless, he had been wrapped in a plaid at harvest time and left by his mother in the shelter of a stook as she gathered sheaves in the wake of her man's scythe; in another croft, in the Mearns, he passed his impressionable boyhood. There are other places where one can seek the facts of those early farmtoun days, in *Johnny Gibb of Gushetneuk*, for instance, which gives its own interesting insight into the life in the mid-1800s. But in none does the feel for farmtoun and landscape come so strongly together as in *Sunset Song*.

Looking back, another fine Scottish literary figure, the novelist Neil Gunn, recognized this; Gibbon, he said, gave "a voice to the land". Taking stock, near the end of that first book of his famous trilogy, of the farmtouns of his beloved Mearns, Gibbon sees "the last of the Peasants, the last of the old Scots folk". Looking round him, he realizes:

> A new generation comes up that will know them not, except as a memory in a song, they passed with the things that seemed good to them with loves and desires that grow dim and alien in the days to be. It was the old Scotland that perished then and we may believe that never again will the old speech and the old songs, the old curses and the old benedictions rise but with alien effort to our lips.

It was almost a valediction to the days of the old farmtouns and he could not have been unaware of it.

# XXVII

## *Finale for the Old Touns*

B<small>Y THE START</small> of the 1930s the great days of the old farmtouns were on the wane; their era was almost at an end. They had had their own kind of charisma, bred their own legends. Once their names had rung through the bothy-talk like the names of crack regiments and deference would be paid to a man who had in his time strutted through one or other of their famous closes or driven one of their Clydesdale pairs. Now their greatness was a muted thing and their remarkable feats of labour excited something less than admiration. But their rise and their reign had not been in vain. Their contribution through the latter half of the 1800s and the early part of the 1900s had matched the improvements of the pioneering lairds of a century or so earlier. They threw up great men who rose like comets and left a tail of lustrous achievement behind them; they ordered the landscape; they took agriculture from the days of the sickle into the era of scientific husbandry. Let no one say that was not a significant achievement.

By the mid-1800s young men from the Continent as well as England had been beating their way to the door of that famous toun Fenton Barns, where the kindly George Hope dispensed farming wisdom and the steam plough took its turn with the Clydesdales. The Eastern-Central counties had already established a potato export trade to London and were on the way to making Scottish seed supreme. Shrewd guidance and incentive from the Highland and Agricultural Society was encouraging a study of the breeds, sheep as well as cattle; guano was arriving from Chile and Peru and the new nitrogenous and phosphatic manures would soon be boosting crop yields and making the cultivation of marginal land an economic possibility.

The new artificial feed-stuffs and the use of the turnip with linseed cake and cotton-cake would turn beef production on its head and make the bailie an important man about any farmtoun, even if he never quite had the glamour of the ploughman. And it

was here that the ballad country of the North-East came into its
own. Beef was its triumph, and if one may say: "Where would
the chip-shop have been without Archibald Findlay of Auchter-
muchty's Majestic potato?" one can even more forcefully ask:
"Where was the steak-house without the great Willie McCombie?"
The Galloway perhaps excepted, there was not a single pure cattle
breed in the country as the farmtouns began to function as part of
the new agriculture. But by 1820 or so, the North-East was taking
an interest in the problem and over the next 30 years that beef
trade for which the region would become famous would grow
and the sea shipments from ports such as Aberdeen would increase
phenomenally to become worthy of mention, even a thing of
wonder, in the first travellers' guidebooks.

Yet it was success in the show-ring that burnished a toun's
name and none can have come so easily on to the lips as that of
Tillyfour, that up-country toun and home of the Aberdeen-Angus
breed where McCombie presided, bearded and whiskered like an
Old Testament prophet, a masterly self-publicist it is true but
still and all a masterly judge of beef on the hoof. The shrewd
son of an even shrewder father who had been a well-known figure
at the country's cattle trysts such as Falkirk, McCombie's name
was as familiar in Paris or Smithfield as it was in the markets of
his own North-East Lowlands. He had taken up the pioneering
work of Hugh Watson of Keillor, in Forfarshire, and it was the
Aberdeenshire man's skill that forced the breed to the forefront
and world-wide acclaim. Before then, it had still basically been a
local breed. It was in 1840, at Aberdeen, that McCombie exhibited
for the first time, winning first prize with a four-year-old ox. It
was a modest start but for the next 30 years his name would
rarely be missing from any important show-list. In the same
countryside sat the farmtoun of Sittyton of Straloch, the toun of
Amos Cruickshank; it too would pass as firmly into the volumes of
farming history, as the place where the Shorthorn was brought
from a promising obscurity into the full limelight of farming
achievement. Cruickshank was a different kind of man entirely
but no less sure in his judgement. He was less fond of the show-
ring, less a believer in the infallibility of pedigree. Nonetheless he
gave his working life quietly to bringing to pre-eminence a breed
suitable, in his own words, "to our country, our agriculture, our
people". It was a statement with just a touch of statesmanly

greatness that the shy man himself would not have recognized. The master at one time of a herd of 300—the United Kingdom's largest—the quiet Quaker, his life's work done, lived out the last of his days into his 80s at his famous toun, modestly fattening a few head of cattle and sheep. The Cruickshank mantle would pass down a generation or so to bring the spotlight on another modest tenant farmtoun of the same area, Collynie, where William Duthie, stern master and local banker, entertained the envious bids of millionaire breeders from all parts of the Commonwealth and—the falling shadow of the future—the Argentine and Brazil. Nor did the battle of the opposing breeds fade when McCombie slipped from the scene for The Blacks found new homes, new meccas, among them Ballindalloch on Speyside where, with stock from both Keillor and Tillyfour, Sir George Macpherson Grant carried *their* prestige as strongly into the 1900s as Duthie did the fame of the Beef Shorthorn.

But then there was hardly a frontier on which the Scottish farmtouns did not press forward advance of one kind or another. South from the heartlands of the ballad, the raspberry fields came to ring Blairgowrie and bring it the soubriquet "The Berrypan of Scotland". Here as the soft fruit ripened each year the wandering folk of the countryside gathered for the five or six weeks the picking would last. It was a great festival of folk and with luck and fair weather two train-loads of berries a week would leave Blairgowrie's railhead for the jam factories of Dundee, Perth and Glasgow as well as for the English market, all barrelled and hooped to hold in the crop's freshness. To the South-West, Ayrshire, always a region of milk, became the udder for Glasgow's sprawl and an area where the white-wash brush gave conspicuous charm to a landscape of neat dairytouns.

A toun's stature had a bearing on its folklife: a man from the Shorthorn stronghold of Collynie who saw stetsons every day of his working life and met queries constantly set in the American drawl with the sometimes slower drawl of his own Doric tongue might be less than inclined to call a man from this or that Mains his farming equal, even though the fame of his toun was paying him no better. But that is not to say that these lesser touns were not as soundly-run; their names might be further down the prize-list but their fields were as tidily worked. In any case, a Mains—its steading renewed with the dawn of the farmtoun era—had its own cachet from old association with some noble family or estate. Time and a lack of romantic imagination (never a product of the farmtouns) might have hedged it round with East, West, North, South, Nether and Lower Mainses and any bothy lad with a liking for the district might move round all of them before quitting the parish for good. Some touns had assumed the ancient title, quite justifiably, but with a grievous poetic loss from the proud Gaelic of their past. Bog Gurker got a touch of gentility no doubt by becoming the West Mains of Castle Fraser, but no longer would its name come off the northern tongue like a battle oath.

There were touns that never entered the show-ring; their concern was not with livestock championships but with something more basic: hard, pinching survival. They were the family one-pair touns whose tenants struggled against the caprice of the seasons and the bank's foreclosure, using one as an excuse against the other. If there is little to say for them, there is as little to say against them. They kept their tenants in a permanent condition of anxiety neurosis but as though to make up for it, they had homely names that hid their unbearable tyranny. If these names fall now as enchantments on the ear it is as a guide to the past of the countryside: they are the signposts to days long gone by—Waulkmill (where the cloth was waulked after weaving), Sheelhill (the site, surely, of some old shilling law where the corn was riddled?), Hogshillock, Souterhill, Teuchathaugh and Whauphill (the teuchat was the plover that keened so ceaselessly over the spring work of the fields, the whaup the curlew whose cry broke the silence of summer's dusk). In some cases their heart-tugging warmth would be eroded by the heavy hand of bureaucracy and the terrible correctness of the Ordnance Survey which pickled their fine sounds in impeccable English. Peatiebog lost its savour forever in the unsoftened preciseness of Peatbog; Cauldhame, in the old Scots tongue a warm refuge from the world, as Coldhome became a place of such chill charity that it drove its sons and daughters round the world. And still one wonders about Paddock-hole; whether this, after all, was not a genteel vowel transplant that gave chic to what was once, as Puddockhole, the ill-drained haunt of frogs. Unlike the touns of the North-East Lowlands, those of the South and South-West had little chance to ride to fame on a ballad-line, however derogatory the mention. All the same, they found their own kind of poetry those southern touns in the unmetrical prose of the newspaper mart reports which were also an unvarnished guide to their worth. It is easy at first to imagine a softer naming of the touns, as though that kindlier country had left room for romance with Ravencleugh, Finglandbrae, Larkhill, Hazelrigg and so on. Alas, too soon the eye lights on tell-tale Broomhill, Cowburn, Shankend and Mossfoot. They were never the stuff of high-farming legend. Yet they were, implacably, a part of the farmtoun folk-life.

Soon there would be another new factor on the farmtoun scene, fresh and forward-looking, as yet uncontroversial: science. Increasingly, every aspect of farming would come under its close scrutiny and provide fruitful areas of inquiry. Here, if Scotland did not initially lead, she was singularly fortunate in having men who had money to endow the research establishments where the elements of farming might be studied. These in time would make a vital contribution. Funded by the government and by private donors the famous Rowett Institute in 1920 began its study of nutrition, animal and human, and ten years later became the home of the Commonwealth Bureau of Animal Nutrition. Under Lord Boyd Orr its research sustained the health of Britain through the war years. Probably the wealthiest of individual benefactors, Dr Thomas Bassett Macaulay, President of the Sun Life Assurance company of Canada, returned in 1928 to his ancestral Hebrides and two years later established the equally prominent Macaulay Institute for Soil Research. A year after that, the Hannah Dairy Research Institute began its work at the typical 120-acre dairy farmtoun of Kirkhill, gifted by John M. Hannah and situated appropriately in the very heart of Ayrshire's dairying country. Here again, two strands intertwined: the health of the people and the progress of farming. The institute's immediate aim was to benefit the dairy industry; its research centred on the dairy toun with an immediacy of application; its talk was of profit margins rather than the abstract considerations. It investigated, among other things, feeding standards; the manufacture of milk itself, inside the cow; and breed longevity. But equally important, in an area that supplied the depressed tenements of Glasgow, was the close-linking of its research with the problem of tuberculosis. Its rôle, too, would become critical with the war.

If such things lit hope, it was but feebly in a stilled landscape.

As the years wore on the plight of the farmtouns had become worse. For many it was already too late.

The blow, when it fell, had come from the West. After all the years of blockading Continental corn, it was the cereals from the virgin land of America's Middle-West—grown under a more seductive sun and harvested, ironically, by McCormick reapers—that brought disaster to the home grain market. And on the heels of that, there had come another innovation that would rock the farmtouns to their very foundations: the introduction of the cold-store ships that could bring in other cheap farm products, from as far away as New Zealand. Their future bleak, their rôle diminished, the farmtouns began their inevitable run-down.

Some, the big farmtouns, would ride out the depression years with a kind of grace; a bit of guttering hanging loose from a barn roof might betray the bitterness of the times but their fields seldom did, for they had a kind of in-built professionalism the great touns and a loyalty to the land on which they stood. And World War I helped, as wars tend to do; it gave farming a fillip when it needed it most, in the middle of the difficult years. All the same, there were farmtouns where the poverty showed and the rotten fence-posts swung like beads on the paling wire; there were small tenant farmers as poor as the few men they employed, their own moleskin trousers as threadbare at the knees as those of any hired man. They crushed men those small touns, their tight acreages too limited to juggle with in those desperate times; they bled their tenants of hope even while making sure that they had to do the work of three men just to keep out of the hands of the money-men. Their occupants became the victims, when the time was ripe, of the speculative laird or the auction sale.

With the end of the 1914–18 war many of the Scottish farmtouns struck a very fine balance indeed; from the early-1920s right up to the outbreak of World War II their tenants were men on a tight-rope, walking the brink of bankruptcy, winning crops just in time to avoid disaster. And if the farmer himself was so tight and far-in at the bank what could life be like for his cottar? Not good. But then, it never had been. Even in the boom years the hired men of the farmtouns rarely shared in their wealth. And through the slump things were worse. Many a country teacher's log of the time tells its own sad story with a terse bitterness, reflected in this entry from a small school in the North-East, for a day in May

1919: "Lack of boots reason for much irregularity of attendance."
Into the 1920s there were cottared men still who were glad to see
their children going to the school in parish boots, and even in the
1930s their bairns took the school road not only in hand-me-
downs (which they had always done) but with the conspicuous
patches of poverty on the backsides of their breeks.

For the old ploughmen of the farmtouns looking over the land
in the 1930s one thing was becoming abundantly clear: machines
were to be the chariots of agricultural advance. Their own day,
and that of their Clydesdale pairs, was over. Proud, conscientious
men, they must themselves have been depressed by the state of
once-grand farmtouns, at the barns and byres that went unpainted,
the steading doors that got leave to rot in the smirr rain till they
fell off their rusty hinges. And there was another kind of change:
the dour dignity and symmetry of stone of the old steadings was
already beginning to be diminished by the first of the factory
pre-fab materials. That geometrical rapport between steadings
and fields, that affinity of stone and landscape, that had once so
delighted the eye, began to be lost. There had come a need for
bigger multi-purpose buildings, of warehouse proportions
sometimes, in which the movable partition allocated space
according to crop and livestock need. Silo towers raised blunt
fingers of grey concrete to disfigure the skyline, all justifiably in the
name of progress. And with prefabrication came the obscenity of
asbestos. These were the buildings and the materials of the factory-
age; they helped to destroy the old character of the farmtouns;
concrete block, asbestos sheeting and the girdered frame drew
nothing from the land in which they stood.

Difficult though it is to imagine it now, there were about the
old farmtouns of the 1930s cottars who were almost ashamed to go
from home, their "best suits" were so threadbare. The run-down
of the touns left them even without a place to put their pride.
So there may have been a further strand among all the complex
reasons for the drift from the land: the decline in the countryman's
dignity. In time, and in despair, they moved away these farmtoun
men, to jobs in the town—as milkmen, carters and cleansing-
department drivers, any work where their skill in handling horses
could still be counted an asset. When they went, it was the end of
the old farming way of life, the end of an old song. There died
then a little of man's harmony with the landscape.

And of course there were other forces that drove men away from the ritualized, insular life on the farmtouns. The world of the 1930s impinged on the cottar's house more directly than it had ever done before. It came in on the aerial he strung between the chimney pots. Before that it had come in with the post, in newspapers that came late in the day to the grieve's house or to the cottage of the head gardener and got passed down in time to a neighbour; by the time it reached the cottar's table the world was old and stale. Now it had that magic ingredient: immediacy. Well-meaning men encouraged by the BBC and maybe to curry favour with John Reith tried to keep the ploughman's culture alive by singing farmtoun ballads that lost most of their vigour somewhere out there in the ether when what he wanted to hear was the championship boxing relayed from the far ends of the earth in the early hours of the morning. In the excitement of it all there were dairy bailies who some nights never got to their beds at all. But little they cared about that: they were, for once, at one with the rest of the world, part of the greater community of men. For good or ill, the influence of the kirk and the minister was diminished, diluted by the tinsel world of the cinema. There was hardly a small town within a bothy-lad's bicycle reach that did not have its cinema and its three-night programme. Farmer's boy and kitchen maid alike were susceptible to the glamorous life it depicted; both dreamed of the city way of life and a cinema for every night of the week. There would be few who would mourn the passing of the old farmtouns. But now and then when the drams were in him an old man might draw his chair to the fire to speak of them. And of the hard moustachioed men, in their moleskin breeks and sleeved waistcoats, who worked them.

# GLOSSARY

a': all
aboon: above
aboot: about
ae: one
afore: before
agley: out of line, irregular, gone wrong
ahint: behind
ain: own
airm: arm
aise: fire-ash
ait: oat
ale-wife: woman who brewed ale for sale
amang, amon': among
ane: one
ance: once
arles: money given to confirm a bargain
aucht: eight
auchteen: eighteen
auld: old
ava: at all; ne'er come back ava, never come back at all
awa': away
aye: always

bandster: one who binds sheaves after reaper
bailie: stockman tending cattle; dairy bailie, one looking after
   dairy herd
bait: food
baith: both
banes: bones
beetlin' stone: stone on which clothes were beetled—i.e. beaten
   with a heavy wooden mallet
bellman: one who passed through the town ringing a bell and
   making public announcements
ben end: the best room or front parlour
besom: heather brush, but also used to describe farmyard brooms
biding: staying

bigging, biggin': building

big house: estate mansion

binder twine: twine used in binder mechanism to bind sheaves

bittie: bit

blate: bashful, sheepish, gauche

blawin', blawvin': blowing

blinkit: to become sour, to lose gaiety

boll: a measure of meal or grain. In oatmeal: 10 stone

bonnet: flat cap

bonnie: pretty

bothy: quarters for unmarried farmtoun crew; bothy toun, a farmtoun where single men were so housed; bothy-wife, old woman (usually) who looked after bothy and cooked for men; bothy ballads, songs sung by bothy men, the ministrelsy of the farmtouns

bothan: a cot or hut, usually associated with illicit distilling

bout: once round a piece of ploughing or cornfield

bowie: small water-tub

braeside: hillside

braid: broad

braird: first sprouting of grain

braw: fine, gaily dressed

brawly: very well; brawly kens, knows well enough

bree: juice, liquid

breeks: trousers

breid: bread, but in North-East usually applied to oatcakes

breist: breast

brig: bridge

brock: fragments left in field, usually in potato-lifting

brod: thistle stob

broon: brown

brose: oatmeal-and-water dish of the farmtouns

bught: a pen in which ewes were milked

byre: cattle-shed

byword: well-known fact, indicating fame—or notoriety

ca': carry, transport

caird-tongued: coarsely spoken

cairt: cart

cam': came

cankered: ill-natured

canna: cannot

carlie: little man, often of uncertain temper

cauf: chaff

caul', cauld: cold

catcher: name for Sunday-duty horseman on North-East farmtoun

caup: wooden bowl from which farmtoun men supped their brose

ceilidhs: Highland gatherings at which folk made their own entertainment

chaumer: North-East name for smaller-type bothy

cheils: young men of the farmtouns

chessil: cheese vat

clapshot: mixture of turnips and potatoes

clavers: idle or frivolous talk

clean toun: a toun from which all the crew left at Term-time

clip: a colt or young horse

close: farmtoun courtyard or precincts generally

Clydesdales: breed of horse predominant on Scottish farmtouns

coarse: rude, crude

coggie: small wooden vessel

coo: cow

convoy: to accompany

cornkist: stable chest for Clydesdales' oats

cornkister: bothy ballad

cottar: married farmtoun worker living in tied cottage

cottar-folk: farmtoun families

cottars' market: feeing market for cottar men held about six weeks or so before Term at local mart

cot-toun: small village or hamlet of cottars

countra clatter: countryside gossip

covey: small man

crack: top-notch, the best

crap: crop

cratures: creatures, usually human-kind

craw: crow

creesh: grease

creepie stool: a child's stool, or any small stool

crew: complement of a farmtoun

croon: crown

cruisie: small iron oil lamp

daffin: dallying with intent, teasing

dang on, ding on: come down heavily—snow or rain

daurna: dare not

daut: fondle; dauting, act of fondling

deece: long wooden seat or bench in farmtoun kitchen or croft
   house (a kind of farmtoun sofa)

deid: dead

delling: delving, digging

denner: lunch, mid-day meal

dinna: don't

divot: sod of turf

dominie: schoolmaster

doo: dove

dools: sorrows, ill-luck, depression

doon, doun: down

drag-pole: centrally-located draught-pole on implement

dram: drink (of whisky), the size varying with the humour and
   hospitality of one's host

drover: man who drove cattle from the trysts and fairs

dung: farmyard manure

dyke: stone wall


endrigs: headlands

e'en: eyes

engagement: terms and duration of a ploughman's contract with
   a particular farmer or farmtoun


fa': fall

factor: estate manager, laird's man of business

farmtoun: farmhouse, buildings and land belonging to it

Fastern's e'en: eve of Lent

fee: a farm servant's engagement or contract with a farmer, also
   the sum of money agreed between them; fee home, accepting
   contract to "go home" to a particular toun: feeing, the act of
   negotiating such a contract in feeing market or elsewhere

fern-tickled: freckled

finger-steels: finger coverings, sheaths for protecting fingers

firkin: small barrel or cask

flagon: lidded can for carrying milk

flail: hand implement for threshing grain

fleep: a stupid fellow

fleer: floor

flit: to remove; flitting, the load comprising the furnishings of a
house

forder: further

fore-breast: front panel of box-type farmtoun cart

forefoughten: exhausted

fu', fou: full

frae, fae: from


gae: go; gae's oot, goes out

gaed: went

gang: go

gait: way, direction

gane: going

gar, gars: make, makes; gars ye snore, makes you snore

garron: light horse

gatherer: one who gathered corn into sheaf in wake of sickle or
scythe

gaun: going

genteel: sedate, circumspect, socially inviolable

gey: very, considerable; gey weel, very well (though its nuance
in conversation between Scots can suggest anything from sly
wonder to scandalous outrage)

gie: give

gied: gave

gin: if, should

gill: measure of whisky

girn: complain, moan

girnal: chest for oatmeal

gloamin', gloaming: evening twilight

goon: gown

goushet: small triangular piece of land

gowd: gold

graith: harness

gravat: scarf, muffler

greets: cries

grieve: farm overseer

grippit: stiff; grippit hips, stiffness around hips

grumphie: pig
grun': ground
guid: good
guid-fegs: exclamation of astonishment in North-East, to some
  extent a mincing oath instead of "Good God"
guid-faith: similar exclamation of astonishment
guidman, gudeman: master of farmtoun
guidwife, gudewife: mistress of farmtoun
guidwill: goodwill
gweed: good
gyaun: going, gyaun furth, going outside


hacks: chaps in the hands or feet
hae: have
hairst: harvest; to "take a hairst", engage with farmtoun for
  duration of harvest
hail, hale: whole
halflin: not fully grown, a farmtoun lad in his teens
hame: home
hamespun: spun at home
hansel: to toast, wish well (with a dram of course)
haud: hold
haivers: foolish talk
heid: head
heilin': Highland
heuk: reaping hook
hing, hings: hang, hangs
hinmost: hindmost, last
hoo: how
horseman: man who worked pair of farmtoun Clydesdales, a
  farmtoun ploughman
horse-copers: horse dealers
Horseman's Word: secret word said to make horses (and women)
  complaisant
hun'er: hundred
hup: command to make horse quicken its pace


ilk: every
ither: other

jaud: jade, teasing mischievous girl
jumpit: jumped


kail: colewort (or greens); used to indicate the particular food or
    dish but also meals generally
kailyard: enclosed plot where cottars grew kail as a safeguard
    against scurvy, latterly cultivated as a vegetable garden
kebbuck: a cheese
keely-bags: containing reddish substance made from red ochre,
    for colouring doorsteps, hearths, etc.
keepit: kept
ken, kens: knows
kent: knew, known
kickit: kicked
kick-up: commotion
kirk: church
kist: chest, ploughman's wooden trunk in which he kept all his
    possessions
kitchen maid, kitchen deem: servant lass who did the hard chores
    in the farmhouse kitchen
kittle: to excite, enliven; quick, lively
knowes: small hills
kye: cows


laft: loft
laird: land-owner, usually with estate and country seat
lang: long
lat: let
lauch: laugh
lave: the rest, the remainder; a' the lave, all the rest
lee: lie, an untruth
longboard: plough with long mouldboard
loon: boy, usually one in menial post; the youngest member of
    a farmtoun's crew
lowlan': Lowland
lowse: to untie, unyoke; lowsing time, end of yoking or working shift
lowser: one who unties—the twine binding the sheaves, for
    instance, for the threshing mill
lugs: ears

luggie: small wooden vessel for meat or drink

maiden: farmer's eldest daughter
mair: more
maist: most
mak': make
Martinmas: 28 November Term
maught: mighty, powerful
maun: must
meal-and-ale: end-of-harvest celebration supper and dance
mear: mare
meat: to feed folk
micht: might
midden: farmtoun dung-heap
mishanter: misfortune
moonlicht: moonlight
moss: marshy land where peats are dug
mou': mouth
muck: farmyard manure; to muck, to clean out beasts' stalls, removing dirty bedding straw, etc., to midden
muckle: big, much
mull: mill, usually threshing-mill but sometimes used to denote meal mill
multure: the fee for grinding grain
mure, muire: moor

nae: not
naething: nothing
nane: none
neeps: turnips
neiper: neighbour, neighbouring toun
nicht, night
noo: now
nowte: cattle

oor: our
orra: coarse, untidy, uncouth, trashy
orra-beast: spare Clydesdale, not one of a pair
orra-man: farmtoun jack-of-all-trades capable of many jobs, often abstemious and of upstanding character

oot: out
oot-woman: woman of farmtoun working in fields
out-owre: out of, out over
owre, ower: over
owsen: oxen


packman: pedlar who came round country with his merchandise on
   his back
pair: pair of Clydesdales to which a ploughman was assigned
peer: poor
perquisites: the extras—coal, meal, milk, potatoes, etc.—a cottar
   received in addition to his house and wages as part of his
   agreement with a farmtoun
pickle: a small quantity or portion
piece: snack, taken in fields during harvest, potato-lifting etc.
pints: bootlaces
pit: put
plaid, plaidie: ubiquitous outer garment worn shawl-fashion
pleuch: plough
ploo: plough
ploomen: ploughmen
policies: grounds immediately surrounding mansion house
pouch: pocket
powsowdie: sheep's head broth
prees: kisses
pu'ed: pulled
puff: boast
puir: poor


quarter: 15 minutes; quarter to, 15 minutes to the hour, quarter
   past, 15 minutes after hour
queets: ankles
quintra: country


rarest: grandest
raips: ropes
redd: comb; redd up, tidy up
reek: smoke
refeese: refuse

richt: right

rick: cornstack

rig: strip of land; run-rig, ancient form of strip cultivation

rin: run

roon: round

roup: farmtoun auction, displenish sale of implements and
    household possessions

rug: pull


sae: so

saft: soft, also slow-witted

sair: sore

sark: shirt

sairest: sorest, hardest

sax: six; saxpence, sixpence (old currency)

scarlatina: scarlet fever

scraich: screech

scrankie: coarse-featured; also, lean, lanky

seiging: raging

sharn: cowshit

shaltie: pony, but on farmtouns usually a light horse

shank: piece of knitting; to shank, to knit

shavies: sheaves

shearers: band of harvesters using sickles

sheels: shovels

sic: such

sicht: sight

siller: silver, but usually money generally

simmer: summer

sleekit: sleek

smiddy: smithy

snap: eat hastily or eagerly

snod: tidy

sonsie: plump, healthy, thriving

soor: sour

souter: shoemaker

sowens: farmtoun dish made from meal left in milled grain husks;
    oatmeal flummery

sowff: whistle in a low tone

spads: spades

spaewife: fortune-teller

speired: asked; speired tae bide, asked to stay

spurtle: round, dressed stick (with decorated end) for stirring porridge in the pot

stanes: stones

stankies: roadside ditches

steading: cluster of buildings which, with farmhouse, comprise farmtoun

steelbow (tenure): stocking of farmtoun by landlord

stirk: bullock or heifer between one and two years old

Stonehaven pipe: type preferred by farmtoun men

stook: arrangement of harvest sheaves set to dry in harvest field; to stook, to so arrange sheaves: stookit, a crop or field where stooking has been completed

strae: straw

straik: stroke, also tool for sharpening scythe

strapper: man who drove farmer's phaeton

strath: broad valley through which river runs

straucht, straught: straight

striddlers: women who assisted stack builders in Lothians

swack: supple, quick

sweir: swear

swingletrees: part of the yoke arrangement for plough, etc., to equalize draught

synin': sieving

tacksman: land occupier who re-leased to smaller farmers, crofters and cottars, especially in a clan context

tae: to

tatties: potatoes

tattie drottle: a basic soup of potatoes and creamy milk with leek and onion added sometimes for flavour

tee: to; follows tee, falls to

teem: empty

Term: 28 May (earlier 26 May) or 28 November, Whitsunday and Martinmas

theek: line out, thatch

thocht: thought

thistley: covered with thistles

thraldom: burdened by obligation, bondage

thrang: throng
thrash: thresh
thraw: twist
thrawd: grimaced
ticht: tidy; keeps ticht, keeps tidy
timmer: wooden
tine: lose
tink: tinker, gangrel person
tinkler: tinker
tither: other; the tither, the other
tocher: dowry
tounkeeper: Sunday-duty horseman at a farmtoun
traivel: walk
trumpin': tramping
tryst: large livestock market
tup: young ram
twa: two
twines: twists
tyawvin: struggling


unceevil: uncivil
unco: very


wa': wall
wad: would
waddin': wedding
wadna: would not
wark: work
weel: well
werena: weren't; were not they
weskit: waistcoat
wha: who
Whitsunday: 28 May (formerly 26 May) Term
wi': with
wicht: man, fellow
wime: stomach
winna: won't
wrang: wrong

yer: your

yill: ale

yoking: one work-shift, from morning to lunch-time or lunch to
  suppertime; also act of hitching Clydesdales to implement

yon: yonder